Servants of Satan

Servants of Satan

The Age of the Witch Hunts

Joseph Klaits

INDIANA UNIVERSITY PRESS
Bloomington

Manufactured in the United States of America

Library of Congress Cataloging in Publication Data
Klaits, Joseph.
Servants of Satan.

Bibliography: p.
Includes index.
1. Witchcraft—History.   I. Title.
BF1566.K53   1985   909'.0982105   84-48252
ISBN 0-253-35182-0 cloth
ISBN 0-253-20422-4 paperback.
2   3   4   5   6   91   90   89   88   87

For Frederick and Alexander

Contents

Preface

This book is an extended essay, reflecting on and synthesizing the extensive recent literature on the witch craze of the sixteenth and seventeenth centuries. The chapters began as a series of course lectures designed to help bridge the gap between the interests of undergraduates and the concerns of scholars. I owe a great deal to the students at Oakland University and Catholic University of America whose questions and suggestions forced me to clarify my thinking and improve the presentation.

Many others contributed comments on earlier chapter drafts or led me to materials I otherwise might have overlooked. I especially want to thank for their encouragement and good advice Donald Bailey, Jack Censer, Richard Golden, B. Robert Kreiser, Lawrence Orton, Orest Ranum, Dan Ross, and Timothy Tackett, and to acknowledge the invaluable assistance of the late Marian Wilson. A grant from the National Endowment for the Humanities and sabbatical and research support from Oakland University gave me the leisure and resources necessary to complete the project.

Throughout the years of research and writing, this book has been a family project in our household. It began when Alexander was small enough to take witchcraft even more seriously than did his father. The writing ends with Frederick old enough to do the bibliography. For their inspiration, and for Barrie's, my deepest thanks.

Columbia, Maryland
April 1984

Servants of Satan

Introduction

Belief in witchcraft—harm inflicted by someone employing supernatural means—is one of the most widespread of cultural traits. Our modern skepticism about the efficacy of witchcraft can easily blind us to its importance in the past and in many contemporary societies.[1] Even in the late twentieth century, witch beliefs continue to flourish in Latin American voodoo, among the satisfied patients of African witch doctors, and, not least, in the stories we in the West tell our children.

To most Americans, however, witchcraft suggests a specific and isolated historical event, the Salem witch trials. In fact, the great Massachusetts witch hunt of 1692, which resulted in the death of twenty people, is the one episode between Plymouth Rock and the Boston Tea Party that seems to stand out in our national collective memory of colonial times. Fueled by fictional accounts and an inexhaustible stream of reinterpretations, remembrance of Salem appears perennially adaptable to society's shifting concerns, from McCarthyite inquisitions to hallucinogenic drugs. It is hard to imagine a new theory about a witch trial other than Salem's featured on the front page of the *New York Times*, for this is the only witch panic still vivid in American cultural tradition.[2]

Yet the Salem witch hunt was merely the tip of an immense iceberg, whose shape and substance we are just beginning to appreciate. Thousands of people were tried for witchcraft during the craze that swept over Europe in the sixteenth and seventeenth centuries and crossed the Atlantic with the first white settlers. Exact statistics are unobtainable because of gaps in the records, but over ten thousand cases have been verified.[3] Estimates of the actual total range much higher. Salem, then, was very far from a unique event. The Massachusetts panic closely resembles a multitude of far less famous witch trials. This book explores the core of the great witch craze that lies buried far below our images of Salem. It attempts to map and interpret the social, political, and intellectual dimensions of the age of the witch hunts.

During the era of the witch trials, the Halloween witch we know today had not yet been domesticated, commercialized, and trivialized. Instead, she lived in the imagination as a supremely dangerous, uncontrollable menace. The stereotypical witch evoked the same emotions of fear and

horror that satanic cults like Charles Manson's have inspired in contemporary society. The terrifying witch stereotype current at Salem held that the
accused had made pacts with the devil. In return for their allegiance, Satan
supposedly granted his servants awesome powers to inflict harm on their
neighbors. In the form of spirits or "specters," witches could travel through
the air over long distances, pass through strong walls, and attack their
helpless victims. Even at their trials, it seemed, the witches dared to send
forth specters to torment their accusers. Anguished shrieks and convulsive
seizures in open court were vivid testimony to the dreadful sufferings
experienced by the young girls of Salem whose bodies ostensibly were
possessed through witchcraft.

As frightening as the abilities of the Salem witches seemed to their
contemporaries, witches in Europe could apparently do worse. Witches
regularly were held responsible for sudden death due to illness or accident.
In the overwhelmingly agricultural society of the time, they were apt to be
accused of devastating crops with bad weather or destructive pests. Thus,
witches were charged with blighting the grain, raining down hail on the
vines, or visiting disease on domestic animals. Within the household,
witchcraft might be invoked to explain difficulties between husband and
wife, particularly when sexual and reproductive matters were involved.
Impotence, failure to conceive, miscarriage, stillbirth, and infant death
were conditions likely to be attributed to the witch's curse. In short, witches
were blamed for nearly every kind of personal calamity.

Still more alarming were the other consequences of the witch's imagined allegiance to Satan. Generally the witch was pictured as a woman,
usually middle-aged or older, often poor and a widow. By signing the
demonic pact, thereby renouncing God and Christianity, she became the
devil's servant, a partner in his universal war against all that was good in the
world. Specifically, it was thought in many parts of Europe that these
women showed their subservience to Satan by becoming his willing sexual
slaves. Flying through the air at night to join others of their kind at mass
meetings known as witches' sabbats, the devil's human servants were said
to worship him by blaspheming against God, copulating with their master,
and indulging in orgies of sexual promiscuity with everyone present. Once
returned home, the witch could shelter an animal "familiar," a demon in
animal form, and suckle him at her "witch's tit," the extra nipple given her
when she entered Satan's service. A young witch might receive the sexual
attentions of an incubus, a devil who assumed human shape in order to
impregnate her and thus bring forth a new generation of witches.

Such, briefly stated, was the stereotype of the witch. However unlikely it may appear today, it was a powerful image in the era of the witch craze. Between about 1560 and 1700, thousands of witch trials and executions in Europe and her American colonies were based on this idea of the witch as Satan's servant and accomplice in evil.

Our modern point of view may make us question the sincerity of accusers who maintained this stereotype. Witness our usage of the term "witch hunt" to connote an unfair judicial proceeding of the McCarthyite type, undertaken for cynical political purposes. Were the judges of the witch trials consciously fabricating accusations? In a few instances the answer undoubtedly is yes. The great majority of those charged with witchcraft were poor and powerless, however, and little material gain or political advantage could be hoped for in most trials. The evidence produced in this book will show that the typical judges and accusers sincerely believed that by executing witches society was cleansing itself of dangerous pollution.

Witch-hunting judges were not alone in their acceptance of the idea of witchcraft. It was part of the dominant world-view during the era of the craze. Nearly everyone—from intellectuals to peasants—believed in the reality of invisible spirits, both angelic and demonic. Hardly anyone challenged the universal opinion that supernatural forces constantly intervened in everyday life, rewarding and punishing, blessing or cursing. Most people were likely to attribute to God or to the devil responsibility for events that we are more inclined to ascribe to human actions, natural forces, or sheer coincidence.[4]

Because educated people today generally associate witchcraft with irrationality and superstition, we might expect learned opinion to have led an attack on the witch trials. Indeed, this eventually did happen, but only at the end of the witch craze. For most of the period discussed in this book, the educated were in the forefront of the witch hunts. It was learned men who gave to the Western concept of witchcraft its most distinctive and most disturbing characteristic, the relationship with Satan. In this respect, European witchcraft differs fundamentally from ideas of the witch found in non-Western parts of the world. Nowhere else was the witch considered a servant of the devil. The educated European minority created this demonic image of the witch when it associated harmful magic with religious dissent or heresy. To the ancient folk image of the witch as evil sorceress these intellectual and political elites added the witch's even more threatening reputation as an ememy of God. Thus, the stereotype of the witch combined learned fears of spiritual deviance and the traditional popular motif of the dangerous hag with her cauldron and curses. The resulting psychological compound proved extraordinarily powerful.

Witch hunting unfolded against the background of one of the most creative and dynamic periods in the history of Western civilization, the era of Michelangelo, Shakespeare, Galileo, and Descartes. It was the brilliant age of Renaissance art and literature, of the Protestant Reformation and Catholic Counter Reformation, of overseas explorations and commercial growth, of the establishment of centralized monarchies, and the rise of modern science. At first glance, the simultaneous occurrence of witch trials and these great movements, all of which have been associated with the achievement of modernity, seems a strange contradiction. Yet a closer look can show how the course of the witch craze was directly affected by all these momentous developments. Renaissance culture, for example, contributed much to the formulation of the witch stereotype. The rediscovery of ancient works on magic encouraged the development and enhanced the status of attempts to invoke and control spiritual forces. Renaissance humanists' preoccupations with learned magic and the conjuring of spirits, reacting to the social tensions and religious concerns of the time, produced an environment favorable to the crystallization of the witch stereotype.

Similar linkages tie witch hunting to the other social developments of the time. The witch craze exploded during the era of the Reformation. It would be impossible to overestimate the social impact of this great spiritual outpouring in the sixteenth and seventeenth centuries. The movements of Protestant Reformation and Catholic Counter Reformation touched every aspect of life and thought, and they affected witchcraft in fundamental ways. The missionary thrust of religious reformers was crucial to the advent of witch trials on a massive scale. In seeking to spread their messages to previously untutored rural Europeans, the reformers engaged in a vast struggle against popular religious practices, which they interpreted as satanic in origin. Because many reformers perceived aspects of folk religion as manifestations of the demonic, they were prepared to cast ordinary folk as devil worshipers and witches. Thus, the witch hunts were in part a by-product of the evangelizing ideology of religious reform.

Like the political ideologues of more recent revolutionary movements, those of the Reformation era tried to change behavior and redefine standards of morality. In this period, centralizing secular authorities generally cooperated with clerics in imposing new sets of values on lower social groups. Purifying reformers were particularly concerned with prohibited sexual activity, which they came to view as a symptom of religious deviation. For this reason, church and secular courts vigorously punished forbidden sexual behavior during the age of reform. Predisposed as they were to think of common folk as followers of Satan, religious leaders and the secular authorities they influenced frequently associated the "sinful" sexual behavior of lower-class women with supposed diabolical practices. Thus, reforming impulses cemented the connections between women, popular heresy, and witchcraft. About four out of five witch suspects were females, a preponderance that suggests the intensity of misogynistic feeling in early modern times. Woman-hatred seems to have become particularly prominent then, with monumentally lethal results.

In most witch trials, the judges used torture to obtain confessions. Thousands of coerced admissions of witchcraft attest to the enhanced power absolutist rulers of the time exercised over their subjects. Torture made possible a snowballing of mass prosecutions in witchcraft cases, as each victim was forced to name accomplices. In this way a single confession often led to a large-scale panic. Because of their deep ideological commitment, the authorities needed to win over the hearts and minds of their prisoners. Outward conformity to the rulers' new spiritual and social standards was not sufficient. A true inner rebirth, made manifest by formal confessions and declarations of repentance, was the goal of most judges in witchcraft cases. Their interrogations often tapped deep and powerful unconscious dynamics in the minds of the accused. As in modern cases of brainwashing and moral re-education by states espousing today's ideological dogmas, torture and suggestion were potent forces that few prisoners could resist. In the torture chamber, many a witch suspect was led to believe that he or she was truly guilty as charged.

In all of these ways, the witch craze reflected the imposition on lower social levels of the educated elites' values and standards of behavior. But witch beliefs often responded as well to tensions originating at the lower end of the social spectrum. In poverty-stricken villages only partially adapted to the capitalistic work ethic of individual responsibility, the beggar was often cast as the witch. Her knock at the door frequently evoked a dangerous mixture of resentment and guilt in the mind of an only slightly better off neighbor. When, on Halloween, our outlandishly dressed children ring doorbells and announce "trick or treat," they are re-creating in a pale, innocuous way the fearful role attributed to charity-seekers at the time of the witch trials. Villagers believed that the beggar's trick, if refused her treat, might be to curse the household by means of witchcraft.

The fear of disease and death pervasive in a society that suffered from epidemics, famines, and chronically high mortality rates inevitably prompted deep popular anxieties. Under the right circumstances, such stresses could turn villagers against a defenseless member of the community. The poor in general were subject to witchcraft accusations, but those with certain problematic occupations were singled out most frequently. Among the more vulnerable callings was that of the midwife. Suspect because of her gender, her poverty, and her central role in the often lethal and always anxiety-ridden process of childbearing, midwives became a frequent target in witchcraft cases that originated from the accusations of their neighbors.

The foregoing observations suggest some of the ways that witch trials were organically related to the major forces of historical change in early modern Europe. The witch craze was not an aberration in the history of the sixteenth and seventeenth centuries. On the contrary, witch hunting reflected the darker side of the central social, political, and cultural developments of the time. The end of the witch craze around 1700 likewise signaled important changes in European life and thought.

These introductory remarks dictate the plan of this book. Chapter 1 considers possible frameworks for interpreting the witch trials. Succeeding chapters discuss the rise of the idea of witchcraft in medieval and Renaissance times, the impact on witch trials of the spiritual reformers' concerns with popular religion and sexuality, the origins of witchcraft cases in popular attitudes toward beggars and midwives, the meaning of outbreaks of demonic possession in the witch hunts of Salem and Europe, the spread of torture and its psychological ramifications, and, finally, the reasons for the disappearance of witchcraft cases.

The bleak terrain of the witch trials is both forbidding and depressing. Their vast scale must daunt any writer who hopes to explain the dynamics and significance of witch hunting, while the story of the trials also is bound to provoke discouraging conclusions about the human potential for inhumanity. Yet the witch craze's prominence in the history of the period necessitates the broadest possible treatment, not only chronologically and spatially but also conceptually. Our current knowledge of political institutions, social structure, and patterns of thought should be brought to bear when placing witch hunts in their historical context.

The rise and decline of witch trials can also illuminate matters that remain tragically current. Plainly, we are not dealing with obsolete issues when we consider such problems as the roots of intolerance, manifestations of prejudice against women and minorities, the use of torture by authoritarian rulers, and attempts by religious or political ideologues to impose their values on society. This is why the term "early modern" is an appropriate one for the era of the witch craze. The sixteenth and seventeenth centuries were "early" in the long-term development of today's historical patterns, but the continuity of such patterns shows that these centuries were "modern," too.

A discussion of the witch hunts, then, can tell us not only about the trials themselves and the society that generated them; it also can tell us about ourselves. In this sense, the prominence of Salem in the American collective memory seems completely appropriate. The witch trials remain important now because through them we can hope to understand impulses that are still with us.

I

The Witchcraft Enigma

Were there really witches? Did women attempt to inflict harm on their neighbors by magic? Did they actually gather for nocturnal rites of devil worship? Among modern interpreters of the witch trials, opinions about the existence and activities of witches have ranged from total credulity to complete skepticism. Even the most basic questions lack firm answers, and nearly all the logical possibilities have been upheld: that the idea of witchcraft was a hoax invented by self-interested churchmen and other authorities, that witches not only existed but also possessed supernatural powers granted them by Satan, and numerous intermediate positions. The witch trials constitute perhaps the greatest enigma of the least understood era in modern history. There is still no complete consensus among historians on this subject, but recent scholarship has approached the problem of the witch hunts with a high degree of precision and has achieved notable advances in our knowledge.

Seventy years ago there was little controversy. Numerous studies of the witch trials appeared from the 1880s to the years of the First World War, and scholarship pointed toward a single conclusion. Marshaling mountains of sources, the indefatigable writers of that generation, most notably the German scholar, Joseph Hansen, and Americans Andrew Dickson White, Henry Charles Lea, and George Lincoln Burr, concluded that witchcraft trials were the sad result of medieval superstitious fears and the copious use of torture to elicit confessions. From wide reading in the surviving trial records and demonological handbooks, these scholars became convinced that the authorities, particularly those in the Catholic church, were hypocritically manipulating a gullible public to enhance their own power. Or, alternatively, they classed churchmen and other officials among the gullible—honest but foolish victims of the superstitious belief in witchcraft.[1]

The first generation of witchcraft scholars, whose works are still valuable compendiums of source materials, emerged from predominantly Anglo-Saxon, Protestant milieus, which accepted the near-total identification of medieval Catholicism with ignorance and backwardness. Children of an optimistic age that placed supreme faith in the progress of reason, they confidently consigned witchcraft to the dustbin of history, an object lesson in the folly of irrational religion. The conviction that reason had conquered superstition with the trials' end made it clear to these scholars that here was one more episode in the epic struggle between science and religion, a war that happily concluded with the worldwide triumph of Western values and material civilization at the dawn of the twentieth century. These biases made it easy for them to believe accounts of mass witch trials conducted by the clerical judges of the papal Inquisition in fourteenth-century France and Italy. In fact, we now know that these accounts are fraudulent and that relatively few witch trials were conducted in Catholic Europe during the supposedly dark Middle Ages.[2]

Like all historical models, that of the prewar scholars had its internal inconsistencies. Even when the tales of inquisitorial witch hunts were accepted at face value, it was always clear that most of the witch trials took place not in the medieval era, but after the advent of the Renaissance and Reformation. Protestants had been as active as Catholics in prosecuting witches during the sixteenth and seventeenth centuries, and torture was not inflicted on many of those who confessed to witchcraft. As often happens, however, this prewar interpretation was ultimately rejected not as a result of internal criticism but because of a change in the general cultural environment. By shattering the illusion of moral progress in the modern West, the war of 1914–18 reopened many questions formerly regarded as settled. To the postwar generation, a society capable of immense blood sacrifices to the cults of nation-state and industrial technology no longer seemed self-evidently rational and progressive when compared with contemporary non-Western cultures or earlier periods of European history.

In the general cultural reassessment that characterized Western thought between the two world wars, the role of the ethnographers was very great. Eager to understand non-Western cultures without succumbing to the biases of missionaries and colonists, anthropologists sought out communities that were as free as possible from European influences. The reports they brought back of highly organized societies were well received by intellectuals predisposed to question the values of their own culture. Among the most intriguing findings of the new anthropology was that witch beliefs played constructive roles in many societies. Although differing in some respects from the witchcraft of Europe's past, non-Western beliefs in the harm inflicted and curses effected by ostensibly supernatural means strongly resembled Europe's own experience with witchcraft. No longer was it possible to hold the opinion that the witch hunts were uniquely an instrument or symptom of medieval Catholic irrationality. Clearly, a new framework for interpreting the witch trials was in order, one that would place the European experience in a broader context.

Unfortunately, the first attempt at charting a new direction for European witchcraft studies led to a dead end. James Frazer's monumental collection of folklore, *The Golden Bough*, had appeared just before World War I. Frazer's work and its novel ethnographic consciousness inspired many scholars to look into the European tradition of folklore. In 1921 one such writer, Egyptologist Margaret Murray, published *The Witch Cult in Western Europe*. In this and subsequent books, she claimed that the victims of the witch trials were members of an ancient cult that had originated in Egypt and became the prevalent religion in Europe until the seventeenth century. Murray described Christianity as the religion of only a tiny elite, which had managed to suppress most written references to the majority's faith. She was able to show to her own satisfaction that a fertility cult dedicated to the horned, two-faced god, called Janus or Dianus by the Romans, flourished in Europe until repressed in the great witch trials by hostile Christians who mistook the cult's activities for the worship of Satan. Organized into covens, the worshipers of Dianus attended weekly meetings (called "esbats" by Murray), which she claimed were the basis for the misconstrued stories of witches' sabbats.

Murray's bold theses have been effectively criticized many times over the years, most recently by Norman Cohn, who shows with great thoroughness that her opinions rest on a tangled tissue of highly selective quotations, mistranslated passages, and out-and-out fabrications.[3] Although the popular reputation of Murray's works remains remarkably strong, no serious student of the subject accepts her evidence. Her theories nevertheless continue to provide an imagined historical foundation for members of witch cults today. Such modern witches practice a kind of pagan worship of Mother Earth. They reject completely a belief in Satan and have no connection with the supposed devil-worshiping witches of witch-hunt lore.

It is possible, of course, that although Murray was wrong in her reasoning, her conclusions were correct. A few scholars have continued to point out similarities between accounts of witches' sabbats and folkloric practices devoted to fertility.[4] This resemblance is circumstantial evidence for the existence of organized groups of devil worshipers. The important point, however, is that no one has been able to show that covens of witches actually existed in the Middle Ages or during the period of the witch craze. An occasional historian may still be willing to continue the nineteenth-century romantic tradition of Jules Michelet and assert the reality of peasant devil worship as a sublimated form of social revolt.[5] But in the absence of uncoerced testimonies to the existence of witch gatherings, such assertions must remain unproved.

Thus, two well-known interpretations of the witch hunts seem deficient: first, that they were simply an inevitable consequence of clerical superstition and power hunger; and, second, that the trials reflected the existence of a network of organized societies practicing something called witchcraft. The question remains, then, how can one explain the ubiquitous accounts of sabbats and devil worship? Of course, one option is simply to assume the reality of Satan and the accounts of witch activities. Given these assumptions, such talents as flying through the air and changing one's shape become entirely plausible gifts of the devil. Those who assert the reality of such phenomena, however, clearly pass beyond the bounds of historical scholarship into the realm of theology.[6] Obviously, the axioms of modern historical method—axioms I endeavor to apply throughout this book— make it impossible to consider an interpretation of witchcraft predicated on the devil's existence. This is not an issue that can be addressed profitably in historical discourse.

Somewhat more accessible to historical analysis is the theory that tales of airborne trips to the witches' sabbats resulted from visions induced by hallucinogenic substances. The widespread use of drugs in modern culture has prompted scholars to consider the possibility that trance-inducing plant derivatives may explain the uniform accounts of flying and devil worship.[7] This may be an attractive hypothesis, but, once again, there is no persuasive evidence for the existence of drug cults at the time of the trials. Although witches were often accused of using hallucinatory ointments, we can be certain that at least in some cases such charges were completely false. Particularly impressive in this regard is the evidence accumulated by Alonso de Salazar, a judge of the Spanish Inquisition, who made a thorough study of witchcraft charges in 1611. Salazar conducted experiments with alleged hallucinogens that had been seized from accused witches in the Basque country of northern Spain. When he administered the supposedly potent drugs to animals, the judge found the material to be perfectly harmless. Salazar then learned from the accused that they had tried to satisfy the fantasies of their eager and credulous prosecutors by turning over jars containing such worthless concoctions as pork fat mixed with chimney soot and water. As a result, the inquisitor confidently concluded that there was no use of drugs among the so-called Basque witches.[8] Although some people elsewhere in Europe may have been using hallucinogens, evidence of

drug involvement in witchcraft is extremely sketchy and mostly circumstantial. For example, a recent attempt to attribute the Salem trials to an
attack of ergotism, a disease accompanied by hallucinations and caused by
eating rotten bread, turned out on closer analysis to be based on a long chain
of unlikely assumptions.[9] Nearly all analyses linking witchcraft with drugs
rest on highly suspect testimony drawn from secondhand or more remote
accounts of (often coerced) witch confessions.

Even if they were not drug induced, it is possible that the confessions of
accused witches resulted from psychotic delusions. Some scholars and
physicians have argued that mental illness lay at the root of the witch trials
and have labeled as clinical symptoms the witches' reports of their night
flying and devil worship. No doubt some of those confessing to witchcraft
were suffering from mental illness as we understand the term, but this
explanation cannot account for many of the thousands of cases. In numerous instances enough is known about the victims to make us certain that
they were not insane. Too often, psychiatric explanations of witchcraft have
been based on fundamental misunderstandings—for example, confusing
witches with the possessed—and on psychiatry's tendency to abstract the
behavior of an individual from its societal context.[10]

If delusions lay behind the witch hunts, they appear in most cases to
have originated in the minds of the prosecutors, not the accused. After a
century of witchcraft scholarship, it is at last becoming apparent that there
is no reliable evidence of the existence of devil-worshiping witch cults and
that the relatively few individuals who sincerely believed themselves to be
devotees of Satan typically acquired such beliefs by suggestion from
preachers or prosecutors. This conclusion emerges from the efforts of
recent scholars to explain the witch trials by addressing the other major
activity (in addition to devil worship) usually attributed to witches, namely,
bringing harm to their neighbors by supernatural means.

On the surface, harmful magic may appear an even more mysterious
and inaccessible area than rituals devoted to a devil figure. Yet the abundant
records compiled by modern ethnography enable us to understand much
more about such magical beliefs than was previously possible. Inspired by
E. E. Evans-Pritchard's pioneering work in the 1930s on witchcraft among
the Azande of South West Africa, numerous anthropologists have made
careful studies of witchcraft beliefs all over the world.[11] As a result of this
field work, we can now see many parallels between traditional Western
cultures and others elsewhere.

Medieval and early modern Europe shared with numerous other technologically primitive societies a conviction that unseen forces were re-

sponsible for everyday events. Not only cataclysms like wars, earthquakes, and epidemics, but also the basic conditions of life—weather, birth, illness, and death—were explained by recourse to occult (i.e., hidden) powers. It was widely believed that demonic spirits could withhold needed rainfall, turn milk sour or make the cow dry up, render women sterile and men impotent, and, in general, cause injury, disease, and death to humans, plants, and animals. In the absence of modern medicine, science, and technology, the world seemed filled with mysteries, and quite understandably these mysteries held terrors.[12]

In his monumental study of Western attitudes toward death, Philippe Ariès has pointed out the significance of linguistic variants on the themes of evil and the demonic.[13] In the Romance languages the words for misfortune, illness, and mishap stem from the same root, meaning evil or malign, that is the base of the word for devil. Thus, in French, *malheur*, *maladie*, and *malchance* are all related to the Latin *malum*, from which *le malin* (the word for devil) also is derived. All kinds of suffering were connected linguistically with the devil, the source of all evil. So, too, were the harmful actions of witches, actions known in Latin as *maleficia*, in English as *malefice*. Etymological evidence reinforces the conclusion that, learned or illiterate, nearly all Europeans before the mid-seventeenth century were convinced of the reality of malevolent demonic spirits who caused all manner of misery.

Indeed, every branch of Christianity denounced as heretical the opinion that there are no devils. But few espoused this deviant opinion, not primarily out of fear of religious sanctions, but because there was no other convincing way to explain reality. Whereas the citizens of advanced nations in the twentieth century can rely on a physician in the face of most threatening illnesses, the medicine of the age of the witch hunts was crippled by a mistaken theory inherited from the ancient Greeks. We have meteorology to explain such catastrophes as destructive hailstorms, but the peoples of past times could portray these events only in personal terms—as divine retribution for sin, instances of temptation meant to test the believer's faith, or the actions of evil demons.

Thus, the most important practical matter confronting premodern Europeans was how to protect themselves against environmental forces that constantly threatened to overwhelm them. Religion provided the leading defense against these terrors. Aside from opening the road to spiritual fulfillment for the pious, the Christian churches had a social function in reducing the level of personal and community fear. By availing himself of religious sacraments, prayers, and other rituals and by depending on his faith in God, the congregant believed himself armed against evil. Thus, the rite of baptism is in part an exorcism of demonic forces; the marriage ritual invokes the superior power of God for the protection of the couple; holy water can supplement human resources with divine guardianship; and prayer may offset human weakness with God's strength. These are just a few examples of the ways Christian practice sought to cope with the human sense of powerlessness in the face of threatened disaster.[14]

As a means of understanding and coping with evil, the concept of witchcraft had great appeal to people chronically subject to personal tragedy. Vulnerable as they were, victims often attributed the evils that befell them to the intervention of witches. In Western societies during the sixteenth and seventeenth centuries, most people regarded the witch as the malevolent human ally of ubiquitous demonic spirits. Witchcraft was a convenient way of explaining misfortune. Even more important, it was an explanation that offered the victim an apparent remedy: the witch could be executed.[15]

Certainly there were people in the age of the witch hunts, although perhaps not many, who tried to harm their neighbors through black magic. Thanks to the work of Keith Thomas and other scholars, we now know the importance of "white magic," that is, magic for good ends, in village life. Everywhere in Europe, wizards (also known as cunning folk, conjurers, or simply magicians) attempted to heal the sick, inspire love, foretell the future, and identify thieves so as to regain stolen property. In general, they filled roles now played by physicians, policemen, and social scientists. Conjurers were also hired by villagers to deal with threats to the local economy. They had rituals to get rid of locusts or vine pests and to chase away hailstorms. That these magicians often satisfied their clients will not surprise anyone who knows the effectiveness of a skillful attorney in elicit-ing a confession, of a physician in curing his patient's symptoms with a chemically worthless placebo, or of a futurologist in influencing govern-ment policy. No doubt magical practitioners drew on physiologically effec-tive herbal remedies in treating the sick. Above all, however, the confidence of the community in the magician's abilities contributed to his continuing reputation for success. His power was rooted primarily in his psychological mystique.[16]

Miraculous curative abilities were also ascribed to Christian figures whom religious tradition endowed with divine grace. Christ had healed the sick in biblical accounts, and the church's sacraments were seen as vehicles of God's mercy. There is much evidence connecting the spread of Christian-ity in the Roman empire to miraculous healing associated with saintly churchmen, notably St. Martin in Gaul. Christian converts who witnessed apparent resurrections and the disappearance of disease could not doubt the superiority of the new religion. In later centuries, too, the authority of the Christian churches rested in part on the supernatural attributes popularly attached to their symbols. Famous images and relics became the objects of pilgrimages to shrines associated with curative powers, as is still the case today in Catholic countries.[17]

Perhaps the most dramatic of magical healing rituals was the ceremony of the royal touch, practiced by French and English kings from the later Middle Ages until (in the French case) the early nineteenth century. Scrofula, now known to be a form of tuberculosis affecting the skin, was then regarded as the sacred disease, which monarchs could cure by touching the afflicted. The sacral nature of kingship, said to endow the ruler with divine powers, provided the theoretical underpinning for his curative technique. No one ever claimed infallible or immediate results for the royal touch. Thus, the remission of symptoms in a percentage of cases apparently sufficed to maintain belief.[18]

The royal touch was a special case of the general reverence for the curative potential of holy figures. In his observations on Spanish shrines, William A. Christian, Jr. captured the force of curative rituals built around the relics or images of saints:

> Orthodox theology and modern psychology would agree that on some level people must believe in a saint for the saint to cure them. Once they believe in a saint's power they will invoke it in time of need. And since in a certain percentage of cases they would be cured, freed, or spared (whether by divine intervention, luck, or the psychological boost of faith) these new graces or miracles were in a sense self-generating. An image built up a momentum of miraculousness.[19]

Similarly, belief in a witch's ability to do evil could give her real power. In popular belief the witch figure was the malignant opposite of the benign magician and Christian saint. The anthropological and medical literatures describe many cases of effective "witch's curses" in contemporary societies. These fully documented accounts show that psychosomatically induced symptoms ending even in death have resulted from the victim's conviction that he or she is bewitched. As Evans-Pritchard heard one Azande remark about the English visitors: "Perhaps in their country people are not murdered by witches, but here they are."[20]

In fact, however, such instances of suggestion are not limited to "primitive" cultures. This much is clear from recent cases, in the United States and similar advanced countries, that physicians and psychologists have treated successfully by using faith healers, voodoo practitioners, and other experts in traditional cures. One particularly well-attested case of this kind was reported by doctors at Vanderbilt University Hospital in the early 1970s. A young woman, convinced that her mother-in-law could cast spells, developed regional enteritis after a falling-out with her husband's family. She became certain that she was under a curse of death. Unresponsive to conventional medical therapy, the patient lost weight rapidly until she was taken to a Baptist preacher, who read her biblical passages about the casting out of devils and told her the Lord's power was the greatest of all. After this religious encounter, the young woman began a quick recovery and soon gave up the conviction that she had been hexed.[21]

The victim of supposed witchcraft today has access to both modern medicine and religious cures. The very existence of medical science is enough to create at least a sense of ambivalence about witchcraft in the victim, and this doubt in itself can mitigate the effects of a supposed bewitchment. But no such alternate system of belief was available in the age of the witch hunts. A personalized view of nature, combined with medical ignorance, made it seem that disease and other disasters had a supernatural origin and hence would respond only to supernatural treatment. Although most Protestants came to reject the Catholic rite of exorcism as itself a kind of magic and substituted the remedies of prayer, fasting, and other testimonies to faith, both groups agreed about the reality and powers of witches.[22] During the age of the witch trials, consciousness of witches' ability to wreak havoc in society became extraordinarily intense. Religious remedies did not apply to every malefice and in any case were not considered absolutely infallible. The only certain way to destroy a witch's power was to kill her.

By the sixteenth century, European learned traditions had come to associate malefice with devil worship, resulting in the concept of the witch as a sabbat-attending, Satan-adoring woman who did evil as proof of her rejection of Christianity. The folk magic of the village sorcerer may always have been a source of community anxiety, but this anxiety produced very few trials until the end of the Middle Ages. Only when educated people connected such sorcery with heretical activities did the witch stereotype mature and the witch craze begin. Within the last decade, several scholars have shown how the educated interpreted tales of village malefice in terms of the elites' concept of devil-worshiping heresy. Elite groups- –lawyers and judges, theologians and other clerics, physicians and philosophers, rulers and wealthy landowners—were the ones who vigorously asserted the reality of cults devoted to Satan. By transmitting their fears to the uneducated majority, the authorities transformed the traditional popular suspicion of harmful magic into terror of devil worshipers. Each for their own reasons, then, the learned and the illiterate combined to prosecute and burn thousands for witchcraft.[23]

A preoccupation with heresy was at the foundation of the witch hunts, but the matter is not that simple. Although Christian heresy is as old as Christianity itself, the period of the witch hunts was of much shorter duration. Only a special definition of heresy, one that pictured women as Satan's sexual servants, could have inspired the repressions of the witch hunts. Despite the well-documented four-to-one preponderance of women among accused witches, up to now the sexual dimensions of witch hunting have not been a central concern of witchcraft scholarship. In the chapters that follow, one of the main themes is this sexual linkage and its context in early modern ideological and cultural change. Such an approach requires an investigation of the social psychology of this age, in which fear of malefice and fantasies of the sabbat created the phenomenon of witchcraft. This approach to the study of witch hunting, combining the political and the anthropological, supplies the general interpretive framework of the book.

The witch trials, like the recurrent persecutions of such minorities as Jews, homosexuals, and groups labeled heretical, are an instance of the deep intolerance and hatred that have surfaced repeatedly over the centuries in Western civilization. As John Boswell has observed in his pioneering account of gay people in medieval Europe, "it seems to have been fatally easy throughout most of Western history to explain catastrophe as the result of the evil machinations of some group distinct from the majority; and even when no specific connection could be suggested, angry or anxious peoples have repeatedly vented their negative emotions on the odd, the idiosyncratic, and the statistically deviant."[24] But the witch craze differs in a crucial way from other episodes of persecution involving racial minorities, religious or national groups, despised social classes, and people with unorthodox sexual tastes. Majority cultures have frequently ascribed responsibility for social disaster to heretics, blacks, homosexuals, Jews, and others. Everyone is now familiar with the stereotyping process whereby habits regarded as distasteful and dangerous are associated with such categories of outcasts, even in supposedly sophisticated industrial societies. Preposterous as such beliefs are, they at least bear a marginal relationship to reality, in that they concern existing groups of people. Medieval Christian heretics, for example, did not eat babies, as their Catholic detractors alleged, but there were heretics in the Middle Ages. In modern times, Jewish bankers have not organized a worldwide Zionist conspiracy, but there are Jews in banking and Zionism is a reality.

The witch stereotype, however, was a fantasy in an even deeper sense. It referred to an almost entirely imaginary phenomenon. Scholarship has unearthed no groups of devil worshipers and few individuals who spontaneously saw themselves as servants of Satan. The original witch hunts had even less relationship to reality than do the modern investigations named after them, such as the search for nearly nonexistent American defectors to communism. Everywhere the term "witches" appears in this book it should be imagined in quotation marks, to imply that the label derives only from the accusers.

Until the twentieth century, it could be argued plausibly that the witch craze was the most sustained and statistically the greatest instance of mass persecution in Western history. The fantastical witch stereotype that was the foundation for thousands of trials and executions must have rested on deep and persistent conflicts, with obscure origins hidden in the human psyche. The overwhelming predominance of women among the accused strongly suggests that such psychological conflicts may have been based in large part on sexual fears. Unfortunately, the historian of the witch hunts is not very well equipped to investigate these mysteries, as he must deal with people who can no longer be interviewed, with societies that have since been transformed, and with cultures whose ways of understanding the world are very different from ours. There is an ever-present danger of reading today's conventional wisdom back into an utterly different past. All interpretations should be taken as tentative and provisional when they concern so elusive a problem. Marc Bloch's general observation about the historian's need to draw out the testimony of the past applies directly to the task of interpreting the witch hunts: "A document is like a witness; and like most witnesses, it does not say much except under cross-examination. The real difficulty lies in putting the right questions."[25] To many of the questions posed in the following chapters, the only honest response is that we do not know enough to be certain of an answer. The most that can be hoped is that we have learned to ask appropriate questions.

In the deepest sense, the witch hunts raise issues that go beyond the historian's power—or the power of rational discourse—to explain. The nature of human fear, the origins of intolerance, and the persistence of evil are matters that our crude intellectual constructs cannot fully encompass. Yet, although we still know very little about the witch craze, we know much more than earlier generations did. This knowledge, incomplete as it is, may yet be useful, especially because, although the witch panics stopped long ago, the persecution of other despised groups shows no signs of abating.

2

Medieval Witches

Dissenters and Demons

Witch trials were virtually unknown until the final centuries of the Middle Ages. Through most of the medieval era, churchmen generally held that anyone who believed women went flying about at night was a victim of superstition. But, even as these assertions became formalized in influential collections of the church's canon law, the foundation on which they rested was slowly eroded in the course of the medieval Catholic encounter with nonconformists whom the church perceived to be dangerous deviants.

Jews, heretics, homosexuals, and magicians were among the most important of the nonconforming groups. From the twelfth century on, outsiders came under increasing verbal and physical attack from churchmen, allied secular authorities, and, particularly in the case of Jews, from the lower strata of the population. In the early Middle Ages, a more easygoing acceptance of social diversity had usually been the norm. After 1100, however, new patterns of enmity quickly emerged, and a climate of fear and hostility became frozen into place. Not until the end of the seventeenth century, when ancient hatreds receded somewhat, did a few areas of Western culture temporarily abandon the stress on social conformity and unanimity of belief. But, by the time of this decline in preoccupation with unconventional behavior, the witch craze had run its course.

From this perspective, the six centuries from about 1100 to 1700 can be considered as a unit. Charges that early in the period were directed against heretics, homosexuals, Jews, and magicians were later applied in modified form to people labeled as witches. The dynamics of fear and fantasy were similar early and late, but this is not simply a case of parallelism. There were strong connections between the persecutions of these medieval outsiders and the victimizations of the witch craze. The stereotype of the witch grew directly from the menacing images associated with medieval nonconformists. By the time the witch craze began in the mid-sixteenth century, authorities on demonology had mixed a recipe for witchcraft concocted from parts of the stereotypes long applied to medieval dissenters. The following pages trace this development in the witch craze's medieval prehistory. This chapter is intended to set the stage for investigating the witch craze itself.

Just why pervasive intolerance emerged as medieval civilization approached its cultural and material apex is one of the biggest mysteries in the history of the Middle Ages. A suggestive hypothesis ties intolerance to widespread anxiety caused by a sudden increase in the pace of economic, political, and cultural change after a long period of relative stability.[1] But, if the deeper origins of intolerance remain obscure, the more immediate triggers of hostility are fairly clear. Beginning in the twelfth century, religion seemed to take on a heightened sense of immediacy for many people, and spiritual expression reflected the believer's personal relationship with the leading figures of the Christian faith. Strong feelings of devotion to God inspired perhaps the greatest achievement of medieval civilization, the construction of scores of magnificent churches built by broad community efforts in the newly invented Gothic style. In the sculpture adorning these churches, portrayals of Christ came to depict not the distant, enthroned judge of the early Christian centuries but an emotional, human figure suffering on the cross. Mary, a relatively minor personage in earlier iconography, now emerged in the crucial role of chief intercessor with God, while many artists emphasized her warm, maternal character. These changes indicate that Christian teaching was gaining greater meaning for ordinary men and women.[2]

There was, however, an ugly side to this upsurge in religious emotion. It ended the traditions of pluralism that had characterized the medieval world before the twelfth century. Crusade-minded clerics inspired their audiences to fervent expression of inner belief, often with destructive results for those outside the Christian fold. A more personal spiritual style made it harder to accept the presence of nonbelievers and nonconformists. Jews were among the first to experience the effects of this newly powerful spirit of intolerance. After centuries of relative tranquillity, the Jewish communities of Western Europe experienced repeated outbreaks of mob violence beginning at the time of the First Crusade in the 1090s. The propaganda campaigns that urged crusaders to set off for Jerusalem ignited great bursts of fervor among those who stayed at home. Fifty years later came the first medieval instance of a charge that would persist through the centuries: a family of French Jews was accused of sacrificing a Christian child. From the mid-thirteenth century, Christians began to accuse Jews of desecrating the host. Eventually, popular hatred was transformed into official persecution, as Jews found themselves compelled to wear the yellow star or other distinctive dress. The logical culmination was expulsion, and the Jewish residents of England and the kingdom of France were exiled accordingly in the years around 1300.[3]

The Jews were not the only minority group to come under attack in this period. Homosexuality, widely accepted and apparently widely practiced in twelfth-century Europe, was regularly condemned by theologians and penalized in the legal codes of the later Middle Ages. Typical was the change in English law. Twelfth-century English legal documents did not mention homosexuality when listing sexual offenses. But a hundred years later the royal law grouped gay people, significantly, with arsonists, heretics, sorcerers, and Jews as criminals deserving horrible execution.[4] The decline of tolerance for people of differing beliefs—spiritual as well as sexual—became one of the defining characteristics of late medieval Europe. As we will see, heretics and witches were regularly charged with homosexuality and other departures from sexual norms. They also were said to attend devilish "synagogues" or witches' sabbats at which they practiced infanticide and trampled on the host. A generalized image of the dissenter slowly took shape and expanded to incorporate many kinds of unconventional behavior.

The missionary fervor that inspired campaigns against Muslim or Jewish infidels and sexual nonconformists also was directed against Christian heretics. A persistent mood of intolerance inevitably focused attention on minority religious sects. Ironically, the same ideals that inspired Catholic spiritual renewal fostered the growth of elements that the church labeled as dissident. The so-called Waldensian heretics, for example, took vows of poverty and, after their excommunication in 1181, denounced the Catholic clergy for its material wealth and worldliness. Regarding themselves as the only true followers of Christ, various Waldensian communities persisted in France, the Low Countries, Germany, Switzerland, and Italy for the next three hundred years, despite intermittent and sometimes vigorous persecution. Another heretical group, the Cathars or Albignesians, was centered in southern France and northern Italy. Cathars ("pure ones") took the dualistic implications of Christianity to the extreme, maintaining that only things of the spirit were godly and that the material world was the creation of the devil. The Cathar doctrine drew on Hindu and Buddhist influences in its concepts of reincarnation and animal soul, but its major component was a revival of the Manichean heresy that had been very prominent in the first centuries of the Christian era. The political base of the Cathars was destroyed in the early thirteenth century after a war conducted by the French monarchy with papal backing, but fear of dualistic heresy remained embedded in clerical consciousness long afterward.[5]

The dominant ideology of later medieval civilization justified these violent reactions to heretical movements. The culture of the Middle Ages was constructed on deep religious foundations. Religion explained the individual's destiny; it also told him how to live. Religious authority underlay all social and political arrangements. Further, the hierarchical order of things—in the family, the state, and the cosmos—depended for legitimacy on essentially religious justifications. A challenge to religious authority, then, was supremely dangerous. In the view of nearly all theologians and men of power from the thirteenth century onward, the heretic threatened not only the Catholic church, but all of society. Thus, religious dissidence implied political and social subversion, and heretics were often charged with treason against God and man. As the ultimate criminal, a heretic was deemed to have turned his back on humanity and divinity both.[6]

The proliferation of sects that divided reality into separate categories, one divine and the other demonic, reflects the rising awareness of the devil after 1200. Persecution of such dualistic sects by Catholic authorities in turn reinforced this preoccupation with Satan, for churchmen regarded their opponents as servants of the devil. Cathars were said to worship Satan, and Waldensians allegedly murdered and devoured babies as part of their demonically inspired rites. A papal bull of 1233, *Vox in Rama*, issued against German heretics by Gregory IX, depicts a devil worshiper's initiation ceremony, in which are featured huge toads, half-human and half-feline creatures, and incestuous orgies. The tragically ironic precedents for these wild fantasies about heretical activity were identically defamatory canards circulated against early Christians in ancient Rome and preserved in monastic manuscripts through the centuries.[7] But, no matter how baseless, such stories persisted in the late medieval world. Deviant groups of all kinds found themselves accused of trafficking with the devil. The preoccupation with Satan that developed at this time paved the way for witch trials.

What was the image of the devil in Christian tradition?[8] Satan had played only a very minor role in the Old Testament, appearing in the prologue to the book of Job as a cynical wagerer and in Chronicles as a source of temptation. These late books of the Jewish scriptures depart to some degree from the consistent theme of the earlier works, that one omnipotent and just God is responsible for all that happens, both the good and the bad. Possibly as a result of the influence of dualist Zoroastrian beliefs that originated in Persia and spread through the Hellenistic world, the Jews of Jesus' time were thoroughly familiar with the concept of Satan as the tempter who induced humans to sin. In the books of the Apocrypha, a colorful array of demons appears as tormentors of the faithful. These beings were said to have descended from the union of lusting angels with the daughters of men in the period just after the creation of the world. By the time of the New Testament's composition, Satan had been elevated to the status of prince over these demons, the ruler of a kingdom of darkness. In fact, the Christian books of the Bible see him as nothing less than the personification of the principle of evil. No longer is he the simple "adversary" of God—which is the meaning of the Hebrew common noun *satan*, always preceded by the definite article in the Jewish scriptures. Christ's kingdom and Satan's were now cast as polar opposites in a struggle of cosmic dimensions.

During the first three centuries of the Christian era, the picture of Satan grew steadily clearer. He became associated with the serpent in the garden of Eden and thus took on the responsibility for the fall of man and original sin. His own fall now was placed before the creation and was said to have resulted from an unsuccessful revolt of dissident angels in heaven. As punishment for their rebelliousness, Satan and his followers, here identified as the demons of Apocryphal tradition, were cast out of heaven and condemned to pursue their "wickedness in high places" (the phrase is St. Paul's) in the air just above the earth. This account of the fall of Satan and the demons partially superseded, though it did not fully obliterate, the earlier tradition of miscegenation between lascivious angels and lustful human females.

Despite this crystallization of demonic concepts, the early church did not exhibit the obsessive dread of the devil that later appeared. Fully expecting Christ's imminent return and the final victory of God's kingdom, churchmen stressed the powerlessness of demons against Christians. Thus, in fourth-century Gaul, St. Martin had only to put his fingers in the mouth of a possessed cook to compel the offending demon's departure.[9] As the centuries passed and the Second Coming remained only a hope, Satan and demons took on a more menacing appearance. By the central Middle Ages they were imagined as dangerous tempters and destroyers of body and soul.

In accounts preserved by clerical writers, the devil murdered the innocent and lured people into renouncing their allegiance to God. When he appeared in human form, the devil was said to be a Moor or a black, figures of revulsion in European eyes. Even more frequent was Satan's embodiment in frightening animal shapes. In the twelfth-century reliefs at Conques, the devil appears as a grotesque mass of repulsive body parts: there could be no mistaking the demonic nature of this figure. But, in later centuries, portrayals of the devil endowed him with more subtlety. Many times they showed him taking on the figure of a beautiful young man or woman.

In this attractive guise, the devil was believed to mate with human beings. The male form of such a demon was called an incubus, the female form a succubus. It even was believed that the union of an incubus with a mortal woman could produce children. No less an authority than St. Thomas Aquinas ingeniously explained that a demon wishing to generate a child first transformed himself into a succubus in order to receive human seed, and then became an incubus to implant it in a woman. (This belief no doubt accounts for the fear of incubi among jealous husbands; in accord with the principles of the double standard, much less horror was attached to unions of men with succubi.) Especially fearsome was the ability of demons to invade the human body and possess it, thereby forcing the victim into uncontrollable sin. Several thirteenth-century sources tell of episodes of possession in nunneries and monasteries that prevented the fulfillment of religious duties.

In the terror of these stories the new character of the demonic image is readily apparent. Norman Cohn summarized the change as follows: "The accent has shifted, unmistakably, since the days of the early Church. Now the stress is all on the ubiquity and resourcefulness of demons, the relative helplessness of human beings. Demons are always around us and in our midst, and their cunning is infinite. . . . Indeed, a demon is such a dangerous being that only an exceptionally virtuous person can see or touch one without suffering serious harm."[10] The clerical elite was becoming more aware of Satan's protean guile. Eventually this fear was transmitted to other social groups and provided a crucial prop for witch trials.

During the later Middle Ages, the relationship of demon to human was transformed. Satan and his subordinates had long been pictured as the enemies not only of humanity but also of each individual. For the idea of witchcraft to evolve, it remained for humans to be cast as associates of Satan, themselves bringing temptation, causing destruction, inducing possession, and copulating with the devil. These attributes of what later came to be called witchcraft were first ascribed by churchmen to various groups of heretics. The Catholic reaction to heresy produced a horrifying stereotype that resembled later charges against witches.

How did the terrible image of the heretic develop? To understand this, we should consider the chief institutional response of the church to the challenge of heresy, the Inquisition.[11] Organized under papal authority in the second half of the thirteenth century and staffed in large part by members of the newly founded Dominican order, the Inquisition was the church court that dealt with the crime of heresy. It employed fashionable practices of Roman law, then undergoing revival, including secret sessions and indefinite detention before trial. Defense attorneys were uncommon, the right of appeal practically nonexistent, and, since in theory the Church was initiating the charge, the prisoner had no way either of confronting the person who accused him or of calling and cross-examining witnesses. Testimony about heresy, unlike other crimes, was taken from perjurers, excommunicates, and convicted felons, not to mention individuals who might have harbored a grudge against the accused. By far the most decisive practice of Roman law adopted by the Inquisition, however, was the use of torture to elicit confessions, a subject to be discussed fully in a later chapter.

Eventually this "inquisitorial method" of criminal investigation (from which the Inquisition derived its name) was adopted by most European secular courts. The techniques first used against medieval heretics became the norm in prosecutions of all malefactors, including those accused of witchcraft. The widespread influence of its procedural methods attests to the effectiveness of the Inquisition as an institutional response to the threat of medieval religious dissent.

By producing numerous confessions to such practices as devil worship and sexual deviance, the Inquisition made these charges ever more plausible. In this light, it is not difficult to see how the stereotypical picture of the heretic fed on itself in the later Middle Ages. The inquisitorial judges' preconceived ideas about heresy conditioned their interrogations of suspects. A liberal use of torture enabled them to elicit confessions, thereby reconfirming their assumptions about the crimes of religious dissidents. Thus, by the fifteenth century, the notion of devil-worshiping heretics was deeply imprinted on the imagination of European authorities.

An early set of trials exhibiting many characteristics of the later witch panics took place in France just after 1300, when King Philip IV and his ministers used inquisitorial techniques to destroy the crusading order of the Knights Templar. At the opening of the fourteenth century, the Templars were the wealthiest and probably the most powerful religious order in Europe, but Philip brought them down in a remarkably short time with allegations of blasphemy, devil worship, and homosexuality. Most historians dismiss these charges as totally false. Yet Philip's servants successfully

used confessions extracted by torture to justify the execution and imprisonment of the leading knights. The order was disbanded and its large land-
holdings in France were confiscated by the crown.[12]

By 1300, educated people had learned to associate heretics with prohibited sexual practices and secret rituals devoted to Satan. Such charges
already had been laid against dissident religious groups for well over a
hundred years. Like the Cathars and the Waldensians, the Templars were
subjected to accusations that, as Malcolm Barber put it, had been "part of
the stock apparatus of propaganda used for centuries by church and state to
discredit religious and political opponents."[13] Such charges remained extraordinarily potent long after the Templars' fall. Accusations lodged again
and again, far from arousing a skepticism from overuse, actually drew
strength from repetition. Although those who extorted false confessions
from the Templars perhaps knew the knights' admissions were phony,
stories of the order's crimes were passed on for centuries and were accepted
as accurate accounts. In this way, the Templars' destruction became a
cautionary tale for learned Europeans of later times. The educated became
accustomed to hearing about heretics who practiced secret rites, trampled
on the crucifix and spit out the host, engaged in forbidden forms of sex, and
worshiped an evil master. These same charges were later lodged against
supposed witches in the panics of the sixteenth and seventeenth centuries.

Thus, between 1100 and 1300, elements that later formed the
stereotype of the witch emerged in the European consciousness. But there
were no witch trials as such during this period. After 1300, explicit accusations of witchcraft began to appear. For the next two centuries the image of
the witch grew in complexity and in fearful immediacy. By 1500, we can
find most features of the mature witchcraft theory that provided the underpinning for the massive craze of the period from about 1560 to 1680. Before
turning to the witch trials and witch theory of the later Middle Ages, we
need to consider the origins and outward manifestations of anxiety that
provided the social context for the genesis of witchcraft mythology.

Death and Disease

The most dramatic symptom of psychological distress in the fourteenth
and fifteenth centuries was an obsession with the theme of death. Scholars
have frequently commented on the deep anxieties about mortality that
permeated the religious culture of late medieval Europe. Preoccupation
with death, as expressed in sermons, literature, and the visual arts, betrayed

the profound struggle of many individuals to find some meaning in their existence. Of course, the fear of death is a universal human trait, and fear in a general way may be regarded as a biological necessity without which no individual or species could long survive. But when ordinary instinctual fright becomes an intense and constant dread, we are in the presence of something different, a cultural phenomenon of variable but potentially dramatic impact.

The anxiety that spread through Europe in the later Middle Ages was partly based on the trauma inflicted by the bubonic plague pandemic. From 1347 onward, the Black Death paid repeated visits to most parts of the continent, with devastating results. At least 20 percent of Europe's estimated population of seventy million disappeared in the first onslaught, and the plague returned roughly once each generation for the rest of the fourteenth century.[14] Over the next three hundred years, sporadic but potent outbreaks of plague were a regular feature of European life, particularly in the towns, where lived large numbers of the flea-bearing rats through which the disease was transmitted. In his diary entries for 1665, Samuel Pepys recorded the last major London outbreak of plague, when about 68,000 died. Only after the Marseilles epidemic of 1720 did large-scale plague episodes finally disappear from Western Europe.

Intense panic accompanied outbreaks of the plague. All who could deserted the disease-ridden cities, evading the desperate quarantine measures imposed by officials. While food shortages, looting, and violence afflicted the abandoned, stricken towns, country-dwellers attempted to drive off the dangerously infectious hordes of emigrants. When plague epidemics struck, even the closest social ties might break down: "Then all friends leave us," said a preacher, "then a man or a woman is a stranger to the breath of his own relations. . . . If a man be sick of the plague then he sits and lies all alone."[15]

Of course, medieval Europe had known onslaughts of disease and death long before the arrival of plague. But this new pestilence provoked extraordinary terror. It could take a victim in a day. The calamitous numbers of dead had to be dumped into mass graves before the bodies putrified. The Black Death aroused mass penitential fervor of unprecedented dimensions. Severe psychological trauma led to various forms of extreme behavior, as many turned their pain inward. Some succumbed to a frenzied, trance-like state: groups of people from all social classes were seized by uncontrollable fits of agonized and prolonged dancing. Saint Vitus's dance, as it was known in the north, or tarantism, as Italians called it, swept across large parts of Europe in the wake of the plague. Even more widespread were groups of flagellants who abandoned their homes to wander as pilgrims, voluntarily submitting themselves to regular whippings that sometimes led to death. This type of extreme masochism was new to Christian devotion. Like those suffering from the dance mania, the practitioners of ritual whipping were presumably giving witness to the heavy weight of anxiety and guilt that the plague epidemic left as a bitter legacy to those who survived.[16]

The flagellants were soon condemned by church leaders, who found them impossible to control. Official disapproval hastened their disappearance within a few years after 1350. Outbreaks of tarantism faded more slowly, but eventually they declined too, except in southern Italy, where they occur to this day. For the Jewish communities of Germany, however, the Black Death produced permanent effects. Plague infestations were the occasion for over three hundred massacres of various dimensions, attacks that virtually wiped out the original centers of Ashkenazic Jewish culture. Church authorities explained the Black Death as a scourge sent by God from the treasure of his wrath. But ordinary people apparently felt a strong need for human scapegoats, if only to relieve themselves of the sense of personal guilt that the scourge explanation inevitably entailed. Instead of manifesting psychic stress in such self-destructive expressions as dance frenzy or flagellation, many found a release by externalizing their agony in physical violence directed not at themselves but against a despised minority.

Jews were accused of spreading plague by poisoning the well water, a charge so patently absurd that medical experts and prominent churchmen of the time, including Pope Clement VI, had no trouble refuting it in their many public letters denouncing this popular belief. But, in cities where lawlessness and chaos reigned in the plague's aftermath, the mobs, often whipped up by fiery preachers, were motivated by fear and hate, not cold logic. In Germany, massacres of Jews spread with the plague. Groups were herded into wooden buildings that were set to the torch, walled up in their houses and left to die of suffocation or starvation, or publicly burned in mass executions. On occasion bodies were stuffed into wine casks before being floated down the Rhine. The massacres waned with the plague's passing; by 1351 both had disappeared. But popular violence against Jews had long-term historical importance, as most of the remaining members of Germany's Jewish communities moved east and reestablished themselves in the more tranquil environment of Slavic Europe, which became the center of Ashkenazic culture until the twentieth-century Holocaust.[17]

The catastrophe of the Black Death did not lead directly to widespread witchcraft accusations. When plague first struck, the stereotype of the witch was not yet fully formed. The village sorceress of folk tradition still lacked the diabolical image that might make credible her responsibility for societal calamity. The image of the Jew as Christ-killer and enemy of God, however, nurtured for centuries in the majority culture, made Jews seem believable agents of evil on a cosmic scale. So universal a catastrophe as the Black Death seemed to necessitate an appropriately all-encompassing evil force. The stereotype of the Jew was well suited to fill this bill. Witches, however, rarely played so grand a role. Even at the height of the craze, witches were accused most often of crimes against particular individuals, not of monumental onslaughts against humanity as a whole. Throughout the era of the witch trials, universal disasters such as plagues and wars were seldom attributed to witches. Instead, witchcraft came into play in explaining more personal kinds of misfortune, in which the victim could imagine himself singled out for especially bad treatment. As most victims of witch prosecutions were weak and socially insignificant, the imaginations of their accusers apparently could not encompass the attribution to them of mass destruction.[18] It was otherwise for Jews, who seem to have been cast as a powerful group in Christian popular imagination. But Jews shared with witches and Christian heretics the roles of dreaded outsiders and enemies of society.

Persecution of their Jewish neighbors was the most destructive result of the anxieties afflicting the Christian masses in the later Middle Ages. These killings certainly reveal a society filled with anguish and fear. The onset of plague, however, cannot adequately explain the depth of this anger. Instead, a far more plausible hypothesis is that the Black Death brought to the surface tensions that had long been building. The plague disaster was so obviously cataclysmic that it tends to act as a kind of explanatory magnet for historians, drawing them to attribute all evidence of late medieval social and psychological dislocations to the stresses induced by the plague. Yet in literature and the visual arts there is a pattern of continuous development that began long before 1350 and persisted for at least another century and a half.

A deep concern with and pervasive fear of death was a discernible pattern of European cultural life from the twelfth century onward, particularly among society's upper classes. The plague pandemic reinforced this fear but did not initiate it. Philippe Ariès, in his subtle and comprehensive analysis of changing attitudes toward death, attributes this preoccupation to the rise of individualism in the prosperous, increasingly materialistic society of late medieval Europe. Concern with "one's own death," as distinct from death as the common destiny, began to emerge among well-off people after 1100. Individual tombs, complete with lifelike sculptures and death masks, became common for the first time, supplanting the anonymous graves, ossuaries, and charnel houses of the early Middle Ages. Sometimes images of skulls, skeletons, and gruesomely realistic portrayals of the ravages death inflicted on the corpse accompanied these elaborate tombs.

As the macabre gained hold over the artistic imagination, the motif of the worm-ridden cadaver became a frequent subject of poetry and other literary forms. The stress on the macabre in art was something new. The same sensibility was also expressed in the creation of two novel artistic genres, the danse macabre and the triumph of death. Both depicted a world in which death comes unpredictably and without warning, perversely striking down the young and the vigorous while sparing the sick and the crippled who yearn for death's release. Skeletal figures of death lead the dance or preside over the festive parade marking death's triumph. They escort people of all social classes, each one the equal of all the other victims at the hour of his death.[19]

As "the undiscovered country, from whose bourn no traveler returns," death was a source of deep personal anxiety for an elite that had good reason to love the material pleasures of this world but knew that riches and goods must be abandoned to achieve heavenly reward. The consequent tension between individual aspiration, a hallmark of late medieval and Renaissance values, and traditional Christian ascetic morality produced profound ambivalence, guilt, and a pervasive sense of sinfulness. The intense sadness that Jan Huizinga found in northern European culture as the Middle Ages waned is one indicator of the novel conflicts confronting the upper classes of this time. No longer could such people regard death with equanimity, for death had become something other than what it had seemed in the past (and what it still seemed to most common folk): a natural, welcome passing from an unpleasant earthly life. The extinction of the body evoked profound concern in people now highly conscious of their individuality. Death came to represent the failure that striving Renaissance man most feared. Loving life, Ariès wrote, the upper-class individual "was very acutely conscious that he had merely been granted a stay of execution, that this delay would be a brief one, and that death was always present within him, shattering his ambitions and poisoning his pleasures." The lament of Capulet at Juliet's death echoed the theme of sudden tragedy long familiar in Renaissance arts and letters:

> All things that we ordained festival
> Turn from their office to black funeral:

> Our instruments to melancholy bells;
> Our wedding cheer to a sad burial feast;
> Our solemn hymns to sullen dirges change;
> Our bridal flowers serve for a buried corse,
> And all things change them to the contrary.[20]

The fear of death was not simply fear of the material extinction and decomposition of the body. The fate of the soul became an issue evoking deep dread. The afterlife had not seemed a problem in the early Middle Ages, when images of the Second Coming of Christ portrayed the resurrection of all the dead and the universal elevation of the faithful to heaven. Beginning in the twelfth century, however, to the indiscriminate gathering in of all Christian souls was added a new note, the theme of the Last Judgment, at which Christ redeems the saved but consigns the damned to hell. The increasing importance of hell in the late medieval imagination gave the fear of death its underlying theme of anguish and despair. A prominent topic of preachers' sermons was the torture awaiting the damned, and Dante's vision of the inferno differed from numerous others primarily in its superior literary qualities.

A prayer to the Virgin that the fifteenth-century poet François Villon wrote for his illiterate mother captures the compound of theological pulpit language and the simple human emotions of faith and fear that were the essence of late medieval religious expression: "I am a little poor woman who knows nothing. Who's never read a word. In my parish church I see a painting of paradise, where there are harps and lutes. And of hell too, where the damned boil. One fills me with fear, the other with joy and delight. Grant me that joy, high Goddess."[21]

At a somewhat higher cultural level, the *artes moriendi*, a literary genre giving instructions on the art of a good death, was one of the most important kinds of devotional literature in the first generations of printing. In these works, the Last Judgment at the end of days became transferred to the moment of one's death. The dying man lies in his bedroom, tempted by demons to renounce God and place his faith in the devil's promises of material reward. The Christian must win his salvation by forsaking the devilish things of this world and actively choosing God. Ariès neatly summarized the change: "The last ordeal has replaced the Last Judgment." As it did for Mother Villon, redemption for the dying in the *artes moriendi* usually came after a vision of Mary or another saint.[22]

The menacing figure of the devil loomed over not only the deathbed but also every phase of Christian life in late medieval and Renaissance times. In the culture of the elites, the devil was identified with moral lapses, and, since his temptations were omnipresent, his threat was deemed very great. Reflecting upper-class anxieties about the inevitability of failure, clerical culture in particular had become preoccupied with the role of the devil in the world. Through their sermons, the paintings and sculpture they commissioned, and the new media of woodcuts and printed books that appeared after 1450, churchmen sought to impress on the masses a sense of the overwhelming and dreadful power of Satan. Evil was not to be considered simply a physical fact but also a moral category, identified with the demonic hosts. Thus, misfortune was an effect of sin, and the avoidance of sin—or rejection of the devil—became a moral decision that the church could help each individual to make and sustain. In emphasizing the power of Christianity against the devil, religious leaders conveyed the message that the world is controllable and potential misfortune can be avoided. The sacraments and other rituals of the church were the outward forms with whose help a believer might achieve salvation or at least peace of mind.[23]

Magic and Malefice

The characteristics of late medieval life just described—anxiety about death, virulent epidemics, fear of Satan, mass movements devoted to physical violence inflicted on the self or directed at hated minorities, the resurgence of dissident religious doctrines—all helped to create an environment favorable to belief in the evil power of witches. Slowly, over the course of the fourteenth and fifteenth centuries, there emerged something new in the European consciousness, the widespread conviction that humans in league with demonic forces were threatening good Christian people. To explain this development, we should consider the opinions and practices of the European elites, which included high churchmen and judges, as well as the beliefs characteristic of folk culture. Witchcraft theory—demonology— and witch trials emerged from the encounter of the elites and the folk of late medieval Europe.

In the later Middle Ages there was an upsurge in concern about maleficent sorcery. The attitude of the church on this subject had been set as early as the fifth century, when St. Augustine maintained that malefice could indeed be effective, thanks to the supernatural assistance that demons made available to humans. Augustine saw bodily harm and property destruction carried out through malefice as a form of magic. In this he was following Roman law, which imposed the death sentence on people who intentionally caused harm by conjuring evil spirits with a curse or spell. But Augustine went beyond Roman law when he also denounced other, nondestructive magical activities. To him no magic was benign, because magical arts depended on the devil's aid. Even such apparently harmless practices as the wearing of amulets to ward off evil, the casting of horoscopes, and the use of incantations for healing Augustine condemned as demonic in nature.[24]

With the revival of learning that began in the twelfth century, this latter kind of ritual or ceremonial magic rapidly gained a large following among the educated. Learned men read about magical practices in the recently rediscovered works of the ancient world, and many felt the urge to experiment with magical formulas. This development, combined with the negative reaction of religious authorities to the growing popularity of magic among the educated, helped produce the stereotypical patterns of witchcraft prosecution.

It is not easy to recapture in a scientific age the attraction that magic held for the learned of late medieval Europe. When we find rulers routinely employing court astrologers as late as the first decades of the seventeenth century—after Kepler and Galileo had published their findings about the heavens—it requires an effort of the imagination to explain the force that the occult exerted on the minds of educated Europeans. The key point is that magic was a way of making sense of the universe. Magic was a serious, learned, and practical undertaking; there was nothing frivolous about its pursuit. To a considerable degree, magic fulfilled the social role that science plays in the modern world. Donald J. Wilcox illustrated the practical impact of occult science by pointing to the role of astrology and nature magic in the treatment of illness:

> If a student suffering from tension and exhaustion goes to a twentieth-century doctor, he will most likely be advised to relax, take a vacation, get out in the country, perhaps have an affair. A fifteenth-century *magus* (as practicing magicians were called) would have hardly offered a different prescription, though the reasoning behind his suggested cure would be quite different. The magus would explain to the overworked student that his affliction was caused by the profound influence of Saturn, the planet associated both with intellectual activity and with melancholy. He should therefore avoid animals, plants, and people belonging to Saturn and instead surround himself with things belonging to the cheerful and life-giving heavenly bodies, which are the sun, Jupiter, and Venus. Among things associated with these planets are gold, green, flowers like roses and crocuses, and of course love. Therefore the patient should depart for the country to surround himself with green and flowers, take a vacation to spend some gold, and have an affair.[25]

Magic, then, was a system through which a threatening and mysterious universe might be understood and even controlled. As nearly everyone, from the highly educated to the illiterate, believed in the existence of demons and other invisible spirits, there was no framework available on which to build an effective attack on the philosophy of the occult. In fact, interest in magic developed dramatically among the most advanced thinkers of the age, the Renaissance humanists of fourteenth- and fifteenth-century Italy.

The humanists' revival of the Platonic world-view was probably the most important contribution to the growth of philosophical interest in the occult during the later Middle Ages. Neoplatonism, as taught by the Florentines Marsilio Ficino and Giovanni Pico della Mirandola, among others, portrayed a universe composed of wholly interdependent elements. From the minerals of the ground to God the Creator, and at each level in between, spiritual emanations affecting all parts of the cosmos constantly emerged. The universe was perceived as an animal, moving, feeling, and acting in accord with impulses originating within its various parts or organs. Or, to use another metaphor widely cited at the time, each part of the cosmos resembled a harp tuned to the pitch of all the others, so that when the string of one was plucked all the others vibrated. Thus, the movements of the planets, through the force of their emanations, could affect life on earth. Similarly, the character of a plant or even a rock might influence the mood and behavior of a person exposed to its presence.[26]

In this Neoplatonic view, the role of man in the scheme of things was conceived as both slave and master of these cosmic forces. Most people were merely subject to the influences of the occult impulses around them, but a few, the magicians, might hope to control the powers of the universe. In Pico's *Oration on the Dignity of Man*, one of the most famous texts of the Renaissance, humanity was portrayed as the element of the universe with the greatest latitude. Man might sink to the level of the beasts, prey to uncomprehended forces, or he might rise to a godlike status, unraveling the secrets of the cosmos, controlling nature, and foreseeing the future. Through arduous study, the magician hoped to unlock the powers of rocks and stars. His alchemy and astrology were tools to remake himself by harnessing the fundamental forces of the earth and the heavens.[27]

From this perspective, magic seems a positive and constructive intellectual response to the anxieties brought about by late medieval social conditions. The optimism of Renaissance thought concerning human potential was a trait that encouraged the emergence of learned magic, for the magician hoped to elevate human understanding of and control over the environment. Also contributing to the prestige of magic was humanist admiration of antiquity. In general, humanists reserved their highest respect for works so ancient that they predated even the adored Romans. Thus, the recovery of Plato's writings had a profound influence. So, too, did Christian rediscovery of the Kabbala, the body of Jewish mystical writings believed to have been given to Moses and passed through the generations. Perhaps of still greater influence were the Hermetic works, a group of books actually composed by Platonists in the second century A.D., but thought in the Renaissance to have originated in Egypt before the Mosaic period. As the scholastic philosophical systems articulated in medieval universities were subjected to increasing criticism, humanists became attracted to the formerly neglected world of magic. Plato's works, the Kabbala, and the Hermetic books all achieved wide circulation, especially after the invention of printing, and their availability encouraged a serious philosophical concern with the occult.[28]

Controversy continually swirled around this magical approach, because its Christian orthodoxy was highly suspect. Pico had spoken for many humanists when he wrote that "there is no science which gives more certitude to Christ's divinity than magic and Kabbala."[29] But many churchmen followed the tradition of St. Augustine in remaining unconvinced of a connection between Christianity and the occult. They pointed out that the deterministic qualities of magic seemed to eliminate free will. Astrology, for example, suggested that the stars controlled human life. This kind of determinism appeared to be a direct challenge to the Christian concept of freedom. Yet magicians could answer that the planets only influenced, never controlled, and that the wise man would turn the disposition of these heavenly bodies to his purpose.

More serious was the charge that magic inevitably implied invocation of demons and thus represented deliberate and conscious trafficking with the devil. Writers on magic often were careful to distinguish between their own "spiritual" or natural magic, which was simply a matter of tapping into the forces of the stars or the earth, and the generally disavowed demonic magic. The difficulty, as critics noted, was in the uncertainty of distinguishing accurately between the natural and the demonic. The devil, they pointed out, could make it appear that natural or good spirits were at work when the magician was actually receiving assistance from demons. As there could be no sure way of knowing the source of a magical practitioner's powers, all magic was suspect. Then, too, there certainly were magicians perfectly willing to attempt the invocation of demons to enhance their powers. Marlowe's *Doctor Faustus* could have been modeled on any number of real historical figures.[30]

Churchmen condemned with special vehemence the ritual or ceremonial magic that involved the invocation of demons to carry out human commands. In the view of magicians, invocation was a way of mastering demonic forces for benevolent purposes. The magical tradition taught that spoken or written incantations could conjure up demons who would be compelled to do the bidding of the operator. Commanded to find buried treasure, win a lady's love or the favor of a powerful man, foretell the future, or bestow learning and wisdom, a conjured demon had necessarily to obey. Magicians who practiced such conjurations continually protested that, far from worshiping demons, they were righteous Christians who controlled evil forces for good ends. They maintained that God granted the ability to coerce bad spirits only to those of pure heart, but few churchmen were convinced by this logic.[31]

In the mid-thirteenth century, St. Thomas Aquinas expanded on Augustine's position and denied all possibility of mastering demons. Any apparent control of demons by magic, Aquinas wrote, was an illusion created by the devil to mislead people and involve them ever more deeply in sin. Reflecting the consensus of theological opinion, Aquinas concluded that the conjuring of demons was a kind of heresy because the magician, whether he knew it or not, was serving the forces of Satan. This conclusion held regardless of the results of magic, for demons were not above effecting cures for disease if they could thereby gain the reverence of the magicians. In reality, Aquinas argued, any relationship between magician and demon reflected a pact, whether expressed or tacit.[32]

The connection between magic and criminality was cemented in the early fourteenth century. In several remarkable trials, prominent people were accused of invoking the devil to accomplish evil designs. Like the contemporary persecutions of the Templars, these trials were strongly political, intensely dramatic, and almost entirely fraudulent in their allegations. As show trials, their purpose was heavily propagandistic and the accusations were calculated to shock. Philip IV charged his deceased enemy, Pope Boniface VIII, with invoking demons. The French king also accused the bishop of Troyes of invoking demons and committing murder by image-magic and potions. A few years later, Pope John XXII accused several of his political opponents of efforts to kill him by sorcery. Elsewhere in these years were other allegations of attempted assassination by magic. At Kilkenny, Ireland in 1324, Lady Alice Kyteler and eleven associates were brought before an ecclesiastical court on charges of invoking demons to do malefice, most importantly to murder the three former husbands of Lady Alice. The charges seem to have grown out of aristocratic family feuds over inheritance rights, and so can be classified with other trials of the period as politically motivated.[33]

As was true of the Templars' prosecution, these cases come close to the meaning we now attach to the term "witch hunt." They were loudly trumpeted investigations of corruption, disloyalty, or subversion, but were really meant to destroy the political opposition. The instability of this period, beset as it was with dynastic crises and disputed successions, seemingly fostered an environment receptive to tales of political conspiracy with demonic forces. After 1330, however, with the propaganda value of such charges perhaps depleted through repetition, trials involving prominent people temporarily disappeared, to be revived about a hundred years later.[34]

In fact, after this spate of trials in the first thirty years of the fourteenth century, witchcraft cases practically died out for two generations. Only about twenty-five witch trials took place between 1330 and 1375.[35] But thereafter the pace quickened, as secular courts began to adopt the inquisitorial system. One of the first large-scale witch panics took place in the Swiss Simmenthal between 1395 and 1406. There a secular court of the city of Bern, using inquisitorial procedure, elicited numerous confessions of participation in a devil-worshiping sect whose adherents supposedly killed babies to concoct magical potions and paid homage to demons in church. In these confessions under torture, as in the Kyteler affair, the image of the witch as a member of a group that reveres the devil and foments evil was complete.[36]

The Simmenthal trials are perhaps the earliest example of the pattern that became common in later centuries. The ancient folk tradition of a cannibalistic female figure who steals and consumes babies fused in the minds of learned judges with the devil-worshiping heretic. The result was the witch stereotype. Why did this crystallization occur in the fourteenth century? The answer apparently lies in the increasing association of magical activities with heresy.

In the 1320s, the papal Inquisition first began to investigate cases of ritual magic.[37] By 1400, the Inquisition and the secular courts that emulated its procedure were conducting heresy trials of accused magicians. As in the political trials of the early fourteenth century, the judges increasingly connected maleficent sorcery and demonic magic. Further, they frequently associated the charge of invocation with devil worship. We now know that this was a slow, evolutionary process, not a dramatic innovation of the Inquisition. Predominantly, it was lay judges who gradually refined the concept of witchcraft.[38]

Little by little, the picture of the witch was fleshed out. In 1398, the theological faculty of the University of Paris declared devil-aided malefice tantamount to heresy, because it rested on an explicit or unspoken pact with Satan. This important step was repeated by other authorities, making typical the crucial connection between popular traditions of malefice and learned notions of heretical invocation and devil worship. Increasingly, theologians and judges found evidence of maleficent magic in rural communities, and they could not understand such sorcery without having recourse to the idea of demonic assistance. Familiar as they were with the concept of invocation from their contacts with learned magic, the authorities combined the doer of malefice with the worshiper of Satan. Richard Kieckhefer has shown that sources reflecting peasant views hardly ever mention devil worship in accusations made against suspected witches between 1375 and 1500. Ordinary people were concerned about the witch's malefice, but to the learned judges such malefice seemed inexplicable without demonic assistance.[39]

Although the concept of criminal malefice was well known and condemned in earlier centuries, few people had been formally charged with the offense. It appears that in the early Middle Ages any suspected village witches were dealt with by local vigilantes or through vendettas that were outside formal legal processes. The old "accusatory" criminal law procedure, which was the universal practice before the triumph of inquisitorial methods, had made charges of malefice extraordinarily risky. Before the development of inquisitorial procedure, ordinary criminal charges were brought by aggrieved private citizens, not by judges or prosecutors. The trial was a kind of contest between plaintiff and defendant. An accuser who could not secure a conviction was deemed the loser and himself became subject to criminal penalties. This so-called *lex talionis* no doubt served to maintain community stability by discouraging frivolous accusations and those charges meant to slander or defame. But as malefice was notoriously difficult to prove, only a rash accuser would bring such a charge. The introduction of inquisitorial procedure, however, made charges of malefice safer for the accuser and easier to sustain.[40]

Devil worship, too, was taking on a more vivid appearance in the imaginations of the authorities. Very instructive in this connection is the change in official attitudes toward the ancient folk belief in women who rode out at night for secret rites. In the twelfth and thirteenth centuries, the learned still regarded as absurd the notion of a human being traveling to nocturnal gatherings for devil worship. The position of the church on this matter was expressed in the Canon Episcopi, a tenth-century document later incorporated into the official collections of canon law. The Canon Episcopi (so known because of its first word, "Bishops") noted that "some wicked women perverted by the devil, seduced by illusions and phantasmes of demons, believe and profess themselves, in the hours of night to ride upon certain beasts with Diana, the goddess of the pagans, and an innumerable multitude of women, and in the silence of the dead of night to traverse great space of earth, and to obey her commands as of their mistress, and to be summoned to her service on certain nights." Labeling this belief "an error of the pagans" because it challenged the unique divinity of God, the Canon Episcopi implied (correctly) that such ideas were a remnant of pre-Christian folk beliefs. The important point drawn in this document is that, since no one can do such things without God's miraculous assistance, beliefs in night riding have no basis in reality. They are only imagined, as in dreams. "Who is there," asked the writer of the canon, "that is not led out of himself in dreams and nocturnal visions, and sees much when sleeping which he has never seen while awake?" Counseling, then, was prescribed as the remedy for women who believed they rode out at night to serve Diana. Clergymen should preach to them about the devil's ability to produce such illusions and so cure these unfortunate victims of their fantasies.[41]

Although it surely would be too much to call the Canon Episcopi "rationalist" in spirit—it attributes illusions to the supernatural power of the devil—the document explicitly rejects the physical reality of night riding and heathen rites. Until the fourteenth century, the educated were unanimous in describing these beliefs as the fantasies of deluded women. Had this attitude remained dominant, the frame of mind requisite for witch trials might not have emerged. But, after 1400, the pre-Christian popular image of the night-riding woman, condemned centuries before as an illusory belief, was revived, treated as a reality, and attributed to many alleged practitioners of witchcraft. The full-blown witches' sabbat, or synagogue, as it was originally known, begins to appear in learned accounts after 1400, although it did not become the central image of witchcraft until the sixteenth century.[42]

With increasing regularity there emerged a characteristic pattern of trials for witchcraft. An old woman was accused by her village neighbors of malefice in one of its two most common forms, bodily harm or love magic. She then was subjected to inquisitorial procedure, usually but not always involving torture, during which it was suggested to her that she had made a pact with Satan, agreed to worship him and reject Christianity, copulated with an incubus, and used the devil's powers to harm her neighbors. Blended here are popular ideas of malevolent magic and the intellectuals' ideas of devil worship. The combination remained at the heart of the witch trials for over two centuries.[43]

The pace of prosecution for witchcraft rose dramatically in the last three-quarters of the fifteenth century. Between 1365 and 1428 there were only 84 verified witch trials, but the next seventy-two years saw at least 354 cases. The actual change was of even greater magnitude than these figures reveal, because the later trials tended to involve more suspects.[44] Some of the fifteenth-century trials even foreshadowed the mass outbreaks of witch prosecution that became common afterward. Such large trials typically involved charges of Waldensianism lodged by inquisitors, bishops, and secular judges in the French and Swiss Alps and in northern France. Indeed, in the minds of the authorities, the Waldensian or Vaudois heresy was now conflated with witchcraft, as can be seen in the name they assigned to this heretical activity: *vauderie*. Waldensianism, which first had helped to inspire fears of the devil, now became entirely identified with witchcraft. Or, to put it the other way around, witchcraft was now deemed coterminus with heresy.[45]

The crystallization of the witch stereotype from learned and popular elements in the fourteenth and fifteenth centuries seems to have been catalyzed by lay and clerical officials' increasing concern about dissident practices and nonconforming beliefs. To clerical suspicion of learned magic were added upper-class fears of revolutionary popular heresy. As church and state were now trying to exert more control over rural society than had officials earlier in the Middle Ages, members of the elites had considerable opportunity to come into contact with folk beliefs. Once they had been incorporated into learned cultural traditions about the demonic, such popular ideas became the basis for the elites' stereotype of the devil-worshiping and maleficent witch.

The trial of Joan of Arc in 1431 offers an example of the psychology linking heresy and magic. Joan's English accusers and their clerical allies could not believe that divine inspiration might prompt a young woman to take up arms and lead the French king's armies. They saw her instead as a demon or Satan's human accomplice. Accused of invoking evil spirits, idolatry, and apostasy, Joan was perceived by her enemies as a kind of magician who had triumphed through supernatural force. This was far more than propaganda. Such explanations gave the defeated English a psychologically convenient way of understanding their setbacks. Thus, two years after Joan's execution, the Duke of Bedford wrote in a private letter to the government of London that Joan of Arc was "a disciple and limb of the Fiend . . . that used false enchantment and sorcery" in combat.[46] Almost two centuries later, when trials for witchcraft were far more common, Shakespeare had his Salisbury, the English commander, express the same sentiment in *Henry VI, Part One*:

> Devil or Devil's dam, I'll conjure thee,
> Blood will I draw on thee, thou art a witch;
> And straightway give thy soul to him thou servest.[47]

Although the word "witch" was never used in the accusations lodged against her at her trial, all of Joan's heretical activities were associated with the practice of black magic.[48]

Joan of Arc was a peasant girl, but her accusers were thoroughly familiar with learned opinions about demonic magic. This generation saw other accusations of sorcery lodged against politically influential people in France and England. Several years after Joan's execution, her comrade-in-arms, Gilles de Rais, was forced to confess to murdering numerous children and making sacrifices to the devil. Accusations of treason were accompanied by charges of sorcery in several other fifteenth-century political trials. As had occurred one hundred years earlier in the politically inspired trials of the Templars' time, the rich and powerful portrayed their enemies as instruments of Satan. With the fearsome reputation of demonic magic more fully developed by this time, it was easy for the accusers to convince themselves that supernatural evil was responsible for their rivals' success.[49]

Aside from these political trials, the most famous fifteenth-century witch cases occurred in the northern French city of Arras between 1459 and 1462. Thirty-four people were accused of witchcraft, and twelve were executed. At issue in these trials was devil worship or, as the prosecutors put it, attendance at the "synagogue" of the Vaudois. Only in one case was malefice against men and animals alleged. All the Arras trials stemmed from the accusations of one man who confessed under torture and went on to implicate two others, a prostitute and a noted poet and painter, as participants in the synagogue. These two were tortured and in turn accused several more people who, also put to the question, involved still others. Tricked into confessions by false promises of leniency, five prisoners were burnt despite their cries of innocence as the flames rose around them. Still the arrests continued, and psychological terror reigned as citizens wondered who would be charged next. After the imprisonment of a number of rich and prominent merchants, the businessmen of Arras found their credit was no longer good in other cities. Fear of confiscation and bad debts was crippling the town's commerce. Meanwhile, two Dominicans presided over the continued prosecution. One was the chief subordinate of the bishop of Arras—the bishop himself was in Rome when the trials began—and the other, Jacques du Boys, was a doctor of laws and dean of the general chapter of the Dominican order. Du Boys regularly preached frenzied sermons declaring that anyone who opposed the burnings must himself be a witch.

At last merchants of the town undertook an appeal to the duke of Burgundy at Brussels. He received inconclusive advice from the theologians at the University of Louvain, who could not agree about the reality of sabbats. But the duke sent a representative to attend all interrogations, whereupon the arrests stopped. Four more people were still to be convicted, yet only one was executed. Despite continued vigorous urgings by the two local Dominicans, the ecclesiastical inquisitors refused to prosecute any more of the numerous people implicated and awaiting trial. Meanwhile the Parlement (or royal court) of Paris, acting on the appeal of one of the prisoners, ordered that most of the jailed be released, and the bishop of Arras, lately returned from Italy, freed the rest. Denounced by the archbishop of Reims and other prominent prelates, du Boys immediately went mad and died a few months later. Finally, in 1491, after a typically snailpaced investigation, the Paris Parlement declared that all of those accused and condemned had been innocent of the charges. Although nearly everyone involved was long since dead, the Parlement's decree pardoned those convicted and ordered the erection of a large cross at the place of execution. To pay for the cross and also for masses on behalf of the departed victims' souls, fines were levied against those few of the prosecutors still alive. At Arras the decree was celebrated in grand style with outdoor theatricals and sermons very different from those of Jacques du Boys.[50]

This remarkable story demonstrates the strong ripple effect a single accusation could produce when it was powered by an inquisitorial procedure in the hands of judges convinced of witchcraft's reality. In the mass trials of succeeding centuries, all too similar scenarios were played out repeatedly.

The Witches' Hammer

By the middle of the fifteenth century, trials for witchcraft had taken on many of the attributes characteristic of the witch craze that began a hundred years later. We have seen in this chapter how the witch stereotype and the institutional apparatus used against witches developed. After 1100, Europeans, especially those in positions of authority, came to fear that things were "going wrong, that is, departing from the natural and moral order," in the formulation used by Philip Mayer to explain the preconditions for witch beliefs.

> There are some cosmologies into which the concept of witchcraft does not fit at all, because they represent everything that happens as being fundamentally right, proper, or natural. Some religions, for instance, teach a Job-like submission to a divine will which brings about everything and is always just. With similar effect, Rationalism teaches that everything may be interpreted as the outcome of natural causes. In neither of these idea systems, if consistently held, is there any room for the witchcraft idea. Witches can only have place in a cosmology that admits to the possibility of things going wrong, that is, departing from the natural and moral order.[51]

Changes in medieval views are evident in the growing intolerance of such dissenters as heretics, homosexuals, and Jews. For religious and secular leaders, and in popular psychology, such deviant minorities were not simply annoying nonconformists. They were demonized, cast as manifestations of Satan's power in the world. The precise reasons for the rise of intolerance remain somewhat obscure, but there can be little question that fear and hatred of the dissenter made him seem supremely evil in the later Middle Ages. As in other times before and since, anxiety-ridden persecutors denied the humanity of despised minorities.

A preoccupation with death, perceptible from the twelfth century and greatly magnified by the arrival of plague in the mid-fourteenth century, led many Christians to fear the end of life as the moment of Satan's victory. Dissent, death, and the devil became interlinked in late medieval traditions. Finally, in the fourteenth and fifteenth centuries, the stereotype of the witch slowly emerged as the focus for this complex of fears.

At the same time, the ancient corpus of magical practice underwent a renaissance among the learned, thus reviving old theological doubts about magic. The magician who claimed to use the devil's power was conflated in the minds of the authorities with the witch who was used *by* the devil. Lay and religious leaders associated the popular lore of the evil-doing, night-riding village hag with their crystallizing image of the satanic magician. Thus, by 1450, the newly formed stereotype of witchcraft—harmful action performed by a human agent of the devil—had been added to the list of dissenting activities condemned by church and secular officials.

As witch trials began to proliferate in the fifteenth century, the theory of witchcraft also approached maturity. We can show this by considering

the most influential treatise on witchcraft ever published, *Malleus Maleficarum*, or *The Witches' Hammer*, first printed about 1486. The *Malleus* was
composed by two Dominicans, Heinrich Kramer and Jacob Sprenger, who
had spent years as inquisitors in southern Germany. Between 1481 and
1486, Kramer and Sprenger presided over nearly fifty executions for witchcraft in the diocese of Constance. Their witch hunting met with considerable opposition from local ecclesiastical authorities, but the Dominicans'
efforts were greatly aided by the apparent support of the papacy. Kramer
had taken the precaution of obtaining from Innocent VIII a papal bull,
Summus desiderantes, calling on German officials to cooperate in the witch
hunts. Although this document went no further than the pronouncements
of earlier popes on the subject, it lent prestige to the inquisitors' campaigns.
Even the *Malleus* seemed to benefit from papal sanctions, as each edition
reprinted Innocent's bull as a preface to the work. There were many
reprints, for of all the newly written works published in the first generation
of printing, the *Malleus* may have been one of the most extensively repub-
lished over the next two hundred years.⁵²

The *Malleus*'s appeal surely owed nothing to the book's literary style,
which is highly scholastic and uninfluenced by humanist ideals of belles-
lettres. Instead, the work's strength is its convenient handbook form, well
suited for use by judges in cases of witchcraft. The *Malleus* begins with
definitions, first explaining the nature of witchcraft (heresy), outlining its
effects (malefice), and identifying its practitioners (mostly female). Part 2 of
the book goes on to describe in detail what witches do, and part 3 systematically sets out the legal procedures to be used in bringing them to the stake.
For judges, the practical value of the last part was inestimable, as it supplied
a step-by-step guide to conducting witch trials. In later chapters we will
discuss the *Malleus*'s lasting influence on the sexual and legal aspects of the
witch trials. Here the primary concern is with the theory of witchcraft
propounded by the two Dominicans.

Kramer and Sprenger methodically disposed of competing explanations for such misfortunes as disease, death, impotence, and crop failure,
and concluded that in many cases they must be attributed to witchcraft.
The authors did not disregard entirely the possibility of natural causation,
but they thought it most improbable that what they saw as the rampant
disasters of their time could stem from natural origins exclusively. Nor did
they believe it plausible that such widespread evil could be coming directly
from God as a test or a punishment of Christians. Instead, they used the
confessions elicited in earlier trials as evidence for the vast scale of witches'
activities. Although the authors thought witchcraft a phenomenon as

ancient as the world, in the first part of their book they argued that until the recent past the devil had usually recruited his servants against their will. Only since 1400, they wrote, had large numbers of people actually volunteered for satanic service. Thus, Kramer and Sprenger found witchcraft a growing affliction in their time.

As for why witches were flourishing so hideously just then, the two Dominicans explained the question in conventional moralizing fashion: people had become more sinful, thus more likely to fall into temptation by Satan. The devil always preferred to do evil through witches, Kramer and Sprenger continued, despite Satan's undoubted ability to cause misfortune without human assistance. In contracting with a witch, he redoubled his evildoing. In the first place he damned a human soul, always an objective of the devil. In addition, by impregnating witches Satan could produce a new generation willing to continue his work. Above all, the recruitment of witches enabled the devil to sow discord in Christian society and in this way to fulfill one of his primary goals. For all these reasons, the *Malleus* states, the devil had always been alert to the possibilities of recruiting humans as his servants, and, since sinfulness was then rife, he was exploiting his opportunity. Kramer and Sprenger combined these theological speculations with total credulity about folk beliefs concerning witchcraft. Their book recast popular traditions in the framework of scholastic argumentation to create an image of the witch drawn from diverse cultural levels.

The *Malleus*'s importance, then, does not lie in its originality. In fact, like most works of synthesis, *The Witches' Hammer* broke little new ground with regard to substance and none whatever with regard to method. The inquisitors' technique of reliance on the authorities of the past to authenticate each assertion is typical of the scholastic approach and of all intellectual discourse of the time.[53] But, in bringing together systematically so much of the fifteenth-century witch finders' experience, Kramer and Sprenger produced the classic work of the demonological genre, one that stood not only the test of time but also that of religious persuasion. Not all theologians were immediately persuaded of the *Malleus*'s view of witchcraft. But, two generations later, in the stress-filled era of the Reformation, there emerged an environment more favorable to witch hunting. Long after Protestants had triumphed in parts of northern Europe, the *Malleus* continued to be read and followed by people otherwise separated from the traditions of the Roman Catholic Church. Although Protestant commentators sometimes took Kramer and Sprenger to task for their "papist" errors, they generally accepted their central arguments.[54] The *Malleus* became a book of rare ecumenical power in an era of bitter doctrinal warfare.

The modern mind finds the sweeping assertions of the *Malleus Male-ficarum* so absurd that the book's influence may seem incredible. But, seen in light of the developments sketched in this chapter, its popularity should not be especially puzzling. For one thing, the cosmological assumptions of the time made effective criticism difficult. Nearly everyone believed in the reality of magic and demonic forces. Further, the prestige enjoyed by the authors of the past was very great, so that few could seriously entertain the possibility that all the experts cited by Kramer and Sprenger might be completely mistaken. Limitations of substance and method, then, meant that the available intellectual tools were insufficient to successfully chal-lenge the axioms underlying the witch stereotype. The occasional critic who tried to dispute the idea of the witch from a medical, philosophical, or theological point of view was unable to find convincing arguments, a point to which we will return in the last chapter of this book.

A second way to explain the *Malleus*'s influence is by focusing on the general social environment that fostered the witch trials. The witch craze of the sixteenth and seventeenth centuries cannot be adequately explained by pointing to the more powerful intellectual apparatus available to those who advocated trials for witchcraft. Their arsenal of ideas was pretty much in place by about 1400; certainly it was well entrenched by the time of the *Malleus*'s first printings in the 1480s. Yet witch trials, although they became more frequent in the fifteenth century, remained relatively rare by later standards. Only after 1560 did the pace of witch prosecution begin to skyrocket.[55]

The *Malleus* was one of the most frequently reprinted original works of the late fifteenth and early sixteenth centuries. It ran through at least fourteen editions between 1486 and 1521. But there is absolutely nothing to indicate that this apparently widely read book increased the pace of witch-craft prosecutions, which at this time remained at the relatively low levels first reached in the mid-fifteenth century. Plainly, the *Malleus*'s appearance did not begin the witch craze. After 1521, interestingly, the *Malleus* dis-appeared from the presses of Europe for fifty-five years. Then, from 1576 to 1670, it experienced a dramatic revival in popularity and was reprinted no less than sixteen times. This extraordinary publication history—two "best-seller" phases separated by a long period of total neglect—may very well be unique in the first two centuries of printing.[56] The *Malleus*'s period of eclipse after 1520 can be explained in part by the lack of interest among the new Protestant leaders in the work of two Dominicans, but this obviously is not a complete explanation. Europeans of this generation seem to have temporarily lost interest in witchcraft; from 1526 to 1554 only two new demonological works appeared.[57] When thorough studies are made of the trials that took place in the period immediately preceding the great witch hunts, it may be possible to reach a more satisfying answer.

More important than the temporary decline of interest in demonology was its revival after 1560. As witch trials began to increase in frequency, many readers became interested in learned opinion on the subject. The *Malleus* was soon joined on the booksellers' shelves by about a dozen major new demonological works published between 1564 and 1612, mostly in multiple editions.[58] These later writers repeated much of the lore well known from the *Malleus*, but they also added new features to the witch stereotype, especially the vivid sexual imagery of the sabbat.

By the 1580s, when the *Malleus* was reprinted at least five times, there was clearly a market for witch-hunting manuals. Canny publishers surely knew about this market before they risked printing new editions. The witch craze, then, commenced before demonology became a booksellers' boon. The demonologists' works influenced the witch craze but did not create it.[59] Where, then, if not from the printed handbooks, did the impetus for massive witch hunting originate? The next four chapters propose various ways to approach this question.

3

Sexual Politics and Religious Reform in the Witch Craze

Why did the number of witch trials in Western Europe increase greatly after about 1550? Why did the crime of witchcraft, familiar for centuries, suddenly appear so much more menacing that thousands of trials unfolded between 1550 and 1700, whereas only a few hundred seem to have occurred earlier?

These questions have been posed by many writers on the witch trials over the past century. But they have taken on fresh urgency recently, in light of the findings (discussed in the previous chapters) of Norman Cohn and Richard Kieckhefer concerning medieval witch trials. These scholars, working independently, have uncovered convincing proof that previously accepted accounts of large-scale witch hunts undertaken by the Inquisition in fourteenth-century France and Italy were based on modern forgeries and other fraudulent evidence. Their discoveries have necessitated a complete revision of the chronology of European witch hunting. Until now, the mainstream of scholarly interpretation suggested a continuing flow in witch prosecution from the fourteenth to the seventeenth centuries. Periods of flood may have alternated with relatively dry spells, and there were some especially spectacular inundations around 1600, but in the accounts of earlier scholars the channel of witch hunting remained intact over the centuries, with few and minor changes of course. Thus, Henry Charles Lea could devote nearly half of his massive digest on witchcraft to the period before the mid-sixteenth century. And, as recently as fifteen years ago, H. R. Trevor-Roper could argue that the witch craze was primarily an extension and magnification of earlier witch hunting.

Kieckhefer and Trevor-Roper exemplify the two main lines of scholarly interpretation in discussions of witch hunting's development, interpretations that may be labeled internalist and externalist. On the one hand, Kieckhefer stressed the internal changes in the definition of the crime of witchcraft from 1300 to 1500, but he did not dwell at length on the social forces that may have contributed to these changes. In his analysis, the stages of witch hunting almost take on a life of their own, independent of the broader environment. Trevor-Roper's approach, on the other hand, treats witchcraft as a relatively static monolith. His essay is all about the social variables acting on the constant of witchcraft. In brief, he saw the tensions engendered by the Reformation as the dynamo that powered the massive witch-hunting industry, although the raw materials were available much earlier.

Both internal and external approaches plainly have merit, but neither one is completely satisfying in explaining the explosion of witch hunting in the late sixteenth and seventeenth centuries. Changes in definition beg for a broader context if they are to be properly understood. In any case, Kieckhefer's book stops in 1500, at least fifty years before the witch craze began. Trevor-Roper, because he was mistakenly convinced that witch trials were common in late medieval Europe, did not look into the important differences between these late medieval and early modern witch prosecutions. Believing in the antiquity of the crime of witchcraft, he, like most scholars, failed to recognize the novelty of the deep fixation on the witch in early modern consciousness. Because his sources led him to conclude that witch hunting was not something particularly new in Reformation times (only somewhat more common than before), he was satisfied to point to rather vaguely delineated social stresses engendered in the Reformation era as sufficient explanation for the increase in witch prosecution.

My approach, in brief, is to extend the internal and external analyses exemplified by these two writers, and in the process to try to close some of the logical gaps in our knowledge of the development of witch hunting. I adopt Kieckhefer's method of considering the evolving definition of witchcraft, but, unlike him, I continue well past 1500 into the witch craze proper. I also emulate Trevor-Roper in pointing to the social tensions provoked in the Reformation, but with a bit more precision than Trevor-Roper allowed himself in his landmark essay.

In this chapter I single out one variable as a bridge between internal and external explanations: attitudes toward sexuality. My thesis is that changes in sexual attitudes can help explain both the metamorphosing definitions of witchcraft and the role of reforming religious ideologies in creating the environment in which witch hunting flourished.

Consider first, by way of review, the stages of evolution in the concept of witchcraft. Kieckhefer argues persuasively that the meaning of witch-craft changed around the turn of the fifteenth century. Before 1375 or so, witchcraft almost always meant sorcery, i.e., maleficent magic. In the early trials of this period, the crime was defined as harm inflicted on a victim by such magical means as spells or potions. Making an image of the victim and then breaking off a leg to cause a neighbor's lameness or inducing recipro-cated affection by administering a charmed drink—these were the typical offenses of fourteenth-century witch trials. Usually in these early trials there was no mention of the devil or demons. When a demon did appear, it was generally as the servant of the witch, who had invoked demonic aid to accomplish evil magic.

After 1375, and especially during the last two-thirds of the fifteenth century, a new definition of witchcraft emerged. In some clerical treatises and torture-elicited confessions, witchcraft was pictured as a combination of traditional sorcery and a novel diabolism. The witch was no longer merely a worker of malefice. She was also a servant of the devil. Clerics explained a witch's supernatural powers as the manifestation of abilities granted her by Satan, a point of view that conformed well with Aristotelian views of causation. It seemed implausible to these writers and judges that witches could do their mischief without demonic assistance, and they cast the witch as worshiper of the devil. This new definition of the crime of witchcraft overlay the older one of the witch as sorcerer. Kieckhefer's very careful readings of the trial records reveal that in the initial stage of a trial, when one villager accused another, only sorcery was attributed to the witch. But, when elite authorities intervened, they introduced the issue of devil worship into the proceedings. By the 1480s, when the classic witch-hunting treatise, the *Malleus Maleficarum*, was first published, the image of the witch as evildoing devil worshiper was firmly established in elite conscious-ness.

An analysis of Europe's witch craze can begin either at the top of society or at the bottom. One may choose to emphasize changes in the outlook of the educated elites, both clerical and secular. Or one can stress the role of popular agitation for witch trials. But these mirror-image interpretive frameworks need not be regarded as mutually exclusive. It seems entirely reasonable to expect that the witch craze, like most other complex historical episodes, cannot be explained in accord with a single theoretical model, no matter how thoughtful or sophisticated. Instead, this book argues that witch-hunting impulses both trickled down from society's leaders and rose upward on a tide of popular anxieties.

Moreover, the cultural distance between elites and populace was not at all fixed. Especially in the later stages of the witch craze, ideas and practices characteristic of society's upper echelons had penetrated deeply into village life. Thus, higher and lower cultures should be regarded not as separate compartments but as overlapping categories with many points of contact. Witch hunting was one of the most dramatic areas of overlap. In the witch trials, members of the elites and ordinary folk found a common cause.

This chapter discusses the impulses for witch trials that came from the educated and the politically powerful. It dwells on the concerns of the elites with spiritual reform in general and sexual reform in particular. The intention here is to show the impact that changing values among the educated had on ordinary folk, who were at the receiving end of reforming religious evangelism and made up the great majority of witches and their accusers. In the next chapter we will turn to the popular origins of witch trials.

Sexuality and the Witch Stereotype

Had Kieckhefer continued his analysis into the sixteenth century, he might have detected a further shift in the definition of witchcraft. After 1550, most European witch trials were of criminals who were said to be not only Satan's worshipers but his sexual slaves as well. Occasionally in the fifteenth century we read in learned treatises of witches who engage in perverse sexual practices. It was only during the witch craze itself, however, that the charge of sexual abuse became a normal component of a witchcraft indictment. As in the case of the introduction of devil worship in the fifteenth century, charges of sexual trespassing were introduced from above. They appear only rarely in the initial accusations but were raised by prosecutors predisposed to see the witch as a sex offender. A preoccupation with the sexual side of witchcraft is the feature that most clearly differentiates the witch stereotype of the sixteenth and seventeenth centuries from the earlier era of small-scale witch hunting.

The ways in which people dealt with sexual matters had an enormous impact on witch trials. The witch craze often has been described as one of the most terrible instances of man's inhumanity to man. But more accurate is a formulation by gender, not genus: witch trials exemplify men's inhumanity to women. The sexually powerful and menacing witch figure was nearly always portrayed as a female. For example, the authors of the *Malleus Maleficarum* were convinced that the great majority of witches were women. And, like a self-fulfilling diagnosis, women comprised the over-

whelming bulk of the accused during the witch craze. Evidence from about
7,500 witch trials in diverse regions of Europe and North America during
the sixteenth and seventeenth centuries shows that nearly 80 percent of
accused witches were female, and, in parts of England, Switzerland, and
what is now Belgium, women accounted for over nine out of ten victims.[1]
This disproportion was far greater than in earlier witchcraft trials, when
men had comprised close to half of the accused. Further, these numbers
understate the predominance of women, because many of the accused men
were implicated solely due to their connection with female suspects. Thus,
in the English county of Essex, where only twenty-three of 291 accused
witches were men, eleven were either husbands of an accused witch or were
jointly indicted with one.[2]

Everywhere, witchcraft was a woman's crime. Those who advocated
witch trials saw nothing remarkable in this sexual imbalance. It conformed
perfectly with the dominant notions of female inferiority, while it confirmed
the legitimacy of woman-hatred with each new case. A circular process of
great force, the dynamics of the witch trials were one expression of deep-
seated misogyny in early modern times. Indeed, this chapter will argue that
the witch trials were symptomatic of a dramatic rise in fear and hatred of
women during the era of the Reformation.

To illustrate the centrality of sexual imagery in the picture of the witch
during the peak period of witch hunting, consider one of the most influential descriptions of a supposed witches' sabbat. This account comes from
Pierre de Lancre, counselor in the Parlement of Bordeaux and prosecutor,
under King Henry IV's commission, of hundreds of female witch suspects
in the predominantly Basque region of the Labourd in south-western
France. In 1609, de Lancre sent more than eighty women to the stake in one
of the largest of the French witch hunts. Three years later, he published his
Tableau de l'inconstance des mauvais anges et démons. This is a lengthy work
describing the evil deeds of the Basque witches, and prominently featured
in it is an extended report on the witches' sabbat.

De Lancre portrayed the sabbat as a lurid affair attended by numerous
witches who flew in from considerable distances on broomsticks, shovels,
spits, or a variety of domestic animals. Some sabbats were attended by as
many as twelve thousand witches, though most meetings were of more
manageable scale. The devil might appear to his congregants as a three-
horned goat, a huge bronze bull, or a serpent, but, whatever his guise,
de Lancre's informers rarely failed to mention his large penis and scaly
testicles. A festive air prevailed, reminiscent of a wedding or court celebration. Generally, the proceedings began with the witches kissing their mas-

ter's rear. Then each witch reported malefice she had carried out since the last sabbat. Those with nothing to report were whipped. The business meeting concluded, a work session followed, during which the women industriously concocted poisons and ointments out of black bread and the rendered fat of murdered infants. Having built up an appetite, they next banqueted on babies' limbs and toads, foods variously reviewed as succulent or awful-tasting. Then the devil presided over a parody of the Mass. Finally, the social hour: the naked witches danced lasciviously, back to back, until the dancing turned into a sexual orgy that continued to the dawn. Incest and homosexual intercourse were encouraged. Often the devil would climax the proceedings by copulating—painfully, it was generally reported—with every man, woman, and child in attendance, as mothers yielded to Satan before their daughters' eyes and initiated them into sexual service to the diabolical master (Plate I).[3]

Such was de Lancre's account of the sabbat, boiled down from his two hundred pages of detailed description. In this portrayal the sexual elements are of course very prominent. The powerfully sexual nature of the dominant imagery begins with the broomstick ride, continues with exciting whippings, the fascinating close-up look at devilishly huge sexual organs, the baby-eating (possibly sublimated incest or infanticide?), and, finally, the frenzied orgy itself.

The important place of the sabbat in de Lancre's book and in other demonological works of the late sixteenth and early seventeenth centuries is all the more striking when we note that the witches' sabbat was not a prominent feature in earlier formulations of the witch stereotype. The sabbat does not appear, for example, in the *Malleus Maleficarum*, the most widely circulated demonological treatise of the fifteenth century, and it is encountered infrequently before 1500. Earlier, the image of the witch was that of a rather isolated individual. Witches might get together in small groups to stir their cauldrons, as in a 1510 engraving by Hans Baldung Grien (Plate 2), but, until the era of the Reformation, few writers thought in terms of large prayer meetings devoted to the adoration of Satan.[4] The *Malleus*, like other early demonological works, had discussed witches' ability to "tie the knot" and cause impotence. It also pictured witches as the sexual partners of demons in human form. In later witch-hunting treatises, sexual overtones became the leading theme of demonological imagery, and the sabbat emerged as the central focus of the witch hunters' fantasies. Not only de Lancre but nearly every continental demonologist of the era of the witch craze laid great stress on the sabbat as the occasion for witches to express their perverse sexuality.

PLATE I. Pierre de l'Ancre (De Lancre), *Tableau de l'inconstance des mauvais anges et démons* (Paris, 1612). Frontispiece depicting the witches' sabbat. Folger Shakespeare Library, Washington, call number 176711.

PLATE 2. Hans Baldung Grien, *The Witches' Sabbath*, Chiaroscuro woodcut (1510). Museum of Fine Arts, Boston, bequest of W. G. Russell Allen.

Along similar lines, witch-hunting judges regularly warned that a sure sign of witchcraft was the presence on a woman's body of the so-called devil's mark. This was an insensible spot or anesthetic scar with which Satan branded a woman (like a slave) when initiating her into witchcraft. Related to this idea, though somewhat less common, was the belief that the witch had an extra nipple through which to suckle her familiar or incubus. Any wart, mole, or other skin growth on the accused's body might be identified as a devil's mark or witch's tit. Since the devil would of course do his best to hide the evidence of his servant's fidelity, it was deemed necessary to conduct a thorough, formal search. In practice, this meant stripping and shaving the accused's entire body before meticulously examining and pricking every part of her. Such inspections were usually conducted by physicians or surgeons, but sometimes by midwives or other women, before an all-male audience. In Scotland, witch pricking was the specialty of men who made a profession of the search for the devil's mark. There, as in some other places, it was common for suspects to undergo repeated examinations until a devil's mark was discovered. The devil's mark was unknown in popular beliefs about witchcraft, and even early demonologists like the authors of the *Malleus* had never heard of it. After 1560, however, the search for the mark became an ordinary feature of witchcraft investigations, particularly in Protestant lands, where strong emphasis was placed on the witch's pact with the devil.[5]

In the republic of Geneva, this ceremony of stripping and probing took place regularly in the more than two hundred recorded trials of women for witchcraft, although failure to find a devil's mark on the accused often sufficed to save her from a death sentence in Genevan courts. The Genevan judges' unusually high standards of proof were condemned by commentators of the time, who no doubt would have been even more critical had they known that only about one-fifth of the republic's accused witches wound up at the stake. This was one of the lowest execution ratios anywhere in Europe. Genevan witch suspects, however, were typical of their counterparts elsewhere in their preponderantly rural origins. About half of Geneva's accused witches were peasants from the city's rural dependencies, even though these hamlets accounted for only about 20 percent of the republic's total population.[6] That an urban, reformed patriciate regularly subjected country women to the rape-like humiliation of the search for the devil's mark is an indicator of elite suspicions about rural sexual habits and of the dehumanizing consequences that such suspicions could produce, even among relatively careful and lenient judges.

Another sign of the authorities' preconceptions about female sexuality was their association of the devil's mark with women's genitals. Demonological experts warned judges that women often bore the devil's mark on their "shameful parts," "on the breasts or private parts." As a seventeenth-century handbook for English justices of the peace pointed out, because "these the Devil's Marks . . . be often in women's secretest Parts, they therefore require diligent and careful Search." One witch suspect in the Swiss canton of Fribourg contemptuously chided her judges for their naivete about female anatomy. After the prosecutors discovered what they took to be a devil's mark on her genitals, Ernni Vuffiod informed them that "if this was a sign of witchcraft, many women would be witches."[7] The same part of the female body received careful attention from judges at the Salem witch trials. The women examiners employed by the courts reported that they found on three suspects "a preternatural excrescence of flesh between the pudendum and the anus, much like teats, and not usual in women."[8] A Scottish witch always was searched with similar thoroughness to discover "marks . . . between her thys and her body." During his years in Scotland, King James VI (later James I of England) was especially fascinated with the details of the search for the devil's mark, no great surprise in a man who consistently displayed a prurient interest in the sex lives of his courtiers and relatives.[9]

By about 1560, the witch stereotype had taken on all its menacing features. The witch was not only what she had been for centuries in popular imagination—a source of mischief and misfortune. Now, in the eyes of learned judges, she was much more—one of a vast number of devil worshipers who had yielded to Satan in the most repulsive ways and become his sexual servant. This newer definition of the witch as sexual servant and member of a large devil-worshiping cult became even more frightening to those in authority than the witch's power to inflict malefice. The change can be measured in the law. For example, the *Carolina*, the German imperial law code promulgated in the 1530s, punished alleged witches more severely if they could be shown to have brought harm to their neighbors. But the Saxon criminal code of the 1570s, which was widely imitated throughout Germany and Scandinavia, mandated death by fire for *any* dealing with the devil, regardless of whether the accused had brought about harm by magical means.[10]

This reformulation of the law of witchcraft reflected the new view, frequently expressed in witch hunters' manuals published after 1560, that the real root of the witch's crime was her allegiance to Satan. The change can be dated precisely in Scotland, where the statute on witchcraft passed in 1563 defined the crime as malefice. It made no mention of dealings with Satan. But, by the 1590s, the decade of the first large Scottish witch hunts, the meaning of witchcraft had been altered. As on the continent, the offense now lay in the witch's pact with Satan and her promise of servitude. Accusations of malefice usually were not enough to condemn a suspected witch. Because evidence of the demonic pact was essential for conviction, the search for the devil's mark became an inevitable part of Scottish witch trials.

In a discussion of witch trials in the Cambrésis region along the border of France and the Spanish Netherlands, Robert Muchembled has asserted that charges of devil worship, with their attendant pattern of sexual deviance, were never lodged in the initial accusations by peasants. Suggestions of copulation with Satan were regularly introduced at a later stage, by the elite judicial officials who presided over the trials. "Sex plays a starring role," Muchembled observed, in the accusations leveled by professional judges after 1550. The prosecutors elicited from each suspected witch the admission that she gave Satan "a hair from her private parts" to symbolize her subjection. Similarly, Christina Larner has shown that seventeenth-century Scottish indictments followed a common form that included accusations of "carnall dealling or copulations with the devil" and taking "his marks upon your bodies," even though in most cases nothing of the sort had been alleged in the initial charges of malefice lodged by the suspect's neighbors.[11]

The triumph of this updated image of the witch as the sabbat-attending sexual servant of the devil coincided with a dramatic rise in the rate of witchcraft prosecution. For all of Europe during the last two-thirds of the fifteenth century, about three hundred witch trials have been verified. Between 1560 and 1680 Germany alone experienced thousands of such trials. The important changes in the meaning of witchcraft and the tremendous increase in trial incidences during the era of religious reform have sometimes been played down by scholars searching for the medieval origins of witch hunting. We should remember, however, that the new stereotype of the witch current among the elites seems to have evoked far more intense fears than had earlier images of witchcraft. This redefinition set the stage for the witch craze.

It was not simply a matter of more witch trials; specifically, more women were accused of trafficking with the devil. Before 1400, when witchcraft meant sorcery, only a bare majority—50 to 60 percent—of accused witches were women. In the fifteenth century, as witchcraft became equated with diabolism, Kieckhefer found the proportion of female accused rising to between 60 and 70 percent. During the witch craze itself, the preponderance of women increased still further. Over Europe as a whole in this period about 80 percent of witch suspects were women, and in some places women accounted for more than nine out of ten accused witches.[12]

These figures suggest that originally witchcraft was not viewed specifically as a woman's crime. The stereotypical medieval sorcerer said to engage in image magic, spell casting, or the concoction of love potions was frequently perceived as a male figure learned in the arcane and dangerous science of ritual magic. As the crime was redefined in the fifteenth century to stress servitude to the devil, however, witchcraft became a gender-linked offense; women, the witch-hunting manuals repeated, were morally weaker than men and therefore were more likely to succumb to satanic temptation. The linkage thus forged became even stronger when, during the sixteenth and seventeenth centuries, lay and clerical elites came to see the witch as Satan's sexual servant. The one-fifth of witch suspects in Scotland who were men, for example, do not appear to have been accused of any sexual relationship with the devil, unlike their female counterparts. As witchcraft became identified with sexual trespasses in the minds of reforming witch hunters, its gender-linked status was greatly reinforced.

Satan and Spiritual Reform

The coming of the witch craze was one manifestation of the impact of spiritual reform in the sixteenth and seventeenth centuries. The twin movements of the Protestant Reformation and the Catholic Counter Reformation (referred to collectively, for convenience, as the Reformation) created a new ideology that profoundly affected all aspects of European life. The reformers—both Catholic and Protestant—saw spiritual matters as the core of human identity. In this they resembled earlier Christian leaders, but they broke decisively with the medieval past in their systematic, persistent attempts to Christianize peasants and other ordinary folk. In the reformers' ideology, Christianity was not just a matter for a few religious specialists, such as monks or priests, as had been the de facto situation in the Middle Ages. Instead, the reformers believed that each member of the community should lead a Christian life. This conviction gave all branches of reform their great stress on missionary work. As evangelists spreading the faith, the godly reformers preached and taught at all levels of European society. Their educational efforts met with considerable success, for members of the lay elites and even lower social groups adopted the values and habits required by the new doctrines of spiritual reform. In this way the ideology of the religious elite came to be a potent political and social force. Embraced by rulers, judges, and other authorities and imposed on popular classes, the ideas of godly reform penetrated deeply into European culture during the era of the witch craze. A "Christianization" of Europe in the sixteenth and seventeenth centuries was probably the major long-term result of the upsurge in spirituality that occurred during the Reformation era.[13]

The reformers, whether Catholic or Protestant, were militants who saw the world as the scene of cosmic conflict between forces of good and evil. They were inclined to detect evidence of deviant practices everywhere. The new stereotype of the witch reflected the religious and lay authorities' concern with religious dissidents in strife-torn Reformation Europe. The witch hunters' image of collective devil worship at the sabbat undoubtedly derived in part from their knowledge of secret religious services that persecuted minorities were resorting to in many areas of Europe. Authorities predisposed to suspicions of clandestine conventicles gathering under their noses were ready to believe that large numbers of devil worshipers were also in their midst. Worth noting in this regard is the symbolism of the witches' sabbat, which reveals the authorities' belief that devil worshipers were reversing Christian ceremonial. Making an obscenity of the holy kiss, turning consecrated bread into devil's food—these, like the diabolical stigmata of the devil's mark, were the blasphemies that the orthodox expected from their heretical enemies, whether they were labeled Catholics, Protestants, or witches.

More generally, the Reformation was the occasion for renewed concern with the power of Satan in the world. Leading Protestant and Catholic reformers, continuing the tradition of late medieval Latin Christianity, laid great stress on satanic imagery. For example, in the catechism of the leading Jesuit reformer Peter Canisius, the name Satan appears sixty-seven times, four more than Jesus' name. Martin Luther believed that the devil was lord of this world; in almost Manichean fashion, he held that visible reality and all things of the flesh belonged to Satan. The great reformer, as he confessed, could not "shake off Satan as I desire," "although I be a doctor of divinity, and have now preached Christ, and fought against the devil in his false teachers a great while." And John Calvin, who saw humans so yoked to sin that they could do nothing to save themselves, pictured human will as the captive of Satan's wiles, in most cases abandoned by God to the devil's power. As Luther's reference to the devil's "false teachers" implies, preoccupation with Satan was fed by the bitter sectarian strife that poisoned the emotional atmosphere of Reformation Europe.[14]

Mainstream reformers and religious radicals seem to have been equally deeply concerned about Satan. John Rogers, the seventeenth-century English sectarian, admitted to seeing devils in every tree and bush. For years he slept with his hands clasped in a praying position, so that he would be ready if Satan came for him during the night. As a boy Rogers was haunted by "fear of Hell and the devils, whom I thought I saw every foot in several ugly shapes and forms, according to my fancies, and sometimes with great rolling flaming eyes like saucers, having sparkling firebrands in one of their hands, and with the other reaching at me to tear me away to torments."[15]

It may be hard to take seriously today the idea of a personal devil who brings bad weather, illness, or other misfortune, but the image was vividly real to the religious reformers and those who came under their influence. Keith Thomas notes that "the Puritan Henry Holland attributed the plague to evil spirits, while the mid-seventeenth-century clergyman, Thomas Hall, knew that his chronic insomnia was the work of Satan, because it was always worse on the night before the sabbath or a religious fast."[16]

Belief in the devil proved a psychological necessity for many people, as the intensely introspective habits and preoccupation with sin encouraged by all branches of reformed Catholic and Protestant Christianity apparently heightened feelings of inadequacy and moral responsibility. Thus, there was created powerful psychological pressure to project the resulting guilt feelings onto an external personage, the devil, if not onto the devil's human servant, a witch. Meanwhile, the Reformation era's profound political and social upheavals seemed clear proof of Satan's increased activity. Rival groups regularly cast their enemies as representatives of the devil, just as they viewed themselves as fighters on the side of God.

After 1560, clerics and other members of the elites who were influenced by reforming ideals came to interpret many folk practices as devilish and heretical. The representatives of reformed religion had little tolerance of the folklorized Christianity that had been the everyday religion of most people in the Middle Ages. Imbued with a new sense of doctrinal purity, they sought to root out all popular practices that did not flow from official teaching. Reformers labored to inculcate Christian doctrine and moral codes of behavior formerly unheard of in the European countryside. These strong missionary efforts brought the reformers into conflict with deeply traditional folk practices. In such combat the godly saw themselves fighting on one of the many fronts in the war against heresy.

Partly because elite culture laid so much stress on satanic imagery, the reformers were predisposed to find heretical dualism in the folkways of the uneducated. What they discovered in the backwoods horrified the missionaries. In Brittany, for example, peasants believed that buckwheat was not made by God but by Satan. When they harvested this grain, the staple of the poor family's diet, they threw handfuls into the ditches around the field as a thanksgiving offering to the devil. Many purifying missionaries were alarmed to discover rural folk who believed that Satan was coequal with God or that good and evil stemmed from separate forces.[17] This was the old Manichean view that remained a perennial subtheme throughout the Christian centuries. Any doctrine that placed weight on a personification of evil tended to invite the deification of that personage, and Christian clergy regarded this tendency with an alarm bred from ages of conflict with Cathars and other dualist heretics.

The folklorization of the devil was evident throughout European culture. Extraordinary features of the landscape, from giant boulders to the equally superhuman-seeming Roman roads, monuments, and bridges, were attributed to satanic origin. The devil was believed to have built the Pont du Gard, for instance, demanding as his reward the first living being to cross it, but he was cheated when the local residents arranged to have an animal cross before any human.[18] That such an outlook has survived to the present will be clear to anyone who has toured rock-strewn river gorges, from the Tarn in France to Minnesota's St. Croix, and heard the guides describe impressive formations as "Satan's pitchfork" or the like. Even in a scientific age, the U.S. National Park Service supervises monuments called the Devil's Postpile in California and Devil's Tower in Wyoming. These names are vestiges of a widespread way of looking at the world that survived, though often in much weakened form, the transatlantic emigration of European settlers.

That any such vestiges survived at all is testimony to the persistence and powerful psychological functions of folk beliefs. Although the Catholic church prescribed sacraments and exorcism for warding off Satan, and Protestants counseled prayer, ordinary people had invented their own remedies. The Breton peasants' buckwheat offering was typical of popular techniques for controlling evil. In general, Satan was not nearly as horrifying in folk imagery as he was in the minds of most theologians. Popular theatricals in medieval towns had featured entertaining demon-figures who danced on the scene amid exploding firecrackers. Yet these devils were defeated by Christ before the final bows. In the popular plays, even the most degenerate sinner could escape hell through a simple act of devotion to a powerful saint like the Virgin Mary.[19]

Folklore stressed Mary's ability to cheat the devil even of his rightful prey, but to the reforming elites of the sixteenth and seventeenth centuries this was too easy a solution. Even the Catholic Counter Reformation, which, unlike Protestantism, retained the cultic veneration of saints, imagined the devil as a dreadful personage whom God permitted to operate in the world as appropriate punishment for the misdeeds of sinners. Michelangelo's depiction of the Last Judgment in the Sistine Chapel reflects the pessimistic spirit of the reformers in its representation of Christ and demons cooperating in sending the damned to hell, while Mary turns away from the doomed sinners' desperate pleas for intercession with her son. After 1560, the godly reformers labored hard to impress on the populace a much more menacing image of the devil. Popular religious plays were suppressed, and the semicomic folk-demon of the later Middle Ages was replaced by the deadly Satan long familiar in elite culture.

The rise of the demonic to prominence in popular consciousness is clear from the chronology of witch trials in Scotland. The first witchcraft trial for which a detailed indictment has survived is that of Janet Boyman of Edinburgh, accused in 1572 of conjuring up demons to perform cures as well as malefice. She vaguely characterized the demonic force as a whirlwind that could acquire human shape. This description is so inexplicit that it may not have been meant to refer to Satan at all. Even twenty years later, when some witnesses spoke clearly of a fully developed devil figure, others were more ambiguous. Only in the first years of the seventeenth century did the figure of Satan become completely standardized in Scottish witchcraft confessions.[20]

Witch hunting spread with the arrival of spiritual militancy in backwoods Europe. The connection between witch trials and religious reformers' efforts to obliterate traditional popular folklore about the devil can be illustrated in the Roman Inquisition's long campaign against a group of Italian peasants called *benandanti*, studied by Carlo Ginzburg.[21] In the isolated mountain villages of the Friuli region northeast of Venice, the *benandanti* ("people who go out to do good") consisted of a select number of peasants whose special role was to protect the crops against the depredations of witches. In the eyes of the community, these individuals had magical powers because they had been born with part of the amniotic sac around their heads. Throughout their lives they carried a bit of the preserved sac on their bodies as an amulet to protect them against the devil's servants. Folk belief held that the *benandanti* entered into a trance-like state and went out in spirit on the first night of each season of the year to do battle against demonic witches. A successful outcome would ensure a good harvest.

When the Inquisition first became interested in the *benandanti*, toward the end of the sixteenth century, the ecclesiastical judges had a hard time understanding how peasants could fly out at night without themselves being witches. Although the *benandanti* claimed to be adversaries of the devil, the learned judges were convinced that their practices must be heretical. Popular vigilante action against witches was certainly neither necessary nor effective, according to official Catholic teaching, and by then the culture of the elites associated any night riding with witchcraft and other deviations from the faith. Under the influence of the Inquisition, the peasants of the Friuli gradually abandoned their previous conviction that the *benandanti* were a force for good. By stages, even the *benandanti* themselves came to reinterpret their actions and beliefs through the eyes of the Inquisition. Although it appears that no *benandanti* were ever tortured, in the 1630s they were admitting to having attended sabbats as observers. Twenty years later they regularly confessed to full-scale participation in devil worship.

The story of the *benandanti* shows how, during the age of the witch trials, folklore became assimilated to the cultural values of the elites. Counter Reformation clerics imbued with a missionary fervor and a horror of popular religious superstition discovered a harmless and socially functional folk belief in a remote mountain region. Determined to root out error, the authorities not only punished the *benandanti* but also convinced them of their criminality. In the end, a local cult was transformed by the powerful acculturating force of an official religious institution. And this process took the form of trials for satanic witchcraft.

The *benandanti* were unusual only in their principle of collective organization. All over Europe, individual men and women carried out roles similar to those performed by the Friulian nightwalkers. Whether known as wizards, magicians, or cunning men, these were the leading therapeutic operatives of pre-Reformation rural Europe. As was described in chapter 1, they were called on by peasants to heal the sick, recover stolen property, or foretell the future. In general, they functioned as protectors of the community against the invisible world of demonic evil. Magicians used herbal medicines, amulets, incantations, and elaborate rituals as their stock in trade. Although generally illiterate, they could rely especially on keen insight into human psychology, playing on feelings of guilt to trap wrongdoers, and they possessed intuitive understanding of the relationship of the psychic and somatic in illness. Although they must have had a high rate of failure, in the absence of competent physicians, an adequate police force, and scientific tools for predicting the future these rural magicians performed crucial social tasks. Above all, they thrived by giving their clients a sense of control, however limited, over a threatening environment. Small wonder that such practitioners were in demand: in England's county of Essex during Queen Elizabeth's reign, no village was more than ten miles from a cunning man.[22]

The existence of popular magic as a universal feature of medieval and early modern village life is testimony to the failure of institutional Christianity to penetrate into rural Europe before the Reformation era. The functions of protection and reassurance carried out by these popular practitioners paralleled certain of the functions of sacramental Christianity. Many Christian rituals were based on the invocation of God's protection for the participants, as in the priest's blessing of a maritime village's fishing fleet before the boats set out to sea. But, because the pre-Reformation clergy tended to be highly neglectful, the psychologically necessary protective role was often performed by magicians. By turning to these practitioners, the populace was in effect rejecting institutional religion. This, at any rate, was the conclusion drawn by the newly energized reforming clergy in Protestant and Catholic Europe during the sixteenth and seventeenth centuries. In this period individual magicians were regularly denounced and sometimes, like Janet Boyman and the *benandanti*, prosecuted for sorcery. In the duchy of Lorraine, where demonologists were especially adamant about the criminality of magical healing, judges threatened and tortured witch doctors until they admitted satanic origins for their curative skills. This was one side of the war on popular religion waged during the Reformation era, as clerical and lay elites associated folk magic with libertinage, atheism, and heresy in general.[23] Paradoxically, the authorities' campaigns against these practitioners of "white magic" may have strengthened the impulse to hunt out witches. For, if recourse to magical healers was denied, an effective technique of self-help against misfortune disappeared. Only the machinery of official witchcraft trials remained to protect the bewitched and the fearful from malefice.

Witch Hunting and the New Misogyny

The foregoing analysis may help explain the rise of a new form of the witchcraft stereotype in the environment of confessional antagonisms and revivified spirituality characteristic of the Reformation era. Yet such a line of argument is really too general to get at the issue of women and witchcraft. The problem remains: why was it generally a female who was identified as the witch? To approach this question from another angle, let us consider some of the main points of Christian tradition on the subjects of woman and sexuality.

Traditions of woman-hatred long antedate the era of the witch craze, of course. Many cultures of the ancient world regarded women as second-class members of humanity or worse, and the male fear of female domination is reflected in myths of diverse cultures. Christian traditions echoed this bias. Despite the strong emphasis placed on the equality of all Christians before God, from earliest times the Catholic church limited the priesthood to men, stressing, as Pope Paul VI reaffirmed in 1977, that the original models of Christian action, Jesus and the apostles, were all males. Although the cult of Mary developed in the Middle Ages, the church insisted that only the status of virginity and the role of motherhood could glorify the female condition. In the serious business of sanctification, even motherhood has disturbed Catholic leaders; there have been very few female saints who were not virgins throughout their lives. Thus, there is no paradox in Jacob Sprenger's leading role as founder of the first German lay confraternity devoted to the rosary. For the coauthor of the misogynistic *Malleus*, idealization of the Virgin Mary merely highlighted the failings of nearly all other women.[24]

In Christian ideology, antifemale bias is closely linked to fears and suspicions of sexuality. Historically, mainstream Christian teaching has been more or less hostile to the sexual side of humans. Inheriting this characteristic from the Hellenistic world in which it developed, early Christianity was greatly affected by St. Paul's emphasis on a two-sided human nature consisting of a mortal body and an immortal soul. Although rejecting the extreme dualism of the Manicheans and later the Cathars, groups believing in the diabolical character of the flesh, Christianity portrayed the body, and particularly its sexuality, as an obstacle to salvation. In St. Augustine's view, which emerged as the representative Catholic teaching, sexual pleasure could be justified only by a married couple's attempt at procreation, and some medieval and early modern Catholic authorities thought sex sinful even for reproductive purposes. Although during the Reformation Protestant moralists rejected the ideal of celibacy and elevated marriage to new heights of respectability, suspicion of sexual pleasure remained a characteristic of all mainstream Christian teaching in the sixteenth and seventeenth centuries.[25]

Jesus' warning, in the Sermon on the Mount, that lusting after a woman in the heart is an adulterous sin became, in the hands of the church fathers, grounds for blaming women for their sexual attractiveness. Origen allegedly castrated himself, an eminently logical solution. But most of the other church fathers, when they found it impossible to banish sexual desire, projected the fault on women, the forbidden objects. Thus, Jerome, who has been called the patron saint of misogyny, discovered that only by studying Hebrew and working on his Bible translation could he sublimate his passion and be rid of the tormenting visions of dancing girls. He characterized woman as "the gate of the devil, the path of wickedness, the sting of the serpent, in a word a perilous object." This view was typical. Tertullian told women, "you are the devil's gateway," and John Chrysostom called the deceptively beautiful female body a "white sepulcher."[26] These early images established a pattern. In the Middle Ages and the Renaissance, women were consistently portrayed as the more lascivious of the sexes, forever dragging men into the sin of lust and away from the ascetic spirituality of which they might otherwise be capable. The reverse of the Victorian idea of female asexuality, the Christian tradition regarded women as quintessentially sexual beings.

Many such misogynistic ideas were compiled in the *Malleus Maleficarum* for perpetuation in subsequent witch trials. Women, wrote Kramer and Sprenger, are inferior physically, mentally, and morally. Their imperfections cause women extraordinary difficulty in warding off temptation. They have an "insatiable carnal lust," are inclined to deception, resist discipline, and lure men into sin and destruction. Such are the characteristics that make them likely targets for the devil; hence, the preponderance of females among the devil's servants. The authors of the *Malleus* rested their assertions on a jumble of historical half-truths, disfigured etymologies, and mistaken medicine. They derived the word *femina* from *fe* and *minus*, to show that women have little faith. The fall of kingdoms and of virtuous men they blamed on females. Naturally, they attributed to Eve's initiative the fall of the human race in the Garden of Eden. Adducing the accumulated wisdom of the ages, Kramer and Sprenger quoted widely from biblical and Roman sources.[27] Only if all of these authorities were wrong could one deny the inferiority of women. And, once female biological deficiency was accepted, the foundation was set for accusations of witchcraft on the ground that women lacked the moral fortitude to resist temptation.

The antifemale prejudices of the *Malleus* were echoed repeatedly in the many demonological treatises that appeared during the age of witch trials. Nicolas Rémy, a judge who prosecuted many witches in Lorraine during the 1590s, found it "not unreasonable that this scum of humanity, i.e., witches, should be drawn chiefly from the feminine sex," for women had always been famous as sorcerers and enchanters. And King James explained the disproportion of female witches by reference to Genesis: "The reason is easie, for as that sex is frailer than man is, so it is easier to be entrapped in these grosse snares of the Devile, as was over well proved to be true, by the Serpents deceiving of Eve at the Beginning," which, he thought, had given Satan ready access to women ever since. In the same vein, Henri Boguet, a witch-hunting prosecutor in the Burgundian Franche-Comté, thought it natural that witches should confess to sexual liaison with Satan. "The Devil uses them so," Boguet explained, "because he knows that women love carnal pleasures, and he means to bind them to his allegiance by such agreeable provocations; moreover, there is nothing which makes a woman more subject and loyal to a man than that he should abuse her body."[28]

This highly unflattering image of women was not limited to a small number of enthusiastic witch hunters. The social order of the elites reflected universal and almost entirely unquestioned assumptions about the inferiority and dangerous attributes of females. The best medical opinion, like that of religious thinkers, associated women with sinful sexuality. Dr. François Rabelais gave this idea its classic Renaissance literary formulation in his *Gargantua and Pantagruel*. Expressing the standard medical view, he described the womb (*hysterus* in Greek) in graphic terms as the seat of woman's sexual passion and the dominant part of a literally hysterical female organism:

> For Nature has placed in a secret and interior place in their bodies an animal, an organ that is not present in men; and here there are sometimes engendered certain salty, nitrous, caustic, sharp, biting, stabbing, and bitterly irritating humors, by the pricking and painful itching of which—for this organ is all nerves—and sensitive feelings—their whole body is shaken, all their senses transported, all their passions indulged, and all their thoughts confused. So that if Nature had not sprinkled their foreheads with a little shame you would see them more insanely chasing the codpiece than ever the Proetides did, or the Mimallonides, or the Bacchic Thyiades on the day of their Bacchanals.[29]

Although by 1600 advanced medical opinion, spurred by improved understanding of female anatomy, led most leading physicians to discard this Platonic image of the migratory uterus, the female's excessive desire for coitus remained a medical truism. "Woman's unnatural, insatiable lust," as the medically learned Thomas Burton put it, was proverbial, and her well-known capacity for multiple orgasms prompted the belief that she habitually exhausted and ran down her mate in satisfying her carnal appetites. As physicians held that only moderate expenditure of semen was compatible with good health, female sexual demands seemed a physical as well as a moral threat to men. But, although women were seen as suffering from overwhelming sexual passion, experts on biology denied them an active role in the reproductive process. Aristotle's theory that semen holds all that is necessary for generation still held sway, and the woman's part was imagined as the entirely passive one of providing a nurturing environment for the developing fetus.[30]

Neither was there much sympathy for woman among other leaders of early modern culture. Theologians, lawyers, and philosophers were nearly unanimous in asserting her inferiority to man, even if a few legal scholars, like some physicians, seem to have been a little embarrassed about expressing antifemale opinions. The occasional intellectuals who spoke out in favor of female equality, including the philosopher Guillaume Postel and the physician Paracelsus, were such general nonconformists that they were denounced as heretics. Given their legion of enemies, women could have done without such friends.[31]

A good indicator of the notion of women that was widespread among the intellectual elites during the age of witch trials comes from Jean Bodin, the famous lawyer and political theorist who also penned a ferocious tract denouncing witches. Bodin began his masterpiece, *The Republic*, with a description of the model household. In it the wife was at the bottom. As the ultimate dependent, she came not only after her husband in the domestic order of things, but also behind the children, servants, and apprentices.[32] Bodin's scheme may have been a bit extreme, but almost no one in the sixteenth and seventeenth centuries, not even early feminists, challenged the need for male superiority in the household. Unlike our modern democratic assumptions, the universally accepted conventional wisdom of the time was that hierarchy was necessary for every kind of social arrangement. As God presided over the universe, as humans were lords of creation, and as kings ruled their states, so it was believed that, in the family, men must be the dominant authorities and women their subordinates. Lawrence Stone, in his comprehensive study of marriage, sex, and the family in early modern England, found that a high degree of patriarchal control characterized upper-class family life until the mid-seventeenth century, and that utilitarian needs and a sense of duty, not affection, were considered the best foundation for relations between spouses. The law, too, reflected women's dependent status. In Scotland, for instance, women were barred from appearing as witnesses in criminal cases, and a special act had to be passed in 1591 to permit their testimony in witchcraft trials.[33]

Acceptance of the principle of male superiority and its embodiment in family life, law, and all other social arrangements meant that, throughout European culture, disorder was associated with women on top. The inversion of morality that was a general feature of the witch stereotype is reflected clearly in the lack of dependency on men exhibited in supposed acts of malefice and in night riding to the sabbat. To men, the reversal in sex roles was probably among the most disconcerting elements in the image of the witch. Among theologians, lawyers, and philosophers, discussion of women was almost always linked with marriage. Thinkers seemed unable to imagine a social role for unattached females. This psychological blind spot is one way to explain why a disproportionately high number of accused witches were widows and other unmarried women not under the rule of men.[34]

In some exceptional parts of Europe, however, the social structure allowed married women a high degree of independence, in large part because their husbands and fathers spent long periods away from home. The fishing villages of the Basque country along the border of France and Spain furnish an example of a society in which the men were absent for months at a time. In this region, women were accustomed to running household and community affairs themselves, a situation that profoundly shocked godly reformers who visited the Basque country.[35]

This brings us back to Pierre de Lancre. He became convinced that Basque women were an immoral and unfaithful lot when observing their social arrangements during his witch-hunting expedition. De Lancre was especially horrified at the leadership roles in religious services taken by Basque women, the very women among whom witchcraft was rife. Like many others imbued with religious idealism in the Reformation era, de Lancre was appalled by popular religious practices. To the godly missionaries who sought to instruct rural folk in Christian teachings, peasant religion was filled with demonic or pagan "superstition," by which expression they meant false religion, not irrational opinions. Thus, de Lancre's witch hunt can be interpreted as a kind of missionary crusade in the name of godly reform.

In general, the religious strife of the Reformation probably had the effect of increasing fear and hatred of women. Females had been singled out as the progenitors of heresy in medieval times, and such accusations resurfaced in the sixteenth century. In fact, earlier dissident sects, including the

Cathars, had encouraged women to assume active religious roles, in striking contrast to strict Catholic application of St. Paul's dictum that women must remain silent in church. And enthusiastic sects of the Reformation era regularly featured women among their leading spirits. De Lancre's horror at female participation in religious services betrayed a characteristic tendency of mainstream church and secular authorities of Reformation times to associate women with religious deviance.[36] This association reinforced traditional Christian fears of women and helped to fuel the misogyny that underlay witch hunting.

Of course, de Lancre was not a unique case. If an argument can be made for witch trials as a manifestation of intensified misogyny in the late sixteenth and early seventeenth centuries, the proliferation of witch-hunting godly reformers is among the most impressive kind of evidence. As we have seen, a prominent feature of all branches of reforming Christianity, Catholic and Protestant, was the evangelical impulse. In spreading Christian doctrine to the backwoods, reformers were fighting popular religious practices, including what they saw as witchcraft. The witch hunts spread with the arrival of spiritual militancy. Trials in northwestern Germany and in Luxembourg and other parts of the Spanish Netherlands, for instance, proliferated with the growth of Jesuit influence in these regions and the publication of works by such local Jesuit demonologists as Martin Del Rio and Peter Binsfeld.[37] Huguenot leader Lambert Daneau published what seems to have been the first French-language book on witches in 1564. The Scottish Presbyterian church adopted the continental image of the witch as the servant of Satan and successfully urged state authorities to initiate witch trials as one way of cleansing rural society of its pervasive immorality.[38]

It is important to realize, however, that this preoccupation with witchcraft and peasant religion was not limited to clerics alone. As the example of de Lancre suggests, such concerns spread to the laity as well. Many of the most active demonological writers and judges were laymen who had become imbued with the values of spiritual reform. For example, the Lorraine witch hunter Nicolas Rémy was a bitter enemy of lax priests and spoke out against the residues of pagan beliefs in Catholic folk religion. Even Jean Bodin characterized witchcraft as "superstitious religion," the same term the godly used to denounce peasant beliefs. And Bodin was far from an orthodox godly reformer in his private religious preferences and his public calls for religious toleration. The imagery of the sabbat, devil worship, and sexual servitude underlay the demonology of many other lay judges. Thus, witch hunting demonstrates the success of reforming efforts to energize the lay elites with the ideology of spiritual purification.[39]

The sexual prejudices expressed in witch hunting are one of the best indicators of this success. The sixteenth century was the first in which it was acceptable for laymen to discuss sexual topics. Secular writers' adoption of traditional Christian ideas about women and sex suggests the considerable degree to which religiously based notions were absorbed into lay culture. Predisposed as they were to identify women with sinful sexuality, lay and clerical authorities came to express misogynistic sentiments on an unprecedented scale in their campaigns against popular religion. In the process, they gave traditional fears of women a new and sharper focus. Thus, the encounter of high and low cultures in the era of the Reformation became an occasion for transforming the ancient, conventional misogyny of the Western past into a murderous set of prejudices. The witch craze's slaughter of women was the result of the spread of woman-hatred in the spiritually reformed elites and its application in the reformers' campaigns against folk religion.

Changes in the visual arts also appear to indicate that distaste for women was becoming a more prominent theme during the sixteenth century. As was the case earlier, the many representations of the Virgin Mary served only to draw a contrast between idealized femininity and the defects of real women. But the contrast became explicit in French engravings made during the second half of the sixteenth century, the high tide of witch trials in Western Europe. A careful study has revealed that in these engravings women frequently personify all or nearly all of the seven deadly sins. When portrayals of virtuous women appear, they almost always are shown in the nude, as remote allegorical figures. But when, as was more often the case, an artist drew a woman engaged in some vice or crime, she was clothed in contemporary garb, thereby associating the sinful woman with the females of everyday life.

Particularly brutal were portrayals of older women as ugly hags who were the embodiments of vice and the special allies of Satan. The Neoplatonic mystical linkage of beauty to goodness that underlay much Renaissance visual art—and which does not appear to have had any practical benefits for real women—had as its inverse an association of ugliness with evil. And the typical victim of witchcraft accusations was just such an ugly old woman, the Halloween witch still familiar today. In the Jura region of Switzerland, in parts of England, and in northern France, for example, the median age of suspected witches ranged between fifty-five and sixty-five. Thus, it seems plain that artistic representations, philosophical opinions, and legal procedure all were manifestations of the same set of stereotypes.[40]

The predominance of older women among witch suspects also

stemmed from the social conditions of early modern village life. As will be explained in the next chapter, accusations of witchcraft mirrored both sexual biases and social tensions. Sexual prejudice linked witchcraft to females, and specific social circumstances made certain kinds of women particularly liable to witchcraft prosecution.

That prejudice against women was based on sexual fears and guilt feelings can scarcely be doubted. Women were regularly depicted as predators, with sexuality as their weapon. Many literary and pictorial representations associate female sexuality with evil, as in Michelangelo's portrayal of the serpent with a woman's breasts in the Sistine Chapel panel on the Temptation. To twentieth-century observers, nothing could be clearer than the erotic emotions that led men, for example, to undress women publicly and minutely examine their genitals. Few people in those days thought in terms of unconscious sexual symbolism, so the possible presence of libidinous impulses in respectable judges was rarely mentioned by contemporary writers. The appeal of sexuality and violence, the mixture of pleasure and pain that we call sadism, was usually not expressed consciously at the time of the witch trials. Still, Philippe Ariès has asserted that this blend of the erotic and the violent, although not characteristic of medieval Europe, has grown steadily since the sixteenth century, finally becoming explicit in the era of the Marquis de Sade. And Lawrence Stone connects the rise of flogging as a form of schoolboy punishment with sadomasochistic sexual tastes among the English upper classes. At least one observer in the era of witch hunting noted the prurient interests that witchcraft investigations could bring out. An astonished eyewitness at Salem recounted how the Puritan divine Cotton Mather publicly exposed and fondled the breasts of a seventeen-year-old girl as she lay writhing in a fit of ostensibly demonic possession.[41]

Sixteenth-century artists gave witness to this unconscious sadism in their depictions of Death and the Maiden, a subject that received many treatments during the later Middle Ages and the Renaissance. Before 1500, artists had tried to suggest moral reflections about the worthlessness of human vanity and the transience of all physical things by showing a beautiful girl engaged in self-admiration while the skeletal figure of death lurks in the background, hourglass in hand, ready to summon his victim away. But, after 1500, treatments of Death and the Maiden became much more explicit. Death no longer hangs back, out of the young girl's sight. He grasps her breast and thigh, runs bony fingers through her beautiful hair, or kisses her on the mouth. And the women, though horror-struck, are also helplessly fascinated. They undress themselves so as to better receive the figure of Death. In one portrayal, a richly clothed lady passionately kisses Death's decomposing skull while she lifts her long skirts and guides his skeletal hand between her legs. These pictures show Death attacking his victims in sexual ways, merging Eros and Thanatos into a newly formulated, powerful compound.[42]

An artist of the early sixteenth century who produced several progressively more explicit variations on the theme of Death and the Maiden was Hans Baldung Grien.[43] His career brings together many of the themes discussed in this chapter. Baldung Grien was active between 1505 and 1545, mostly in Strasbourg. There he developed close contacts with leading humanists and Protestant reformers, many of whom wrote or preached on the subject of witchcraft. Because of these ties, and perhaps also because he came from a family of distinguished jurists and legal scholars, the artist frequently depicted witches in his paintings and woodcuts. More than any other artist of his generation, he seems to have been affected by the imagery of witchcraft as it was expounded in the *Malleus* and other works of the demonologists. His woodcuts illustrate the first German-language treatise on witchcraft, *Die Emeis*, published by Johann Geiler von Kaysersberg in 1517. Baldung Grien's portrayals of witches emphasized such aspects of official theory as their lasciviousness, their ability to fly, and their responsibility for bad weather.

This fascination with witches, however, was only one aspect of Baldung Grien's consistent concern with the evil nature of women. In his several treatments of the fall of man in the Garden of Eden, Eve usually plays the active part. She is depicted as the temptress who brings a passive Adam to sin, and this sin is explicitly associated with death. Baldung Grien was the first artist to represent the fall as an overtly erotic act. He interprets Adam and Eve's sinning as a surrender to lust, and in her body language Eve makes it clear that she is a lewd and sensual creature (Plate 3). The artist returned often to the theme of woman dominating man through her sensuality, as in his woodcut of the legend of Phyllis and Aristotle, showing the lascivious woman clad only in a warrior's helmet, riding atop the aged philosopher's back. Like many Renaissance artists, he was preoccupied with death, which he connected with the sensual power of women and their ability to corrupt men. His image of the witch, then, was a natural extension of his fundamental vision of woman as the progenitor of lust and the explanation for man's perennial failure to rise above bestiality. Later in the sixteenth century, this image of the woman as witch became a staple of demonological symbolism as the spirituality of religious reformers encountered the culture of rural Europeans.

PLATE 3. Hans Baldung Grien, *Adam and Eve* (*Der Sundenfall*) (1511). National
Gallery of Art, Washington, Rosenwald Collection.

Cultural Clash and the Reform of Morals

To understand the predominance of women witches, then, it is not enough to cite the misogynistic sentiments of witch-hunting prosecutors. All too often earlier writers, both clerics and laymen, had given vent to traditional Christian ideas about the inferiority of women. What was new in the Reformation era was the connection of these traditional prejudices to full-fledged ideologically based movements for reform. Catholics and Protestants undertook massive campaigns to alter popular behavior, particularly sexual behavior. The relatively weak social controls characteristic of late medieval Europe were replaced by far more stringent codes and effective enforcement mechanisms.

There are many clues to the meaning of the newly enhanced sexual character of witchcraft in the clash of elite reforming impulses and popular values. As the reform of elite society progressed, many members of the upper classes came to sense a growing distance between themselves and the masses. Traditional attitudes of universal brotherhood gave way to an imagery of social cleavage built on cultural differences. By and large, the European elites grew contemptuous of popular ways and associated them with everything they had learned to despise. The manners of the upper classes, to begin with externals, were becoming notably different from those of ordinary folk. At table they used the newly invented fork instead of their fingers. It was now the mark of a gentleman to carry a handkerchief on his person at all times. In upper-class domestic architecture bedrooms were turning into private retreats for the first time, with the corridor introduced as a by-pass.[44]

These elite expressions of individuality were founded on a sense of privacy and self-discipline that made the physically spontaneous appear dangerous and low. That which was "natural" did not seem necessarily desirable, for human nature had an animal-like side that had to be overcome in order for man to lead a moral life. Infants, therefore, were not allowed to crawl in seventeenth-century upper-class households, because this habit reminded adults of four-footed beasts. Almost inevitably, then, popular culture was associated with bestial naturalness and lack of restraint. In particular, the most subjugated groups were consistently linked with moral licentiousness. Children received hard discipline to drive out the devil in them. Blacks had a reputation for sexual potency because of their allegedly low moral status. And women were consistently tied to Satan and sex. It is not hard to see in these stereotypes projections of desires repressed by

European elites ever more thoroughly imbued with the spirit of religious reform.[45]

Here was one of the key linkages underlying the witch trials. As large segments of elite society were becoming preoccupied with self-control, physical restraint, and ascetic demeanor, the sexual aspects of popular culture caused great concern. Elite convictions that plebeian women were likely to succumb to any attractive stranger make understandable the injection of a strong dose of sex into the witchcraft recipe. Women, and particularly women of nonelite social classes, seem to have struck these judges as fundamentally immoral types who, as slaves to their sexual urges, were capable of the worst treason against man and God.

Joan of Arc's enemies had been convinced that she must be a polluted harlot and went to great lengths to prove she was not a virgin. What was a unique case (or nearly so) in the early fifteenth century became the norm one hundred fifty years later, as the reformed elites grew uneasy about the implications of suspected licentiousness among women of lower social classes. "Whore and witch" was the standard characterization of accused women from the villages of Luxembourg, and whore meant a woman who indulged in sex for pleasure, not for money.[46]

The accused witches of Joan's day, and of the fourteenth and fifteenth centuries in general, were frequently males, but the proportion of men continually declined before and during the witch craze, as the crime was reformulated in strongly sex-linked terms. The one-fifth of witch suspects in Scotland who were men, for example, do not appear to have been accused of any sexual relationship with the devil, unlike their female counterparts. As witchcraft became identified with sexual trespasses in the minds of the reforming witch hunters, its sex-linked status was greatly reinforced.[47]

This association may well be indicative of a psychological process by which women, as agents of Satan, were held responsible for male sexual inadequacy and transgressions. Symptoms of what can be termed early modern machismo include a highly patriarchal family structure, an obsession with codes of sexual honor, and the curious stress on the genital-emphasizing codpiece in dress and literary expression. All of these may betray considerable male insecurity. The purifiers' preachments about the close relationship of sin and sex surely encouraged in their audiences a sense of guilt about sexual feelings. If inability to adhere to newly generalized standards of Christian sexual behavior could be blamed on women as a consequence of satanic intervention, the male sense of guilt would be greatly reduced.[48]

In this may be found one of the principal social and psychological foundations for witch-hunting misogyny in the age of religious reform. Robert Muchembled, one of the historians who has argued vigorously for the importance of cultural clash as the impetus for witch trials, speculates that, in the French-speaking territories of the Spanish Netherlands, the villages that experienced witch trials were the ones with parish priests who took religious reform particularly to heart. These clerics' guilt feelings about their repressed physical desires, he suggests, made them harp on sexual themes in their sermons and stress the stereotypical image of the witch as the exemplar of dangerous female sexuality. In neighboring communities with priests who behaved more like laymen, the congregants never were taught to associate women and sex with Satan, and trials for witchcraft did not occur.[49]

Guilt feelings stemming from repressed sexuality and unrealized desires for spiritual fulfillment were not limited to men during the Reformation era. Some of the most dramatic episodes of the witch craze originated in convents, where sisters declared themselves possessed by demons and engaged in behavior regarded as lewd and indecent by scandalized observers. The nuns blamed men for their actions, claiming that they had been bewitched. Like other females who held males responsible for their bewitchment, these sisters were in effect reversing the cycle of repression, guilt, and scapegoating that the clerical establishment had burnt into the European consciousness by associating women and sex with Satan.

On the conscious level, the witch hunters and other leaders of godly reform, like the medieval inquisitors before them, saw themselves as inspired primarily by the desire to save souls. They regarded many members of their flocks as mired in sin, but the attractive Christian idea that even the worst sinner is capable of redemption and salvation spurred on the reformers. This motivation is important to remember, because the horrors of witch prosecutions can easily blind us to their judges' ideals. The art of the Catholic Counter Reformation revived the New Testament theme of the harlot redeemed by Christ, and seventeenth-century artists produced many propaganda canvases showing Mary Magdalene and others, sometimes in the dress of contemporary prostitutes. These paintings display sin as fundamentally sexual, and they associate sexuality with women. Yet also present is the theme of repentance and the ever-present possibility of salvation.[50] In the spirit that inspired this art can be glimpsed the Christian charity that moved the godly elites, even in witch trials. The reformers' deep ideological commitment made them welcome confession and repentance. They saw such changes in behavior as a means of opening the gates of heaven to the sinner. Nevertheless, one cannot escape the conclusion that the witch hunters' identification of women with sin, sexuality, and lower-class mores, combined with their ideological zeal, led them to establish a pattern of judicial excess and gross violations of human dignity.

Ironically, the available evidence seems to indicate that, despite the cultural elites' perception of ever-increasing distance between their ethos and that of ordinary folk, plebeian behavior was in fact changing dramatically in response to pressures from above. Beginning in the mid-sixteenth century, the moderate toleration of sexual license that appears to have been the norm in the later Middle Ages was replaced by a far more repressive spirit, not only among the elites but also at lower levels of society. A few examples can illustrate the changes. For the old ways, consider the Pyrenean village of Montaillou in the fourteenth century. There casual premarital sex was accepted, and about 10 percent of the households consisted of unmarried couples living together. Meanwhile, the local priest set the pace in lechery.

Montaillou was an atypical community because of its Catharist tendencies, but a concubine-holding priesthood was standard in pre-Reformation Europe. In Bavaria, for example, only 3 to 4 percent of the parish priests of the mid-sixteenth century had *not* taken concubines.[51] The efforts of the Catholic reformers, however, soon led to the transformation of priestly celibacy from a pious hope to an actual model for imitation. Reform-minded churchmen vigorously combated formerly widespread patterns of concubinage among the clergy and the upper classes. Those who persisted, unless they were very highborn, were subject to denunciation and eventually to excommunication. As a result, the proportion of illegitimate births attributable to concubinage fell dramatically after the sixteenth century.[52]

Such campaigns eventually produced a marked improvement in the moral quality and educational preparation of parish priests. The spread of Protestantism in northern Europe can be understood in part as a symptom of popular revulsion against a priesthood that was badly trained and morally lax. The Protestant pastor received a systematic preparation that stressed knowledge of the Bible and methods for communicating its teaching to his congregants. One of these methods was setting a personal example of moral behavior. All over Catholic Europe, church leaders were similarly concerned with improving the quality of the local clergy. Under Jesuit leadership, the Council of Trent's strictures about the training and behavior of priests gradually took hold. No longer was the local cleric just another member of the community, a good fellow who might join in a Mardi Gras dance. In reformed Europe he became a sacred figure, separated from the profane society that he was constantly trying to remake in his own new image.[53]

Not only clerics found themselves called to higher standards of sexual behavior. As in today's ideologically motivated revolutionary regimes, the magistrates of the time developed an interest in crimes against morality. The Parlement of Rouen, for example, began to hear frequent cases of adultery, bigamy, sodomy, and incest. These kinds of crimes increased from less than 1 percent of the court's business in 1548–49 to 10 percent in 1604–06. The town fathers of the Lutheran imperial free city of Nördlingen also legislated harsher punishments for sexual offenders after the middle decades of the sixteenth century. From 1590, judges in Geneva and the Swiss Catholic canton of Fribourg, moved by exposure to reformed spiritual ideas that classified sexual deviance as heretical, regularly tried offenders accused of sodomy and bestiality. The General Assembly of the Presbyterian Church in Scotland was instrumental in prompting trials of—note the combination—"incest, adulterie, witchcraft, murther and abominable and horrible oaths." The General Assembly protested to the king in 1583 that without punishment for these offenses "daily sinne increaseth, and provoketh the wrath of God against the whole countrie." Between 1574 and 1696 the Scottish Parliament passed ten statutes condemning blasphemy and swearing and fifteen against sabbath-breaking. Adultery and incest were made capital offenses in the 1560s, at the same time that the Parliament legislated against witchcraft.[54] After 1600, English church courts and justices of the peace also conducted many trials of fornicators. These efforts apparently were effective, to judge from English birth records. As late as Elizabeth's reign, the rates of premarital conception and illegitimacy continued high, yet both ratios dropped by a remarkable 50 to 75 percent under Puritan influence during the first half of the seventeenth century.[55]

The active roles taken by lay judges in these areas attest to the breakdown of traditional medieval spheres of clerical and nonclerical activities. It has often been pointed out that the state's intervention in witch trials reflects the secularization of law in early modern Europe. Equally worthy of note is the extent to which witch legislation and prosecution by state authorities responded to religious concerns. By exercising the power of the newly centralized states in cases of witchcraft and other moral offenses, lay elites showed the deep impact on them of spiritual reform.

The godly not only condemned adultery and premarital sex but also objected to strong passion in the marriage bed. "Never on Sunday" or during Lent was the standard clerical admonition, along with detailed instructions about avoiding "sinful" positions and actions while making love. The first natives to be told of the "missionary position" were the villagers of Europe. Reforming French bishops distributed detailed manuals to parish priests to help them implement approved sexual behavior among the congregants. In these handbooks, learned churchmen established an elaborate hierarchy of sexual sins and recommended appropriate penances for violations that ranged in seriousness from "unnatural" sexual positions, including women on top, to incest and sodomy. The content of this sexual advice was not particularly novel, but the vigorous, well-organized enforcement effort of reform-minded authorities was.

In all of these ways, the moral ideology of spiritual reform was given political meaning in the late sixteenth and seventeenth centuries. The emphasis on sexual repression in society made witchcraft a particularly heinous crime, especially when formulated as sexual servitude to the devil. One sexual offense traditionally ascribed to earlier witches may, ironically, have faded as the new stereotype of witchcraft emerged. Sexual impotence, common in the charges against fifteenth-century witches in the *Malleus* and other early demonological works, seems to have become less typical of trials during the witch craze, a transformation easily understandable given the reformers' frowns on sexuality. To sexually repressive witch hunters "tying the knot" to induce impotence may not have seemed an entirely unmixed curse.[56]

The reformers' antipathy for popular sexual practices was merely one side of their consistent tendency to identify the folkways of ordinary people with sin and heresy. Popular recreations like dancing, gambling, and playacting were regularly condemned as immoral and in some places were suppressed. The great seasonal festivals, including Carnival, May Day, Michaelmas, and Midsummer's Eve, which were grand occasions in the life of the people, came under heavy attack by reformers, who condemned them as lewd and pagan profanations. For centuries the liberties of Mardi Gras and similar celebrations had served as a useful safety valve in the pressure-filled lives of ordinary people. But to the reformers these festivals seemed circuses of sin. Eating, drinking, sex, and violence were the chief themes of such occasions, and many of the organized activities—parades, contests, and theatricals—celebrated these basic human impulses. The carnality of Carnival implied that it was all right to give free rein to bodily pleasures, at least on some special days of the year. Heavy eating and drinking were part of the ritual, and population records show a clear rise in births nine months after festival seasons. Carnival was playtime, but to godly reformers such play appeared the height of sacrilege.[57]

Repressive authorities were tempted to ban all types of group revelry.

In Scotland the church and borough councils repeatedly prohibited large gatherings, such as the "penny bridal" weddings of poor folk who had to ask guests to bring their own refreshment. This kind of deprivation inspired the typical description of witches' sabbats in Scottish and continental trial confessions. The accounts nearly always speak of uproarious disorder—eating, drinking, music, dancing—the activities denied to ordinary people both by their poverty and by the godly elites' suspicion of festive popular gatherings.[58]

In the imagination of the authorities, the witches' sabbat of ordinary folk naturally included unbridled, licentious celebration, because reformers were certain that their social inferiors were greatly susceptible to the enticements of bodily pleasure. Nicolas Rémy linked this human frailty to the satanic witchcraft he discovered in Lorraine:

> Orgies of carnal indulgence and dances form the commonest occasions among mankind for celebrations and banquets; and the Demon is careful to provide all these in order to attract to himself more numerous and more devoted followers. For after he has pandered to their base passions it follows that it is easier for him to plunge them into crimes at which they had shuddered before.[59]

As in the instance of "penny bridals," reform-minded authorities took a particularly severe line with regard to quasi-religious events such as weddings or funerals. Reformers wished to cleanse religious ceremonies of any taint of desecration. They objected to the traditional revelry of marriage celebrations, wakes, and vigils. In accord with the frequent folk habit of turning established custom on its head, popular celebrations mocked all the institutions of the elites, including church festivals. In Strasbourg around 1500, Catholic reformers protested the local custom that allowed a buffoon to spring out from behind a statue in the cathedral and clown his way through the Pentecost service. In the minds of reformers, these parodies were popular desecrations of holy days with profane entertainment. Thus, after 1560, Spanish religious authorities succeeded temporarily in banning bullfights on Sundays and Catholic feast days. Preachers had been upset by such blasphemies for centuries, but with better organization, better communication, consistent support from secular authorities, and, above all, the evangelical fervor ignited by the confessional struggles of the Reformation, the godly now could hope to achieve their spiritual goals.[60]

Backing for these efforts at purification came from secular rulers, who saw religious uniformity and cultural conformism as effective props for centralized absolute government. The motivation for the reform of popular culture was thus partly political. Severely traumatized by the revolutionary episodes and civil warfare that were endemic in Reformation Europe, princes were determined to suppress political and social dissidence among the lower classes. For example, secular rulers became conscious of the explosive potential of popular celebrations, for festivals sometimes sparked large-scale rioting and even full-blown rebellions. With the support of state officials, the churches moved to suppress the popular lay associations that often organized these events and substituted the parish as the main unit of urban life. An important instance was the abolition of fraternities of adolescent males, which had long been one of the central sources of community identity in European towns.[61]

As a result, by the end of the age of witch hunting traditional forms of folk culture had either disappeared or been subdued throughout Europe. As Carlo Ginzburg summarized this development, "with the Counter Reformation (and simultaneously with the consolidation of the Protestant churches) an age opened marked by the increasing rigidity of authority, the paternalistic indoctrination of the masses, and the extinction of popular culture by the more or less violent shunting aside of minorities and dissident groups."[62] It may be overstating the case to speak of an extinction of popular culture. Yet the wild atmosphere of Mardi Gras, the licentiousness of May Day, and the liberation from normal restraints that characterized all folk celebrations survived only in domesticated, decorous form under watchful Catholic establishments, while in most Protestant lands they were abolished as ungodly profanations. Among Catholics, formal religious processions replaced unbridled popular spectacles. In Protestant churches, Bible texts covered the walls to hide the sensual images produced by local artists in the Catholic past, and everywhere there was renewed emphasis on sermons (often stressing the horrors of hell) as the medium by which the masses were to be guided. A more rigidly controlled society emerged, organized around absolutist states and hierarchical churches that intruded into every area of community life.[63] The witch craze was one side of this scene of generalized cultural clash.

Once sexual "deviance" was connected with witchcraft and heresy in preachers' sermons as well as in the law, the campaign against licentious behavior must surely have been easier to win. To the extent that the reformers' war against sex was successful, the elites' efforts to introduce diabolism into the stereotype of the witch were seemingly accepted by the populace. In any case, as the trials proliferated, popular culture clearly received demonic imagery as a plausible extension of the witch stereotype. Satanic stereotypes apparently did not take firm root in the folklore of witchcraft and tended to fade from popular tradition after the trials ended. But during the age of the witch hunts, ordinary people were effectively conditioned by the godly elites to accept the reality of devil worship among their neighbors. This is one measure of how thoroughly elite ideas of witchcraft were imposed on lower cultural levels.[64]

By way of example, let us refer once more to Pierre de Lancre. His informants about the witches' sabbats were about five hundred boys and girls ranging in age from ten to nineteen, who had been recruited to attend the sabbats and bring back detailed reports. Plainly, de Lancre and his assistants were eliciting these accounts from suggestible children and adolescents. The most recent student of the Basque trials on the Spanish side of the border attributes the confessions there to an epidemic of stereotyped dreams that resulted from such potent psychic stimuli as stories of the events in France, fiery sermons, and the impact of a public execution witnessed by thirty thousand. Churchmen's vivid imagery of the sabbat made a deep impression on ordinary people and produced, in the words of Gustav Henningsen, "that dangerous creation which would take high and low by surprise," a witch panic.[65]

Another indicator of the penetration of elite values into lower cultural levels was the widespread acceptance of the sexual stereotype of female witchcraft. The ancient traditions of misogyny, reinforced by a renewed preoccupation among the reformed elites with sexual sinning, were transmitted to the populace through the missionary efforts of godly reformers during the sixteenth and seventeenth centuries. Thus, bias against women, a conventional characteristic of Christian teaching, became uniquely intense during the era of religious reform. In this period alone did the West's traditional misogyny result in the execution of many thousands simply because, as women, they were automatically suspect.[66] Sixteenth- and seventeenth-century reforming impulses found one of their most important applications in the area of sexuality. The quantum leap in witch trials during this era was one outlet for the deep stresses produced at all social levels as the godly reform of sex took hold.

In many regions of Europe, the spread of witch trials accompanied the advent of a reform-minded clergy. These men of God, trained in seminary or university, were apt to see the devil everywhere and to imagine him as the force underlying all heresy. Thus, when encountering peasant beliefs in sorcery-induced illness or crop failure, clerics and lay authorities influenced by the clerical outlook often went beyond the initial charge and began questioning the accused about devil worship and sabbats. The elites placed charges of malefice in a wider explanatory context within which they could understand the dynamics of supernatural evildoing. This kind of bicultural process, overlaying peasant beliefs with learned concepts, began in the relatively infrequent witch trials of the fifteenth century. With the coming of the Reformation and the appearance of a large, well-educated, irrepressibly evangelical clergy in Western and Central Europe, contacts between learned and popular cultures no longer were sporadic and superficial. They became a regular, permanent feature of village life. These frequent contacts made for frequent witch trials.

One way of understanding the witch craze is to see it as a part of the many-sided war on popular culture waged by reforming clerical and lay establishments in the sixteenth and seventeenth centuries. The chronology of witch hunting argues for this thesis, because the onset of large-scale witch trials corresponds almost exactly with the uneven spread of reforming impulses across Christendom. Witch hunts proliferated as the godly began to indoctrinate ordinary people with Christian theological teaching and concepts of moral behavior unknown to country dwellers of earlier generations. In Western Europe, trials for witchcraft became frequent after 1560, but in Poland and the Habsburg lands of Central Europe, where reform commenced later, such trials were rare until after 1600. As for the remote world of Orthodox Russia, Muscovy, untouched by Western spiritual movements, conducted some trials for sorcery but, lacking the concept of the devil-worshiping heretic, never knew a witch craze.[67] Although it is far from a complete explanation of the trials, the evidence for spiritual reform as a precipitant of the witch craze is very powerful.

4

Classic Witches
The Beggar and the Midwife

Clashes of religious confessions during the Reformation, warfare of unprecedented scale and intensity, a doubling of Europe's population, a five-fold increase in prices, and the persistence of plague and other epidemic diseases, as well as changes in behavior imposed by reforming elites—clearly, European communities were confronted by a galaxy of pressures from the mid-sixteenth to the mid-seventeenth centuries.

A witchcraft trial was one of the few outlets for stress acceptable to both the authorities and the populace. A phenomenon as pervasive and widespread as the witch hunts almost certainly answered the needs of more than one social level. Whether seen as malefice by the villager or construed as devil worship by the elites, witchcraft was a reality to early modern Europeans of all backgrounds. For this reason, efforts to see the witch craze exclusively as a kind of elitist conspiracy against popular culture are ultimately unconvincing. Almost a century ago, rationalist historians assumed that the clerical establishment was the sole active agent, imposing witch trials on a passive and inert population. Now there is a tendency once again to neglect the popular sources of agitation for witch trials. No doubt the predispositions of the elites, together with their control of the judicial apparatus, were necessary conditions for large-scale witch hunting. But there is also much evidence of popular pressure to initiate witch prosecutions. The witch craze is an outstanding example of reciprocal influences among higher and lower cultures in early modern Europe.[1]

The Culture of Poverty

Many accusations of witchcraft resulted from ordinary village quarrels. As the skeptical Jesuit Friedrich von Spee reported in his book attacking witch-trial procedures, "among us Germans . . . there are widespread popular superstitions, envy, calumnies, backbitings, insinuations, and the like, which, being neither punished nor refuted, stir up accusations of witchcraft."[2] Especially common in the overwhelmingly peasant economy of the time was the explanation of household misfortune by witchcraft. Thus, when the cow stopped giving milk or a child grew ill, the farmer/ parent might conclude that a witch had cursed the household. A curse was a very serious matter in the eyes of Europeans in this religious age. It was seen as the way a wronged but helpless individual might invoke God's aid against a powerful oppressor. Curses abound in Shakespeare's plays, and they invariably work.[3] Thus, it is striking to find that many victims of witchcraft accusations were poor beggar women who were said by their neighbors to have laid a curse—not God's, but the devil's—on a household in which something had gone wrong. They were said to practice what might be termed "economic voodoo."

Keith Thomas and Alan Macfarlane have shown that a pattern of accusations against supplicants who had been refused charity predominated in English witchcraft trials. In England, the absence of torture helped keep witch panics in check and muted some of the more lurid aspects of the stereotype of the witch as Satan's worshiper and sexual partner. English witchcraft stressed malefice, and Thomas found that in most cases accusations were triggered by a request for charity:

> The overwhelming majority of fully documented witch cases fall into this simple pattern. The witch is sent away empty-handed, perhaps mumbling a malediction; and in due course something goes wrong with the household, for which she is immediately held responsible. The requests made by the witch varied, but they conformed to the same general pattern. Usually they were for food or drink—butter, cheese, yeast, milk or beer. Sometimes, she would ask to borrow money or a piece of equipment. In all cases denial was quickly followed by retribution, and the punishment often fitted the crime. When Robert Wayts refused Mother Palmer a pot of his beer in Suffolk around 1637, his servants could no longer make beer which would keep fresh. After Mary Ellins, daughter of an Evesham gardner, had thrown stones at Catherine Huxley in 1652, she began to void stones and continued doing so until the witch was executed. At Castle Cary around 1530 Isabel Turner denied Christian Shirston a quart of ale, whereupon "a stand of ale of twelve gallons began to boil as fast as a crock on the fire." Joan Vicars would give her no milk, and thereafter her cow yielded nothing but blood and water. Henry Russe also refused her milk, only to find himself unable to make cheese until Michaelmas.[4]

Beggar women were also among the most common victims in trials elsewhere, although outside England patterns of accusation were more complicated and varied. In the Jura region along the French-Swiss frontier, most witch trials originated in charges against an impoverished and quarrelsome neighbor who had repeatedly cursed the accuser. More than half the witchcraft cases in the Finnish province of Ostrobothnia stemmed from disputes about begging or other village quarrels. In Scotland, too, most suspects were accused by their neighbors of cursing their victims after being refused some favor. It is fair to say that poverty and the social reactions to it were fundamental to the dynamics of witch trials everywhere.[5]

These popular fears of the impoverished, maleficent witch originally had no direct connection with the demonic witch concept fostered by the elites. At first they were independent and autonomous. In such fears can be detected the popular bases of witchcraft accusations, though not the ideological qualities that could turn peasant beliefs into witch panics. Villagers and authorities both accepted as plausible the image of the witch as poor and downtrodden, for it seemed obvious to all that better-off individuals had nonsupernatural ways of achieving their goals. Clauses promising that the witch would never want regularly appeared in alleged demonic pacts—a contract that made sense to peasant accusers and educated judges.[6]

The psychology operating in the trials of beggar women shows that both elite and popular mentalities needed to personalize causation. Ascription of misfortune to an impersonal cause—nature or coincidence—is familiar today. But in prescientific early modern Europe, such a view was much harder to accept, even for the learned. The universally held world-view saw God acting everywhere at every moment. The hand of God could be perceived not only in great events like wars but also in the mundane lives of ordinary people. Thus, if things were going well it was God's doing. If things were going badly, it might also be God's way of punishing the sinner or tempting his faithful followers. Alternatively, misfortune could be the result of Satan's machinations or those of his servant, the witch. In any case, the cause of personal events always seemed particular and specific, not abstract or generalized, as in our modern scientific way of understanding causation.[7]

Given this older way of looking at the world, the problem at the time was to explain the inevitable misfortunes that accompanied daily life. The environmental explanation of witchcraft accusations against charity-seekers spotlights the physical and psychological helplessness of European communities in the face of misfortune. An overwhelmingly agrarian society with little understanding of medicine, meteorology, or scientific agriculture was especially vulnerable to disasters that could affect both life and livelihood with devastating swiftness. The threat of poverty hung over nearly all who worked the land in sixteenth- and seventeenth-century Europe, for even the relatively prosperous farmer might see his family starve in famine years. Most peasants lived at the very margin of subsistence, chronically underfed and subject to deadly infections that spread quickly in malnourished populations. A sixteenth-century Englishman who lived for sixty years would experience, on the average, one or two severe mortality crises in his lifetime, caused by plague or other diseases. If he had lived in a large town, where infection was rife, he might witness three or four such calamities. Mortality crises do not seem to coincide with increased witchcraft accusation in individual communities or districts. But harvest failure and epidemics were the sad environmental backdrop of the age of witch hunts.[8]

Even in good times, one had only to look around to find proof of the precariousness of existence. Every village had its chronically destitute, many of whom had sunk into poverty because of illness, disability, the death of a breadwinner, or simply old age. These impoverished souls offered daily reminders of the hazards of life. Especially in an era of rapid and sizable inflation, the causes of which were but dimly understood, constant fear of economic ruin made for pervasive insecurity.

To exist by the charity of their neighbors was the only recourse of the propertyless and enfeebled. Giving alms to the poor was an everyday reality, not simply an abstract religious injunction. The beggar was the typical welfare case of early modern times. Her knock at the door to ask for a bit of bread, butter, or beer was entirely ordinary in a society that relied heavily on individual acts of charity to assist the needy.

Thomas and Macfarlane have argued that the psychology of the accuser was the crucial element in the charging of beggars with witchcraft. Why should the accuser have connected his act of charity-refusal with subsequent misfortune? Saying no to a request for neighborly charity may have inspired a considerable sense of guilt. According to this hypothesis, in the sixteenth and seventeenth centuries the emerging ethic of individualism may have been powerful enough to cause the denial of charity—"I'm always giving you food; go somewhere else," or "Why don't you go out and work for your bread, like me?"—but the old medieval ideal of communal responsibility could still provoke guilt feelings over the refusal. A justified curse was thought always to work, and apparently the ambivalent householder, later regretting his failure to give charity and thereby to forestall the domestic disaster that had subsequently occurred, suffered under a heavy burden of guilt. He believed himself responsible for the death of the cow, the child's illness, etc., and attributed this misfortune to God's righteous judgment against him for his transgression.

Viewed in this light, an accusation of witchcraft was almost a psychological imperative. Instead of blaming himself, the householder could project his guilt onto the charity-seeker: *she* was the wrongdoer who, with the devil's assistance, had caused damage to the household. He need feel no guilt, for his refusal of charity was altogether appropriate. Who, after all, would want to give alms to the devil's servant, the sower of community destruction?

The accuser in this kind of witch trial was nearly always more prosperous than the accused, though both were at the lower end of the social scale. Almost half the husbands of witches accused in Essex were laborers, whereas among their accusers the more prosperous yeoman class formed the largest single category. In Scotland most accused witches did not come from among the dispossessed or from the servant class. They usually had a house and a yard, were tenant farmers or wage-earners. At the bottom of settled society but definitely within it, these people apparently were not helpless indigents. The poorest of the poor were rarely said to be witches, probably because their neighbors considered them truly needy and therefore entitled to charity. It was the moderately poor person, the borderline case who felt she ought to receive help but was denied it, against whom her fellow villager was most likely to bring a denunciation for witchcraft.[9]

Why, ask Thomas and Macfarlane, did a sense of ambivalence, confusion, and guilt about charity seem to arise in the sixteenth and seventeenth centuries? The logic of their argument compels them to ask this question; for, if this ambiguous relationship between charity-seeker and charity-refuser had existed in the Middle Ages, one would expect to find witch trials earlier. The answer these authors propose is that Englishmen of this era were subject to novel psychological pressures that made them uncertain of their social responsibility. These pressures came from the rise of capitalistic agriculture and the disappearance of the institutional apparatus and doctrinal authority of medieval Catholicism.

Traditional Christian ethics taught that charity was a virtue and mutual responsibility was a religious obligation. In medieval times, the Catholic church had been society's only welfare institution. The church encouraged tithing, bequests, and the giving of alms for the support of the poor and disabled. With the Reformation came the dissolution of the Catholic welfare organization in England, as in other Protestant lands, and the state assumed the burden of welfare. The first English poor law was passed by Parliament under Elizabeth at the end of the sixteenth century. From then on, the upkeep of poor people was primarily the responsibility of lay elites, notably the landowning and merchant classes whose taxes went for welfare. In this way, charity became less a duty incumbent on every Christian; the obligation to care for the poor was depersonalized and mediated through the formal institutions of a bureaucratic government. Eventually all Western countries experienced this shift from personal charity given as a religious duty to primary reliance on impersonal secular institutions.

Often when historians describe this transformation from personal to bureaucratic methods of poor relief, they connect it with the rise of an individualistic business ethic. The much-debated "spirit of capitalism," first raised by Max Weber and resuscitated many times since, is said to have fostered a new ethic of individualism. This new value system held that the individual, not the community, was the primary societal unit. The rise of capitalism in early modern Europe thus can be portrayed as the cause (or, alternatively, the result) of an enhanced stress on the values of individual assertiveness and acquisitiveness. As for the poor, in this capitalistic world they were losers, to whom winners need no longer feel any special obligation. The implications of a mature capitalistic ethic for charitable duties were neatly captured by Benjamin Franklin in Poor Richard's adage, "God helps those who help themselves."[10]

It is very difficult, however, to connect witchcraft accusations with the broad economic and social changes implied in a shift from manorial self-sufficiency to capitalistic profit making. To be sure, our continuing uncertainties about government assistance to the poor suggests the extraordinary difficulty an acquisitive society may have in coming to terms with its responsibility toward indigents. But, unless one accepts the mythology of a golden manorial age in medieval times, when ostensibly the whole community was bathed in a spirit of warm fellowship and mutual responsibility, it is hard to believe that the relationship between those who begged and those who gave was ever entirely free of tension. Macfarlane, who first argued for a connection between witch trials and the rise of commercial agriculture in his thorough analysis of witch trials in Essex, recently disavowed this explanation after discovering that as early as the thirteenth century—the date of the most ancient relevant records—English agriculture was capitalistic and individualistic, not communal and manorial. Yet witch trials did not appear in England until after 1540. Further, there were far fewer trials in England than in Scotland or most continental countries, a fact that makes the explanation from social change particularly suspect. For, if witch trials resulted from the ambivalent feelings of country dwellers caught up in a transitional, quasi-manorial, quasi-capitalistic economy, one would expect that in England, one of Europe's commercially most advanced countries, witch hunting should have been particularly common. Yet the situation turns out to have been exactly the opposite.[11]

As this was the age when religion provided the nearly universal framework in which social values were expressed, the historical detective searching for clues to the meaning of the witch hunts must always give strong weight to the importance of spiritual ideologies. Thomas and, to a lesser degree, Macfarlane suggest that religious change helped produce witchcraft accusations in England. The Protestant rejection of priestly exorcism and other protective rituals employed by medieval Catholicism probably did make villagers feel less secure in the aftermath of the Reformation. No longer could the ordinary householder be confident that he was protected from evil by priestly benediction, for Protestants dogmatically maintained that no cleric could speak for God or mediate between man and the deity. At the same time, the Protestants did not reestablish the Catholic welfare institutions and, thus, seemed to lend support to an ethic of capitalistic individualism.[12] These changes in religious ideology can help make understandable the finding that many charges of malefice, in England and elsewhere, originated in disputes between beggars and their usually not very prosperous neighbors. But, of course, they do not help to explain the many witch trials in Catholic places in which beggars also figured among the accused.

When considering the English trials, it is helpful to keep in mind that witch hunts reflected both the stresses in the daily lives of ordinary people and the beliefs of elites increasingly influenced by the values of religious reformers. Witch trials could take place in large numbers only when the authorities accepted the likelihood of cooperation between Satan and his human servants as the explanation for domestic misfortune. As we have seen, this prerequisite was largely absent in Europe before the fifteenth century. English elites, long isolated from legal and theological changes on the continent, began to adopt this imported view with the coming of Protestant influences from Germany, the Netherlands, and Geneva around the mid-sixteenth century. Thus, English witch trials started late. Largely as a result of the prohibition of torture, they never did take on the vivid associations of sabbat-attending devil worship typical of continental trials.[13]

The significance of legal changes should not be underestimated in analyzing the witch trials. As will be explained fully in chapter 6, the reforms of criminal procedure introduced in the sixteenth century enormously increased the potential for witch panics. Norman Cohn has suggested that witch trials were uncommon in the Middle Ages because the judicial mechanisms of the time often made an accuser liable for punishment if he failed to sustain his charge. The law, by making accusations dangerous for both parties, inhibited the use of witchcraft charges as a way of relieving community stress.[14] Of course, other outlets, of the kind discussed in chapter 2, were available to reduce the level of tension in medieval communities. Further, in the violent world of the medieval European countryside, vendetta, vigilante justice, and other private, direct actions certainly were more effective ways of settling scores than formal court cases.

The great advantage of stressing legal changes and spiritual renewal as leading precipitants of the witch craze that swept across Europe in the sixteenth and seventeenth centuries is that these factors can be found operating throughout the continent in the era of the trials. It is true that legal and religious reform were by no means uniformly felt throughout Latin Christendom, but religion and the law developed with far greater consistency than did economic patterns and social relationships. Theodore K. Rabb has defined the problem in a thoughtful essay on European instability during the sixteenth and seventeenth centuries: "The prime difficulty is the persistence of the locality or the region as a relatively autonomous and self-sufficient economic unit."[15] He concluded that because "regional variation was enormous . . . sharp [economic] patterns and well-defined waves of movement are unlikely to crystallize in the quicksilver experiences of Europe's localities."[16] Rabb is still inclined to see the witch panics as a symptom of widening economic cleavages at the local level and the disruption of closeknit communities. Of course, it would be foolish to deny the significance of social stress in the dynamics of many witch accusations. But, as a complete explanation, or when taken as the chief ingredient in the making of the witch craze, the economic interpretation will not do. Either it turns out to be excessively narrow, accounting for witch trials in only one country, or, equally unsatisfactory, it requires the construction of a model of economic change that greatly simplifies the immensely varied social scene of early modern Europe.

As an example of the difficulties, consider northern France. There Robert Muchembled found abundant and uniform evidence of endemic life-threatening social disasters. But witch trials did not occur everywhere in that region. The Cambrésis had many trials, while neighboring Artois had few. Even within the Cambrésis, some villages were untouched, although adjacent communities burned numerous witches.[17] In a general way, economic change surely contributed to a sense of malaise in the crisis-ridden Europe of 1560 to 1680. But macroeconomic analysis cannot adequately explain witch trials; their dynamics were as personal, individual, and variable as human emotion itself.

Measuring relative levels of social stress in past times is a task that lies somewhere between the extraordinarily difficult and the downright impossible. The root of the problem is the inability to establish that ups and downs in destructive behavior reflect changes in stress rather than changes in record-keeping or the attention paid to such behavior. Likewise, attempts to judge the intensity of stress by disruptive symptoms (witch trials, suicides, pogroms, etc.) tend to run to circular argument. (How do we know there was social stress? Because there were witch trials, suicides, pogroms, etc. Why were there witch trials, suicides, pogroms, etc.? Because of social stress . . .) To avoid the tautological and the unverifiable, one can suggest that social tensions occupied one part of the early modern scene, though not necessarily a new or more prominent part than in earlier times. Medieval society certainly gave witness to widespread anxieties, but not through large numbers of witch trials. A diligent searcher can always find evidence of anxiety and outlets to relieve it, for stress is one of civilization's unavoidable discontents. The key question, however, is why tension and its release take on particular forms in given historical situations. In the case of the witch craze, it appears that anxieties felt at the lower end of the social hierarchy were focused by the upper strata into distinctive patterns of scapegoating.[18] In some places, the elites made witchcraft accusations a newly acceptable outlet for tension. We can illustrate this interaction of high and low cultures by showing how institutional mechanisms could organize the inchoate, desperate fears of everyday life into credible charges of witchcraft lodged against an unusually vulnerable victim, the midwife.

The Midwife as Witch

Elderly females were represented among the dependent poor in disproportionately high numbers, for the old woman was the member of society least likely to be self-supporting. Such poor, old women were the prime targets for witchcraft allegations: evidence from France, England, and Switzerland shows an average age between 55 and 65 for accused witches. In the psychology of witchcraft accusations, the old, impoverished woman was a stock suspect because she seemed entirely helpless, lacking even the physical strength a man might use to avenge himself on his enemies. It appeared plausible that she would resort to supernatural assistance as her only source of power.[19]

Aged single women were especially vulnerable and ran a greater risk of witch charges than did their married neighbors, partly because the widow or spinster was more likely to fall into poverty and thus fit the stereotype of the witch.[20] Also, as discussed in the previous chapter, the woman who lived alone and independent of male control could be a threatening figure in a patriarchal society. There is good evidence that, due to changing marriage patterns, the proportion of single women was growing at the time of the trials, possibly disturbing the delicate balance of community relations. In societies with an atypically small number of unmarried women, such as the French colony in Canada, witch trials were infrequent. Women also lived longer than men, despite the dangers of childbirth. In French communities, there were often two or three times as many widows as widowers. Social bases of popular suspicions about old, poor, and unattached females, when combined with the misogynistic prejudices of the elites, created the image of the witch as an apparently helpless individual who was nevertheless supremely dangerous.[21]

The poor widow lived on the margin of society. Like her, other marginal individuals were good candidates for witchcraft accusations. Outsiders and newcomers inevitably aroused suspicion in a rural environment that held stability, tradition, and immobility as essential parts of the community's self-image, even if, in reality, that society was becoming increasingly fluid and mobile. Certain occupations were particularly dangerous. When we find prostitutes, procurers, and tavern keepers identified as witches, we can see a reflection of the threats to family and community stability that were most feared in early modern Europe.[22]

Midwives were especially vulnerable to charges of witchcraft. These women were marginal in multiple senses. Those charged with malefice were generally old, poor, and unattached to a man. Because they had no other means of earning their bread, they eked out a meager livelihood by assisting at childbirths. Scorned by academic physicians because of their lack of formal training in medical theory, the usually illiterate midwives were nevertheless in demand. Their rough-and-ready practical experience was the only kind of professional assistance available to most childbearing women.

Until the eighteenth century, a lying-in was almost always presided over by women. Scant attention was paid to gynecology and obstetrics in the textbooks of early modern physicians. Most male medical practitioners seem to have considered it undignified and degrading to assist a woman giving birth, and women's desire to avoid embarrassment no doubt also contributed to the exclusion of males from obstetric practice. It has been argued that the casting of midwives as witches was part of a campaign of male medical practitioners to usurp from women their traditional obstetrical and healing roles. This, however, seems unlikely, as the rise of male midwives did not gain strength until after the witch hunts ceased. Yet, as one of the few important events in the life of the community that was given over entirely to female control, birthing may well have been a source of unsettling emotions for men accustomed to supervising every aspect of women's lives. Accusations of witchcraft lodged against midwives are a possible indication of male discomfiture with the competent female.[23]

Certainly childbirth was a moment rich in contradictory emotions for the mother. It was the central event in the fulfillment of her most important social role, that of reproduction. As such, a lying-in promised deep satisfaction and the ultimate confirmation of female identity. Yet childbirth was also exceedingly dangerous. Without knowledge of antiseptics and the dynamics of infection, death of the mother was commonplace. Perhaps one mother in ten did not survive childbirth, a rate one hundred times higher than in advanced countries today.

Even more frequent were stillbirths or infant deaths shortly after birth. Between one-sixth and one-third of all newborn babies died before reaching age one, and a high death rate persisted throughout the childhood years. In one altogether typical English parish in Elizabethan times, only about seventy of every hundred newborns lived to their first birthday, just forty-eight survived to their fifth, and a scant twenty-seven to thirty achieved their fifteenth. An infant death rate of three in ten exceeds even the appallingly high mortality figures of today's most deprived populations. Infant death was more common in Shakespeare's England than among the chronically malnourished populations of present-day sub-Saharan Africa, where about 20 percent of babies never reach age one. Worldwide, one of ten children now dies in infancy, while, in the most wealthy and egalitarian societies, such as Sweden and Japan, fewer than one child in a hundred fails to survive its first year, rates completely unimaginable before the medical advances of the twentieth century.[24]

It is wise not to underestimate the degree of psychological trauma an infant's death might provoke in parents and others, despite the high incidence of such tragedies in early modern Europe. Divine providence could explain infant death, but only at the risk of inducing a heavy burden of parental guilt. For, if God had withheld from a family the universally acknowledged blessing of children, then the parents, and especially the mother, could hardly escape a feeling of responsibility. Fear of the inability to produce healthy children, probably one of the most universal female anxieties, may have been particularly intense in early modern Europe, when high mortality rates combined with the emphasis placed by many reformers on individual responsibility for the rewards or punishments God ordained for each Christian.[25]

To the midwife was regularly attributed responsibility for deaths in childbirth or infancy. Grieving parents could ease their own guilt feelings by blaming the midwife, who thus risked being charged with murdering the newborn. Often ranked below barber-surgeons and the despised execution-ers, midwives could provoke great ambivalence. Their services were re-quired and solicited, but suspicions of "malpractice" always lurked just beneath the surface.[26] Even among her patients, then, the midwife was a potential scapegoat whenever misfortune struck. In the aftermath of a personal tragedy, the midwife's claim that her endeavors were directed only toward good ends, never evil ones, was not always persuasive. Thus, when the midwife Ursley Kemp of Chelmsford, England, maintained that "though she could unwitch she could not witch," the servant girl Grace Thurlow responded that Ursley had successfully delivered Grace's child but had later caused it to fall out of its cradle and break its neck.[27]

Midwifery became an especially dangerous occupation when the au-thorities connected the supposedly murderous midwife with the devil-worshiping servant of Satan. As early as 1499, Fernando de Rojas described the title character of his long play, *La Celestina*, as a witch "whose principal occupation for sixteen years was midwifery."[28] An element of the elites' stereotypical witch belief was that witches killed unbaptised infants, thus depriving them of salvation. After murdering the child, the witch sup-posedly delivered its flesh to the sabbat, where it comprised the main course in the banquet served to all present. Such beliefs reflect the myth of the baby-devouring heretic that remained part of the cultural baggage of early modern Europe. Together with other charges lodged against heretics, it was applied to witches in the *Malleus Maleficarum* and other demonological works and became a standard accusation in witch trials presided over by elite judges. Learned treatises on witchcraft also maintained that midwives used the fat of murdered infants as an ingredient in the ointment that they were said to rub on their bodies in order to fly to the sabbat.[29] Prosecutors familiar with these ideas turned them into actual accusations of murder. Thus, in 1630, two midwives in the archbishopric of Cologne were charged with laying curses on babies at the baptismal font. Of twelve accused witches in the Cologne panic of 1627–30 whose occupations are known, seven were midwives.[30]

Unusually outspoken women who practiced midwifery were liable to

accusations of witchcraft, perhaps because of their nonconforming behavior. In New England during the 1630s, the dissenting religious views of
the midwife and early feminist Anne Hutchinson eventually led the authorities to expel her from the Massachusetts Bay Colony. She had assisted at
the birth of a deformed child whose "monstrosity" provoked uneasiness in
the community. The chief midwife at this lying-in, Jane Hawkins, was
forbidden to practice medicine because of her "notorious . . . familiarity
with the devil," as one contemporary writer explained it. Far more severe
was the penalty imposed on Margaret Jones, a practicing midwife in nearby
Charleston. In 1648 she became one of the first persons executed for
witchcraft in the American colonies.[31]

Since midwives had regular access to newborn children, and because
they also fulfilled the social stereotype of the witch, women who practiced
this occupation were frequent victims of prosecution. In their neighbors'
eyes, such women were likely to acquire over time a reputation for witchcraft, especially because they frequently combined an uppity, independent
spirit with mysterious skills in the always taboo-ridden area of reproduction. Since ill repute was often sufficient grounds to initiate a witchcraft
case, the midwife, like the quarrelsome, cursing beggar woman, all too
often acquired a reputation for malefice. Frequently in witch trials the
accused was someone said to be lacking in deference for her betters. This
was precisely the sort of person of whom it could be believed, in the words
of a Scottish indictment, that she had "shaken off all fear of God, reverence
and regard to the laws of this Kingdome." Such women, who seemed to
threaten conventional opinions of "woman's place," were accused not only
by men but also by other women whose sense of security may have depended on conforming to the standards of acceptable female behavior set
by men.[32]

Another way to explain the identification of the midwife and the witch
is by considering elite preoccupations with popular illegitimacy and infanticide. We have seen that as religious and secular authorities became imbued
with the spirit of evangelical reform they were determined to impose these
values on their social inferiors. Because an illegitimate birth might lead to
punishment in the courts for illicit sex, women quite naturally tried to hide
the evidence. But with birth control practically unknown and abortion
highly dangerous, killing off the newborn was almost the only available
technique. During ancient and medieval times, infanticide apparently did
not evoke in most people the sense of deep wrong that it does in the modern
West.[33] One element of Christianization in the Protestant and Catholic
Reformations was the attempt to instill such a sense of wrong in the

population at large. Thus, prosecutions for infanticide rose rapidly, and the death of babies came under close scrutiny in secular courts. For example, infanticide cases rose from 1.4 percent of the docket of the Parlement of Rouen in 1576 to 8.4 percent thirty years later.[34] Such statistics provide a very poor measure of the actual rate of criminal activity, but they reveal clearly the changing concerns of the enforcement authorities. So, too, does Jean Bodin's linkage of infanticide and the demonic. In his treatise on witchcraft, he maintained that so heinous a crime as infanticide could only result from a pact with the devil, which destroyed "all natural and human affections and piety."[35] Midwives were vulnerable to elite suspicions of foul play and witchcraft because of their lack of professional prestige and the authorities' conviction that they were likely to conspire with the mother to keep the birth secret in order to protect their standing among their neighbors and prospective clients.

In the oaths that the authorities frequently required of midwives after the mid-fifteenth century, they had to swear before God never to murder the newborn or to disguise maternity. The statutes regulating the profession often explicitly forbade the midwife to engage in witchcraft and sometimes demanded a security check to make certain that no prospective midwife had ever been suspected of witchcraft or heresy. Almost without exception, such licensing codes coupled witchcraft with prohibitions of "superstitions and incantations." This combination of forbidden practices hints at what the authorities most feared. To the reformed elites, "superstition" meant popular practices that were not sanctioned by official religious doctrine. The folk magic associated with childbirth now was perceived as heretical; hence, the appearance of statutes, licenses, and oaths to impose religious orthodoxy on early modern midwives.[36] The linkage of devil worship and popular religion was, as we have seen, a fundamental connection in the imagination of the European elites during the age of religious reform. To judge from the frequent repetition of prohibitory statutes, many midwives did employ magical words, acts, and gestures to achieve a healthy birth. For the authorities, the use of such "white magic" was enough to suggest the possibility of black magic, as in the case of Ursley Kemp, who admitted to "unwitching" abilities. In any event, the churchmen generally condemned both types of "superstition" as heretical.

A convenient example of the gap between folk and learned perceptions is the attribution of magical qualities to the placenta by the *benandanti*, as discussed in the preceding chapter. The preserved afterbirth, when used as an amulet by the *benandanti*, struck the Inquisition's judges as suggestive of heresy and devil worship. So, too, the midwife's use of the cord or placenta to magically assure a successful birth seemed to the authorities proof of religious deviance at least and perhaps even of witchcraft. Midwifery statutes from various parts of Europe frequently allude to folk beliefs in placental power and ban the midwife from keeping or giving away the afterbirth and umbilical cord. But reverence for the caul remained widespread. In England, as late as the middle of the seventeenth century, a backwoods country gentleman might regard his caul as a treasure to be preserved and passed on to his heirs.[37]

In brief, both the learned and the unlearned held midwives in ambiguous regard. Performing a necessary service, one disdained by more exalted practitioners, the typical midwife nonetheless remained poor and on the margin of society. She often was feared by clients, who displaced onto her their own guilt feelings. And she was hemmed in by oaths, statutes, and licensing procedures that reflected the elites' deep suspicion of her intentions and misgivings about her competence. For these reasons, the midwife became a standard victim of witchcraft accusations.

Especially revealing is the trial of one German midwife, as reported in a contemporary newsletter. Walpurga Hausmännin, executed at Dillingen in 1587, was accused by her neighbors of causing every imaginable type of misfortune associated with pregnancy and childbirth. During her nineteen years as a licensed midwife, she was said to have brought about numerous stillbirths and deaths of newborns and mothers in parturition. She was also blamed for the loss of children through accident and disease months or even years after their births. Her neighbors produced no less than forty-three counts of malefice against her, many referring to events ten or more years before the trial. A widow for three decades, Hausmännin was further charged by her former clients with inducing repeated miscarriages "in order to cause disunion between two spouses."[38]

Popular anxieties about sexuality and reproduction are evident in these accusations. It seems clear that onto the midwife was projected the unconscious sense of guilt felt by those unable to produce healthy children. The record of Hausmännin's trial contains so detailed a list of charges brought by a large number of her neighbors that we may be confident of this midwife's role as scapegoat for widespread community frustration. Yet, to the judges who tried her in the Dillingen municipal court, such crimes made sense only when placed in the context of devil worship. Under torture Hausmännin was made to confess that she had accepted the devil as her master and paramour. She claimed to have flown on a pitchfork to nocturnal trysts with Satan, where she renounced God and the sacraments, blasphemed against the Virgin Mary—this was a Catholic community—and consumed the flesh of innocent children. According to her confession, she admitted that her malefice, including the killing of cattle and manufacture of hail, was carried out at Satan's behest.

The Hausmännin trial demonstrates how, under the right circumstances, deeply felt popular stresses could produce the need to attribute misfortune to the work of an evil magician. It also suggests how such diffuse popular anxieties, when focused by the demonological fantasies rife in elite circles, might lead to the execution of a helpless elderly woman whose only apparent "crimes" were her poverty, her widowhood, and her dangerous occupation. Significantly, Hausmännin's former clients did not blame her publicly for infant deaths when they occurred. Only after nineteen years and forty-three tragedies did charges of foul play arise. Whatever latent feelings of guilt and hostility the grieving parents had felt very likely were suppressed at the time of the deaths. Presumably the mourners told each other that the losses were the result of God's providence, the traditional explanation for misfortune. But the authorities' new acceptance of witchcraft theory added another possible explanation, one that was less psychologically threatening for parents who had lost a child. Elite receptivity to charges of malefice made such an interpretation thinkable. Thus, feelings of resentment that may have been buried for many years came into the open once the conventional wisdom of municipal officials inclined them to take accusations of witchcraft seriously.

This time lag between supposed malefice and public indictment was common in witchcraft cases. It took time for a woman to build up an evil reputation among her neighbors, and, in the absence of a situation conducive to criminal charges, villagers might harbor uncertainties and suspicions for many years. Frequently present in the accusations of neighbors were characterizations of the suspect's "ill fame" or "evil repute." Those who "had long been suspected of witchcraft" were vulnerable to formal charges from fellow villagers when clergy, landlords, and judges came to regard such claims seriously.

The lengthy period required to establish a convincing and widespread reputation for witchcraft helps to explain why older women were most frequently accused. A young woman would not have had the time to acquire an image of maleficence. In Scotland, the young were almost never accused of witchcraft except during epidemics of multiple accusation. For similar reasons, men were not often accused there or in Germany, except during large panic trials. The stereotype of the witch was somewhat elastic. On occasion it could stretch to include nearly every kind of individual. But at its center was the woman whose habitual activities had given her over time a bad image in the neighborhood.[39]

The accusations against midwives show how each element of the image of the witch reflected social prejudices, at elite or popular levels. Where these levels of prejudice joined there were accusations, trials, and executions. Although higher and lower cultural groups often attached different meanings to witchcraft, there was enough common ground for all to take part in the process. A modern analogy lies in the role of the German masses in the persecution of Jews under the Nazis. It appears that most rank-and-file members of the Nazi party (not to speak of nonparty members) never took seriously the official racist ideology that cast Jews as subhuman. Yet, these same party members acquiesced in Jews' subjection to the demeaning Nuremberg laws, participated in the destruction of Jewish property, and accepted the subsequent roundups for deportation to the death camps. At the popular level, ancient religious bigotry and economic stereotypes were the motivators, while the Nazi elite dealt in the pseudoscience of racist anthropology. But on the plane of action there was unity, and, from the viewpoint of the victims, whether in gas chambers or at the stake, this must be the transcendent fact.[40]

Like Jews in modern times, midwives and beggar women were ideal scapegoats for the frustrations felt by ordinary people in everyday life. In tension-filled villages, ridding the community of these unsettling figures presumably had a cathartic effect and reduced psychic stress. Such lonely, helpless women could easily have touched the subconscious anxieties of villagers who saw in their isolation the worst fears they had for themselves. At the same time, ordinary folk were receiving the message of the spiritual reformers, a message heavily laden with antifemale sentiments and distaste for sexuality. Midwives were thus the focus for projected fears of higher and lower social groups. Marie-Sylvie Dupont-Bouchat has neatly summed up this interpretation:

> It is undeniable that accusations of witchcraft, as shaped by the preachers and reinforced by judicial practice, offered villagers an excellent means of resolving their internal conflicts, by excluding the one held responsible for their misfortunes. They were caught between their centuries-old beliefs, with which a few scraps of Christianity had been slowly combined, and the response proposed to them by the new religious discourse. In the midst of their uncertainties and their anguish, villagers were ready to accept and to collaborate in the purge.[41]

Although the great majority of beggar women and midwives of the time were never charged with witchcraft, the potential for accusation was always present. Given the preconditions of widespread poverty and high mortality, trials could be precipitated at any time by the presence of lay and clerical ideologues receptive to the idea of demonic witchcraft. Walpurga Hausmännin's experience as a midwife was no different from that of many others who died in their beds. For an unlucky few, however, even the best sociological analysis must conclude that they were simply in the wrong place at the wrong time.[42]

When helpless beggars or midwives were singled out for persecution, witch trials could serve the psychological and social needs of many kinds of people. A witch hunt focused the anxieties of villagers on a definite object and thus provided an explanation for the miseries of everyday life. Trials also helped persuade those in authority that the sufferings of their subjects were the result of demonic forces, not the rulers' own inadequacies. Relatively prosperous peasants could justify their refusal of charity-seekers when so many beggars turned out to be witches. Like other objects of scapegoating before and since, witches took people's minds off their troubles and validated the authority structure of society. The persecution of the heretics might divide a community, but a witch hunt had the potential to unite it. No wonder the new demonic imagery of witchcraft took root at the popular level. When the law accepted witchcraft as a reality and influential religious ideologies cast witches as traitors to God and the state, the endemic fears of ordinary folk could take shape in witchcraft accusations.[43]

We can get a clearer view of such fears and ideological principles by considering a special category of accusers, those individuals said to be bewitched by demons. In most witchcraft cases, the accusers seem shadowy figures whose motives can only be guessed from indirect, circumstantial evidence. But people thought to be possessed by demons often received careful attention from those around them. For this reason, we know much more about this type of accuser than about most others. The next chapter examines the connections among the demonically possessed, those accused of bewitching them, and the authorities who used witch trials as a defense against the satanic demons tormenting God's faithful servants.

5

Classic Accusers
The Possessed

Demonic possession became a leading theme in witchcraft trials of the late sixteenth and seventeenth centuries. The idea itself was ancient by 1600. In the gospels, Jesus cures several individuals possessed by "unclean spirits," and his early followers banished demons by uttering the Savior's name. During the Middle Ages, stories of people whose bodies had been taken over by demons circulated in numerous manuscript collections.[1] Eventually such tales became a staple of early modern works on demonology. But only as the witch craze reached its climax in Western Europe and North America did possession regularly move from the theoreticians' pages into the real lives of hundreds, if not thousands, of men, women, and children.

To introduce the subject, consider a typical case of seventeenth-century demonic possession and witchcraft. This dramatic episode unfolded around 1620 in Lorraine, where witch trials had long been common. Elizabeth de Ranfaing, daughter of an upper-class family, had exhibited considerable religious feeling from early childhood. In order to dampen her disquieting piety (or so it would appear), her parents married her off at age fifteen to a professional soldier forty-two years her senior. Her husband treated Elizabeth with brutality. When he died some nine years later, she was left with six children. The young widow's religious fervor was still strong, and she went off on a pilgrimage to Remiremont. After finishing her devotions, Elizabeth stopped to rest at a local inn, where she met a well-known doctor named Charles Poirot. Poirot bought her food and drink in which, Elizabeth later recounted, there was mixed a love potion that placed her under the doctor's control. His very breath was enough to cast a spell over her, and she soon was invaded by "the Other," who caused her to sink into convulsive seizures and utterly outrageous blasphemies. The local apothecaries could only recommend further treatment from Dr. Poirot, whom Elizabeth regarded with a mixture of fascination and horror. At last the village priest sent her to Nancy, where exorcists cast the devils out of her body. Elizabeth remained cured until she chanced to meet Poirot again. Her symptoms immediately returned, and this time exorcism was ineffective. Representatives of various religious orders sent their best men in hope of reaping the honor that would go to the healer of the demoniac of Ranfaing. But each specialist eventually had to admit defeat.

The devil thought to be inhabiting Elizabeth's body was capable of remarkable feats. With his help, the woman could converse in numerous languages, read letters through sealed envelopes, and identify the consecrated host among a stack of wafers. Elizabeth exhibited all the classic symptoms of possession listed in the Roman ritual of exorcism, issued just a few years earlier. She sometimes shrieked the filthiest curses at her exorcists, risked her life by walking the parapets of the church, and, in cataleptic trances, held the most contorted postures for hours on end.

This behavior continued for years, until one day Poirot was passing through Nancy and foolishly dropped in on an exorcism session. Elizabeth saw him and at once denounced Poirot as the source of her bewitchment. The doctor was arrested. Under orders of the magistrates of Lorraine, he was interrogated, shaved, and searched for the devil's mark. The search turned up nothing, and at first Poirot refused to confess. But several months later he was accused by a peasant girl suspected of witchcraft. This time examiners found a mark of the devil on Poirot's body. An elite jury of twenty-four respected judges declared the prominent physician guilty, despite the interventions of powerful supporters on his behalf, including King Philip II's daughter. He and the peasant girl were strangled and their bodies burnt at the stake.

In the following years, Elizabeth made a slow recovery. She went off on elaborate pilgrimages and eventually seemed to have succeeded in conquering the devil. This triumph gave her a reputation for sanctity. In 1631, so firm had her image of holiness become that she was named mother superior of the newly established convent of Notre-Dame-du-Réfuge in Nancy, and Elizabeth made her house a model for the order. At her death eighteen years later, the body of the former demoniac lay in state so that the citizenry of Nancy might pay their respects, and, as a final tribute, her heart was sent as a sacred relic to the headquarters of the Order of Refuge at Avignon.[2]

What are we to make of this remarkable tale? A modern psychiatrist who analyzed the documents on Elizabeth's case has proposed a psychopathological interpretation of her ostensible possession and cure. According to this view, neurotic tendencies, a strict upbringing, harsh treatment from her husband, and her own unacknowledged spiritual inclinations brought about her notion of bewitchment and her persecution mania. Accusations of witchcraft and hysterical crises were reinforced by the exorcisms, and, when Poirot died, the symptoms disappeared.[3]

This clinical diagnosis is enlightening with regard to Elizabeth's personal psychodynamics, but it fails to raise some very pertinent questions. Why did the doctors, clergy, and twenty-four prominent judges all agree that Elizabeth was possessed? Why did they continually reinforce the suggestible woman's belief in diabolical contamination? Above all, why did this kind of episode become so common an occurrence in the age of the witch trials? What was the social context for the possession of Elizabeth de Ranfaing, the young girls of Salem, and many others of the time? These are the key questions considered in this chapter. Before attempting any answers, however, it will be helpful to first place cases of demonic possession in the broader context of ecstatic religion and mystical experience. These phenomena provided the background for demonic possession and ensuing trials for witchcraft.

Ecstasy and the Demonic

Many cultures of the world have manifested a belief in ecstatic religion, one form of which is possession by demons. Usually, when anthropologists encounter religious ecstasy, the society in question views it as something desirable, indeed, a condition to be actively solicited or induced. The ecstatic condition is an altered form of consciousness, wherein an individual leaves his normal sensory situations and enters into a trance-like state. For as long as the experience lasts, the ecstatic may exhibit remarkable feats of physical strength or prodigious intellectual abilities. But the most important attribute of ecstasy, the one toward which the entire experience is directed, is some form of superior spiritual insight. This may take the shape of a general piece of moral advice addressed to the community, a specific prophecy or manifestation of clairvoyance, or simply a feeling of peace, internal harmony, and release from all stress. The ecstatic condition is typically interpreted by the person experiencing it and by observers in the religious community as evidence of a benign supernatural intervention.[4]

Religious ecstasy, then, is an ancient, widely known technique through which humans have aspired to contact or even achieve union with the divine. Whether it is induced by chemical substances or the hypnotic effects of private meditation and group prayer, ecstasy is customarily pictured as a way of transcending the normal limitations of physical reality. Through it, men and women of many times and places have sought to make themselves feel at one with what they imagine to be the universal forces of the cosmos.

In the Christian tradition, religious ecstasy has long occupied a distin- guished place. Its chief form is mysticism, the intensely private quest for union with God. Typically, Christian mystics are solitary men and women who attempt to suppress the physical side of existence so as to enhance their capacity for spiritual insight. In accord with the deep Christian suspicion of all bodily and material things, mystics traditionally have practiced physical self-mortification. Sometimes they accomplish such mortification passively through abstention from food, drink, and other pleasures of the flesh, and sometimes they do so by actively testing their faith through whippings, uncomfortable clothing, and similar tortures of the body. One element of the Christian monastic tradition, with its withdrawal from the world and physical self-abnegation, stems from the mystical impulse to attain a sense of closeness to God by escaping physical reality. In this sense, there have been thousands of Christian mystics over the centuries. But the higher levels of the pantheon of mystics are reserved for a much smaller number, those whose subjectively experienced sense of self-transcendence was sub- sequently formulated in words and practices and thus became a model for followers.[5]

Organized Christianity, however, never ceased to consider the mystic with ambivalence. Almost by definition, religious ecstasy is an isolated state in which all other people are irrelevant outsiders. The "I-Thou" character of the mystic's relationship with God has no need of priestly intercession or of the institutional church itself. Even more, the perennial tendency of the mystic is to formulate his message as "I = Thou." When the biblical prophets sank into ecstasy and emerged with warnings from Yahweh, they set a dangerous precedent for the leaders of organized religion, especially since God hardly ever seemed to select members of the institutional estab- lishment as vehicles for ecstatically inspired utterances. Max Weber ex- pressed this opposition in distinguishing between institutions and charis- ma. For Weber, the charismatic leader, most typically the prophet, derives his prestige from personal revelation, as opposed to the priest, whose authority stems from tradition and his position in the official hierarchy. Charismatic mystics have always walked a fine line between sanctity and heresy, and often circumstances, not doctrine, have determined the out- come. St. Francis of Assisi and his followers were folded into the institutional Catholic church during the later Middle Ages, despite their highly radical, almost heretical opinions, but the Franciscans nearly went the way of the excommunicated Flagellants.[6]

Many of the great reformers of the sixteenth century, including Luther, Calvin, and Ignatius Loyola (founder of the Jesuit order), went through private, deeply moving conversion experiences in which they felt a divine call. Yet the perennial paradox presented by mysticism soon became evident to the leaders of reform movements: a personal connection with God is too individualized a phenomenon on which to construct an organized community. Thus, Loyola's *Spiritual Exercises* attempted to channel a novice Jesuit's mystical devotion along collective lines. In his quest for union with God, the brother was to follow his superiors' instructions. Mystical experience was to be sought after, but the leaders of the spiritual reform movements knew that it must be carefully supervised and controlled.[7]

As has been shown repeatedly in previous chapters, with the expanding influence of evangelical reform among the elites and the folk came an expansion of Satan's assigned role. A preoccupation with Satan led many authorities to suspect that the devil's servants were behind all social problems and religious deviations. Some theologians went so far as to speculate on whether the devil had possessed or merely obsessed their religious enemies. These special conditions of the time contributed to the interpretation of mystical experiences as manifestations not of the divine but of the demonic. The origin of a supposed mystic's illumination always had been a matter of dispute: did the light emanate from heaven, or might it have come from hell? Events that before and after the seventeenth century were seen as signs of mystical union with God came to be viewed as expressions of the demonic. Thus, the claims of young girls to have heard supernatural voices led to the career of Joan of Arc in the early 1400s and to the Great Awakening in eighteenth-century New England. But the identical claim, voiced at Salem in 1692 and in many other places in the era of the witch craze, produced accusations of bewitchment.[8]

For a time, the fear of Satan's power rose so high as to make traditional Christian religious ecstasy seem very dangerous to ecclesiastical and secular authorities. Throughout the era of the Reformation, mystical sects stressing interior religion or "enthusiasm" at the expense of outward ritual were suppressed by the establishment. The Illuminists of Spain, the French Quietists, and the German Anabaptist communities, among others, became objects of bitter persecution from official churches and their political allies. Although sects devoted to inner enthusiasm, such as the Quakers, have survived from the seventeenth century, they had to withstand harsh persecution for their rejection of mainstream religious values.[9]

Fear of the consequences of religious factionalism led the authorities of most European states to insist on the conformity of their subjects to a single, officially sanctioned church. This European stress on religious unity and suspicion of pluralistic approaches to spiritual matters crossed the ocean with the first settlers. Nearly all the North American colonies of the seventeenth century had an established religion and considered religious toleration ungodly and divisive. The Massachusetts Puritans came to the New World in search of religious freedom, to be sure. But it was freedom for themselves they sought. Liberty to practice their own faith did not extend to Christians of differing persuasions. The Quaker colony founded by William Penn at Philadelphia, however, did welcome people of all faiths. Pennsylvania was also exceptional among the British colonies in that it conducted almost no witch trials.[10]

Suspicion of all internal, mystical brands of faith, then, became particularly strong in the sixteenth and seventeenth centuries, when kings and other authorities were placing unprecedented stress on outward conformity and visible manifestations of unity. The social ideals of an absolute monarch like Louis XIV pictured France as a unitary hierarchy, in which the king at the top was tied to all his subjects by political, legal, and religious interconnections. The Sun King's motto, "one king, one law, one faith," accurately reflected his conviction that social stability depended on everyone's recognizing the same authorities. The emphasis on courtesy and deference that began in court circles and soon extended throughout upper-class French society was meant to translate the principle of hierarchy into a code of behavior that illustrated the dominant role of personal allegiances in everyday activities.[11]

In such a politicized culture, where all relationships revolved around one's social standing, the mystic could have no place. His internal orientation and complete detachment from society's hierarchies made the seeker of the ecstatic seem threatening to men of power. Thus, Louis XIV's government, like many others of the time, frequently accused so-called fanatics, both Protestant and Catholic, of inciting the popular classes and endangering the social order. Ecstatic prophecy, often foretelling an imminent Second Coming of Christ, flourished when religious revolutionaries gained political power. Such was the case, for example, in Cromwellian England, despite Cromwell's best efforts. The Restoration of monarchy brought with it suppression of prophets and ecstatics.[12]

Whether they labeled the mystic visionary an instrument of the devil or a potential traitor, church and lay authorities were expressing their horror of uncontrolled charismatic religious expression. The interesting paradox is that the increased incidence of episodes of demonic possession in the late sixteenth and seventeenth centuries seems due primarily to the heightened spiritual atmosphere of the time. Ironically, by harping on Satan's powers in their sermons and writings, religious authorities produced the result they most feared. Such vivid imagery encouraged suggestible individuals to imagine themselves in the devil's clutches.

One such victim was a student named Briggs from the north of England. In London during the spring of 1574 he misunderstood a lecturer to say that all faults were sins against the Holy Ghost. Regarding himself as a hopeless reprobate whose prayers were in vain, Briggs fell into a profound depression and several times attempted suicide. Walking toward the Thames, into which he intended to jump, Briggs on one occasion noticed that he was being followed by a large dog who glared at him "with such terrible sparkling eyes" that he concluded that this was no ordinary dog, but was instead the devil, waiting for his soul. Soon afterward, Briggs fell into a trance in the presence of some godly friends. The witnesses eagerly took down part of a dialogue with the devil that issued from the young man's lips. The devil sought to win Briggs's allegiance by maintaining the falsity of scripture. Satan tempted him with promises of valuables and access to an alluring "painted woman" who sang and danced before him. These conversations continued nearly every day for over two weeks, the devil explaining that he took Sundays off for pickpocketing among the congregants at St. Paul's. Briggs's case had a happy outcome, as he was cured by the Puritan writer John Foxe. But Foxe's published account of the episode seems to have influenced the shape of many subsequent instances of demonic possession among Puritans.[13]

Many religious leaders went through periods of depression in which they thought themselves unworthy and damned for their sins, and sensations of demonic possession regularly accompanied such depressive episodes. John Bunyan, author of *Pilgrim's Progress*, experienced agonizing bouts of hopelessness in which he could feel the fiend plucking at his clothes. Ordinary folk, too, were prone to imagine themselves possessed whenever they experienced self-doubt. Keith Thomas has brought to light the casebooks of the Buckinghamshire physician, Sir Richard Napier, which

> reveal that several of his patients thought that they had seen the Devil in human or animal form. In April 1634 they included Ellen Green, "troubled in

mind, haunted by an ill spirit, whom she saith . . . speaketh to her"; Robert
Lucas, "troubled in his mind, despairing, doubteth whether he be not
possessed with an evil spirit"; and Jane Towerton, "mopish and
melancholy . . . and despairing; thought at first she saw a black dog appearing to her and forbidding her to serve God and say her prayers, and go to
church."[14]

Very obvious in these instances is the heavy weight of guilt burdening
Napier's patients. Such manifestations of guilt provide a measure of the
psychic stress produced by reformed religion's strong emphasis on human
sinfulness.

We have seen in previous chapters that guilt feelings could trigger
witchcraft accusations among those exposed to spiritual reform. This
psychology also connected witchcraft with demonic possession. The guilt-
ridden possessed often accused someone of inflicting demons on them.
Thus, while there have been numerous supposed demonic possessions
before and since, in this one period possession was regularly said to have
involved a human intermediary, the witch. In witch trials involving charges
of possession, a victim of demonic powers, such as Elizabeth de Ranfaing,
accused the witch of ordering devils to attack her and inhabit her body.
Such accusations of bewitchment were taken quite seriously by secular and
clerical officials and resulted in hundreds of trials and executions.

Courts were receptive to this kind of accusation, in part because the
authors of demonological tracts had held for centuries that an ability to
order the possession of an innocent Christian's body was one of the powers
Satan granted to witches. The witch was said by these writers to regard the
inflicting of demons as one of her highest duties, because this was one of the
worst forms of malefice. This theoretical underpinning helps to explain the
predisposition of judges and other officials to associate cases of apparent
demonic possession with witchcraft. At least as important in establishing
this association was the dominant ideological stance of sixteenth- and
seventeenth-century elites. Imbued with the spirit of religious reform,
clerical and lay authorities classified people in polarities of good and evil,
godly and devilish. Ideological predispositions almost inevitably required a
personification of the hated and feared satanic enemy, and this an accused
witch provided.

A practical advantage to society of associating demonic possession with
witchcraft was that the connection suggested an effective cure for the
disorder. Executing the witch was an appealing remedy, all the more so
because other ways of dealing with the possessed seemed less reliable. The
traditional Catholic treatment in cases of demonic possession was exorcism,

the ritual in which a priest, acting in the name of God, orders the offending demon to leave the victim's body. Most Protestant reformers were horrified by the idea of exorcism, because to them it signified the belief that a human being could control God. As God had permitted the demon to enter an individual's body, they reasoned, only God could remove the demon. Exorcism reminded Protestants of what they saw as the worst kind of priestly magical superstition, and they steadfastly denied the ritual's efficacy. Meanwhile, however, Protestants continued to accept the traditional belief in demonic possession. Having discarded the standard remedy, they were confronted with the problem of prescribing an effective course of treatment. This was a dilemma they never fully resolved. As in Briggs's case, Protestant leaders spoke of the victim's need for prayer, true penitence, fasting, and other similar manifestations of trust in divine grace. But these methods lacked the dramatic intensity of an exorcism and did not always succeed.[15]

For their part, Catholic authorities often went out of their way to demonstrate the benefits of exorcism. In France, they conducted public ceremonies before large crowds and gave loud thanks to God when, at the rite's climactic moment, the demons departed and the victim's convulsions ceased. Thus, French Catholic leaders made exorcisms a form of propaganda for their faith.[16] Even among Catholics, however, exorcism had its limitations. The ritual was only a temporary cure, for, although it was thought that a demon must obey the priest's explicit command to depart, there was nothing to keep him from returning afterward. For this reason, outbreaks of possession often led to a wearisome round of repeated exorcisms and reinfections, sometimes continuing for months or even years.

Moreover, all experts agreed that exorcists ran a heavy risk. Priests themselves might be invaded by ostensibly demonic forces, as those familiar with William Peter Blatty's *The Exorcist* will recall. Possession was a contagious affliction, and priests who had undergone the ascetic rigors of inward preparation for combat with Satan left themselves highly vulnerable psychologically. Father Surin, the exorcist who cured Joan of the Angels at Loudun, was afflicted with demons for a long time afterward and never did recover his sanity.

Thus, Catholics and Protestants shared a common problem: the techniques of both faiths were not infallible in dealing with the possessed. Hence the attraction of making witches responsible for these mysterious afflictions. A witchcraft trial was one of society's most reliable ways of defeating diabolical possession. In theory, and many times in practice as well, killing the witch ended an epidemic of possession. Of course, the execution of a single witch did not always bring about a complete cure. Sometimes multiple executions were needed to deal with stubbornly reluctant demons. In these instances, accusations of possession could produce mass witch panics.

Possession in the Cloister

These points established, we can turn to the dramatic French convent cases of the seventeenth century. France had a long history of demonic possession in the period of the religious wars, when exorcisms were used as Catholic weapons in the campaigns against Protestant groups. In 1599, for instance, shortly after King Henry IV had granted limited toleration to the Huguenot minority, devils spoke through a possessed Catholic woman in Paris to explain how delighted Satan was with the new royal policy.[17] Many such precedents were the background for a widely publicized episode of demonic possession that unfolded in and around Aix-en-Provence from 1609 to 1611.[18] This case was particularly scandalous because it centered on several nuns, who accused a parish priest in nearby Marseilles of seduction and bewitchment.

The story begins with Madeleine de Demandolx de la Palud, who at age twelve was sent by her noble and wealthy parents for schooling at the newly founded convent of Ursuline nuns at Aix. Madeleine spent the next two years there, together with five other young girls of aristocratic background whose families had destined them for life behind convent walls. But then Madeleine became greatly depressed and was sent back to her parents at Marseilles. Her spirits soon improved, largely through contact with Louis Gaufridi, parish priest and friend of the family, who was a popular confessor for many women in the Demandolx's social circle.

Soon Father Gaufridi's long private visits with Madeleine inspired scandalous rumors. It seems that the fourteen-year-old girl had fallen in love with a priest twenty years her senior, but exactly what transpired between them in private is impossible to say. Then Madeleine entered the convent of the Ursulines at Marseilles as a novice. Almost immediately, she began speaking of intimacies with Gaufridi and was transferred back to the convent at Aix, far from her erstwhile confessor. There, just before Christmas in 1609, Madeleine began to have episodes of shaking and cramps. She saw devils and said that one of them was responsible for her public smashing of a crucifix.

The spiritual director and founder of the Ursuline convents at Aix and

Marseilles was the prominent Jesuit Jean-Baptiste Romillon. He soon diagnosed Madeleine as suffering from demonic possession and proceeded to administer a series of unsuccessful exorcisms to the distressed teenager. Born a Huguenot, Romillon had converted as a young man and rapidly became a leader of Catholic spiritual reform in Provence. The Jesuit was a vigorous critic of clerical abuses. His official biography describes the efforts he made to root out medieval customs that smacked of sexual license among clergymen. For instance, Romillon had tried to ban the traditional celebration that followed a monk's first mass, at which the daughter of a local family acted as the new priest's partner during the festivities. The dancing, kissing, and other liberties customary at such occasions mortified Romillon, but, when he intervened to break up one of these parties, the unreformed monks are said to have waylaid him and beaten him with clubs they had concealed under their robes.[19]

This kind of exorcist naturally was acutely sensitive to accusations of priestly seduction. Although Madeleine had confessed her real or imagined liaisons with Gaufridi to several others, no action was taken against him until she told Romillon. Gaufridi denied any sexual relations with Madeleine, but she continued to accuse him all through 1610. The effects of the exorcist's unintentional provocation of sexual fantasies became manifest when several other Marseilles Ursulines began having convulsions. One of these, Louise Capeau, claimed that Gaufridi had seduced her, too, and that he was now tormenting her body with demons. A baffled Father Romillon finally took Louise and Madeleine to the famous Grand Inquisitor of Avignon, Sébastien Michaelis, who, in his capacity as papal judge, had sent many to the stake for witchcraft over the previous thirty years. Michaelis transferred the exorcisms to the celebrated shrine of Mary Magdalene in the grotto of Sainte Baume, where they were witnessed by large crowds of pilgrims and other curious spectators. But all attempts at exorcism failed to cure the possessed girls of their torments.

At this point, the inquisitor decided on an investigation of Gaufridi, but the effort produced nothing but evidence favorable to the parish priest. Encouraged, Gaufridi charged calumny and slander. He worked through the bishop of Marseilles to have the Ursulines suppressed and the hysterical nuns jailed. But these efforts only succeeded in earning him the bitter hatred of Michaelis and Romillon. Finally, in February 1611, their pressure resulted in charges of witchcraft brought against Gaufridi by the Parlement of Aix.

Madeleine and Louise experienced frequent convulsive seizures at the trial. Alternating between bouts of depression and hysteria, Madeleine several times recanted all her accusations against Gaufridi. Like other victims of possession in the seventeenth century, she repeatedly attempted suicide. A typical day in court found her first confessing that her allegations were "all imaginings, illusions and had not a word of truth in them." But then she proclaimed in Provençal how she yearned for Gaufridi's love, after which pronouncement she was seized with lascivious tremblings "representing the sexual act, with violent movements of the lower part of her belly."[20]

Such courtroom drama no doubt reinforced the judges' belief in Gaufridi's guilt. It was easy for them to dismiss Madeleine's recantations and suicide attempts merely as additional evidence of her possession by demons. Gaufridi, meanwhile, had been chained up for weeks in a vermin-infested dungeon. The court now ordered him shaved, and a search uncovered three devil's marks. Thoroughly demoralized, Gaufridi at last confessed to being the "Prince of the Synagogue." A few days later he retracted everything, but the judges of the Parlement ignored his denials and sentenced him to death at the stake. The execution was unusually cruel. It was preceded by hideous tortures, ostensibly to elicit the names of accomplices. Then, for five hours, Gaufridi was dragged through the streets of Aix, bound to a sled. The only mercy shown him was strangulation before his body was burned.

Louise Capeau's possession continued after the execution of Gaufridi, and her accusations brought another victim to the stake later in 1611. Madeleine is said to have been freed of her demons immediately after Gaufridi's death, but the epilogue to her story proved most bizarre. Over three decades later, at age forty-nine, Madeleine was herself accused of witchcraft. At first the charges against her could not be proved, but they never were dropped. Eventually, she was subjected to physical examination and devil's marks were discovered on her body. Madeleine was fined heavily and sentenced to life imprisonment. Only after ten years was she released, one of the very few who had firsthand knowledge of witchcraft as both accuser and accused.

The possession episode at Aix triggered another at the far end of France. A nun from distant Lille who witnessed several exorcisms while visiting the south went into convulsions upon her return home, and the contagion spread through her convent.[21] Then, in the 1630s, a similar recipe of sexual frustration, reformist religion, and political rivalry resulted in the execution of Urbain Grandier, the priest who was charged with witchcraft by the famous Ursulines of Loudun. Mother Joan of the Angels accused him of inflicting on her a demon who compelled her to blaspheme and behave indecently. When asked in her lucid intervals why she was acting this way, Joan replied that she had no control over her actions but was forced into them by a demon or by the witch Grandier. Later, she recounted her feelings while possessed:

> My mind was often filled with blasphemies, and sometimes I uttered them without being able to take any thought to stop myself. I felt for God a continual aversion. . . . The demon gave me moreover a strong aversion for my religious calling, so that sometimes when he was in my head I used to tear all my veils and such of my sisters' as I might lay hands on; I trampled them underfoot, I chewed them, cursing the hour when I took the vows. All this was done with great violence; I think that I was not free. . . .

> The demons gave me very evil desires and feelings of quite licentious affection for the persons who might have helped my soul, so as to lead me to further withdrawal from communication with them.[22]

Mother Joan's accusations against Grandier were quickly taken up by the priest's enemies in Loudun. The case soon became enmeshed in factional disputes of the French court between supporters and opponents of Cardinal Richelieu, Louis XII's centralizing chief minister. The hapless Grandier found no effective way to defend himself from the powerful forces arrayed against him. After Grandier's execution, Joan was cured of her possession and, like Elizabeth de Ranfaing, acquired a cultic following.

During subsequent decades, there occurred several more trials inspired by episodes of demonic possession in French convents. One of the last, at Auxonne in 1662, is especially notable, because the accused was not the sisters' priestly confessor but their mother superior. Perhaps because public charges of lesbianism in convents were so unusual and scandalous, the Parlement of Dijon took up this case and dismissed all the charges. Meanwhile, episodes of possession had become the normal form taken by witch trials in Geneva and the Burgundian Franche-Comté.[23]

It is clear that in cases of demonic possession, as in other kinds of witch trials, the nature of the accusations stemmed, at least in part, from the assumptions of the authorities. Those assigned to counsel the possessed were usually religious personages who interpreted the sufferer's behavior in accord with their previous knowledge of demonic possession. They began their sympathetic therapy by reinforcing the suggestible victim's fear that he or she was suffering from a supernaturally induced disorder. In this way, psychologically vulnerable individuals had their fantasies channeled by religious authorities into the delusion that they had been possessed by witch-inflicted demons.[24]

In the twentieth century, too, clinical cases often exhibit patterns similar to those of the possessed, but today's psychiatrists, as a clinician reported in the 1940s, propose to their patients a naturalistic explanation of the condition:

It is truly striking that the ideational content of the mental diseases of four hundred years ago is so similar to those of today. Young women, particularly virgins, suffering from dementia praecox (schizophrenia) today also speak of imaginary black men, but they call them Negroes. They also suffer from ideas of persecution and from fear of defloration. They have suicidal trends which at times appear in the form of hearing voices tell them that they should lay their hands on themselves. The hallucinatory voice is more apt to suggest that the afflicted person jump off the roof of a building instead of into a pit of a well, and the imaginary seducer of today appears to her more frequently as her doctor than as Satan, but the psychological substance of this pathological reaction is identical.[25]

The precise shape of early modern and more recent possession fantasies reflects the assumptions of the time and, in particular, those of the therapist, whether he be religious or medical. In late nineteenth-century Paris, to cite another example, Charcot's patients at the Salpetrière mental hospital exhibited symptoms of "grand mal" hysteria because, it now seems clear, the doctor's treatment induced extreme manifestations of illness among his highly suggestible patients.[26]

As explained earlier, the seventeenth century was a period when restraint and self-control were becoming highly valued personality traits. When we recall the efforts of religious reformers to radically alter popular habits by curbing violence, sexuality, and all physically spontaneous behavior, the linkage between spiritual reform and possession episodes becomes plain. The actions of the possessed featured precisely the characteristics that most appalled the godly reformers: loud, violent speech and unrestrained, sexually suggestive verbal or body language were among the most common. The Freudian definition of demons as "reprehensible wishes, derivations of instinctual impulses that have been repudiated and repressed" would seem to fit many of the guilt-ridden, suggestible demoniacs of the witch-trial era.[27] Religious reformers of the time were greatly concerned with getting people to repudiate "bad impulses." Their vigorous condemnations of instinctual behavior promoted the repression of forbidden desires. Unintentionally, the godly also provided an outlet for the unburdening of resultant frustrations. Their preoccupation with Satan suggested that episodes of possession were an acceptable vehicle for the release of tension.

Like most modern psychiatric therapists treating mental disorders, the
clergy who dealt with the possessed in the sixteenth and seventeenth
centuries regarded their charges as victims and sufferers. The dominant
attitude was one of sympathetic concern. This meant that, no matter how
outrageous their conduct, the possessed usually were not held responsible
for their actions. Regarded as demonic in origin and thus beyond voluntary
control, possession could be a liberating experience for the victim. It served
as a socially sanctioned outlet for the repressed desires of people experiencing a considerable amount of social direction from spiritual reformers.

The French mass possession episodes took place in convents where
parents deposited their young daughters for purposes of spiritual elevation
and/or alleviation of financial burdens. The reformed convents' mixture of
asceticism, social isolation, and highly emotional religiosity proved dangerously combustible, as newly founded orders of nuns, such as the Ursulines,
sought to embody the principles of godliness in an ordered way of life.
Constant exhortations to develop habits of introspection, to detect every
forbidden thought, and to confess all prohibited feelings could produce a
charged atmosphere of repressed desires and deep guilt, stemming from the
nuns' sensations of failure, hopelessness, and fear of damnation.[28] These
explosive conditions often found their spark in a male authority figure,
either the nuns' confessor and spiritual director or a surrogate. Onto these
men, it appears, the sisters projected their ambivalent feelings, the forbidden love that their conscious minds repressed. The resultant conflicts can
explain the sisters' ecstasy of possession, when, at least in imagination, all
desires could be fulfilled.

As in cases of possession the world over, the French nuns' demonic
episodes took an overtly sexual form. A vocabulary of erotic love has been
one vehicle for Jewish and Christian mystical expression ever since biblical
times. And the nun's symbolic marriage to God reflects the universal
tendency to parallel spiritual union with human wedlock. The episodes of
possession in seventeenth-century convents, however, did not follow the
benign course taken by earlier mystical episodes. Because the fear of Satan
and witchcraft was so intense at the time, and because sexuality was
consistently identified with the devil, churchmen who counseled the ecstatic sisters led them to label their experience as demonic and to accuse a
forbidden male of bewitchment. Given this demonic interpretation of their
ecstatic experience, it is remarkable that Elizabeth de Ranfaing, Mother
Joan of the Angels, and several other protagonists in these convent cases
later recovered, mastered the spirits (or emotions) that had tormented
them, and, like many earlier ecstatic sufferers, went on to distinguished

careers as holy women much sought after for their insight and therapeutic powers.[29]

The Context of Salem Witchcraft

Possession tended to be contagious in the closed, charged environment of the cloister, but group possession episodes were not limited to convents. In the seventeenth century, clusters of the possessed appeared in places as widely separated as Salem and the village of Mora in northern Sweden. The Swedish possessed numbered upwards of three hundred, and, as in Massachusetts and many of the convent episodes, the bewitched were children or adolescents. Although an element of conscious playacting may have been present among these young people, at least at first, the more important point is that their immaturity made them especially vulnerable to suggestions of bewitchment. As in the instances of the possessed nuns, the authorities in Sweden took the first accusations seriously and in this way inspired more. In 1669, King Charles XI appointed a royal commission to investigate the initial charges from a possessed fifteen-year-old girl. This commission attempted a cure through sermons and mass prayer, for exorcisms were unacceptable to the Lutheran leaders. Thousands of people heard these sermons, whereupon many newly possessed children suddenly appeared. Over the next few years, mass possession spread through northern Sweden and the neighboring Swedish-speaking provinces of Finland. Much the same pattern had occurred in the Basque trials of France and Spain around 1610, when hundreds of children were inspired by powerful, suggestive stimuli to see themselves as unwilling participants in the witches' sabbat.[30]

At Salem, the conviction of Puritan ministers that demons were at work in two tormented girls eventually provoked at least twenty-five others to announce themselves bewitched. Only three people were accused of witchcraft initially, but the authorities' unwitting encouragement resulted in the imprisonment of over one hundred colonists before the panic ended. Nineteen were convicted and hanged, and one more was pressed to death by heavy weights—the method by which the English common law dealt with a suspect who refused to plead innocent or guilty.

One way to understand the Salem trials is to place them in the context of the elites' concerns with demonic possession during the seventeenth century. The Massachusetts panic originated in the household of Samuel Parris, minister of Salem village. His nine-year-old daughter Elizabeth and eleven-year-old niece Abigail Williams, curious about their future marital status, had apparently been experimenting with crystal balls. Their effort to discover "what trade their sweethearts should be of" was one of the most ordinary kinds of fortune-telling practiced by village magicians in England and throughout Europe. It was likewise normal for Puritans and other religious reformers to rail against young people who indulged in this "sinful and diabolical" magic. The patterns of Puritan upbringing in Massachusetts tended to produce a deep sense of personal sinfulness and an intense fear of damnation. The girls' feelings of guilt for having engaged in forbidden behavior turned to terror when they thought they saw a death's head in the crystal. At least, this is the best surmise about what was going on inside their impressionable minds. As they never told anyone, we cannot know for sure.[31]

The external symptoms were very clear, however, and most disturbing to those who witnessed their behavior. In February 1692 Elizabeth and Abigail were regularly experiencing what the adults around them described as "odd postures," "fits," and "distempers." From the girls' mouths came "foolish, ridiculous speeches." Reverend Samuel Parris first called on Dr. William Griggs for medical advice. But the doctor was baffled, informing Parris that he suspected the "Evil Hand." Next, Parris consulted with nearby ministers, who counseled him to employ fastings and prayer and to "sit still and wait upon the Providence of God, to see what time might discover."[32]

As word of the girls' afflictions and their likely demonic origin spread through Parris's circle, others began to exhibit similar symptoms. In all, about ten people were afflicted by the beginning of March. These included two seventeen-year-old girls, Dr. Griggs's maid and the daughter of Parris's next-door neighbor. The twelve-year-old daughter and the slightly older maid of another neighbor also were new victims. In addition, four married women became afflicted; one was mother and aunt to two of the young girls, and all were members of Parris's church. Parris himself was at the center of the growing network of the bewitched. It seems clear that the rituals of prayer and fasting that the minister conducted in his house during these weeks were the source of the contagion.[33]

After weeks of intense questioning from Parris and other adults, Elizabeth and Abigail finally agreed that they were bewitched and named their tormentors: Tituba, a West Indian slave in the Parris household; Sarah Good, a destitute beggar; and Sarah Osborne, another villager who had acquired an unsavory reputation when she took an Irish indentured servant into her bed and attempted to disinherit her children by a previous husband. The three women were arrested and publicly questioned on March 1, 1692, in the village meeting house. Tituba immediately confessed to extensive dealings with the devil, but the others steadfastly denied everything. All three were ordered held at Boston jail, the filth and cold of which no doubt contributed to Sarah Osborne's death "of natural causes" six weeks later. Like others who voluntarily confessed later in 1692, Tituba was eventually released. But Sarah Good refused to admit to any wrongdoing. She was among the first to be executed and cursed her judges from the gallows.[34] By mid-June six women had been tried, convicted, and put to death. The jails were full of suspects awaiting trial. Those charged came from many parts of Massachusetts (and, in at least one case, from Maine), for the afflicted were no longer limiting their accusations to near neighbors. Frequently the accused had never laid eyes on the possessed who charged them. Unlike nearly all earlier witchcraft cases in England's American colonies, the Salem episode did not conclude after the conviction of the first people to be accused. At least eighty-three witchcraft trials had taken place between Massachusetts and Virginia from 1647 to 1691, twenty-two of which had resulted in executions. With one exception, these had all been of the small-scale variety typical of English witch trials. They involved no more than four defendants and did not spread beyond the site of the initial charge. Moreover, since 1662 only two people had been executed for witchcraft in the English colonies.[35]

Why did the Salem trials break these patterns? Part of the answer lies in the charges of demonic possession that produced the trials. Several other cases of bewitchment had been tried in Massachusetts during the preceding ten years. One of them concluded in the execution of an old Irish woman, Goody Glover, a neighbor of three possessed children in Boston. The eminent Puritan divine Cotton Mather had taken an interest in this episode and published a carefully researched book on bewitchment in 1689. Thus, the subject was in the air, a fact that no doubt helps to explain why Dr. Griggs, Reverend Parris, and the other local ministers immediately assumed that the devil lay behind the afflictions of Elizabeth and Abigail.[36]

Parris's mentality in the years before 1692 has become much clearer thanks to the recent analysis of his handwritten sermon notebook, discovered by Paul Boyer and Stephen Nissenbaum. This previously ignored source permits us to be much more precise about the effects that belief in demonic possession had on a leading instigator of the Salem trials. In his sermons, Parris reveals his deep concern with Satan. Frequently he associated his enemies in the community with the devil. There existed, he wrote, "a lamentable harmony between wicked men and devils, in their opposition of God's kingdom and interests." Wrongdoers, Parris noted, go for counsel "to the Devil, to a witch."[37]

Boyer and Nissenbaum's careful and imaginative reconstruction of the social patterns of Salem Village shows that those who accused others of witchcraft in 1692 were in nearly all cases Parris's congregants and supporters in his quarrels with rival factions in the community. The accusers, like Parris, lived on the west side of the village, where the land was poor and the holdings too small to be profitable. Salem Village's accused witches were clustered in the more prosperous eastern sections, close to the thriving port of Salem Town and adjacent to the Ipswich Road commercial artery.[38]

Samuel Parris came to see his successful enemies as people who had betrayed the spiritual ideals of the Puritan covenant for the sake of financial gain. A failed businessman before he entered the ministry, Parris cast his congregants as the besieged defenders of moral righteousness, set upon by cutthroat capitalists who meant to destroy the godly. The patterns of accusations in Salem suggest that Parris and his followers were unconsciously lashing out at their rivals through witchcraft accusations. To Reverend Parris, only diabolical intervention could adequately explain the economic decline of his godly flock. The sermons and prayers he offered before 1692 and during the outbreak of possession suggested to the afflicted the kinds of people who might be accused.

Not all those named by the afflicted were brought to trial. It was common knowledge that many prominent people had been accused, including the wife of the colony's new governor, William Phips. Yet the higher-ups were not arrested, a fact duly noted by those who remained skeptical of the proceedings. William Stoughton, the lieutenant governor who acted as chief justice in the witch cases, refrained from moving against people at the apex of society.

More than the judges' prudence may have been involved here. The afflicted girls apparently did not accuse the leaders of the anti-Parris faction in Salem Village. Boyer and Nissenbaum suggest that because these were very prominent gentlemen with whom Parris and his possessed congregants were well acquainted, a deep sense of deference did not permit charges of witchcraft. Instead, the accused of Salem were surrogates, people identified with Parris's enemies but not in leadership roles. They were for the most part nonconformists, newcomers, or individuals who themselves had exhibited a lack of deference—in short, the people of ill repute who were everywhere the most likely targets of witchcraft charges. But, because the afflicted could not bring themselves to name those they believed to be the prime malefactors, they never achieved the psychological release that witch-craft accusations normally provided to the possessed. Thus, the hypothesis is that they were compelled to go on naming names because of an irresolvable inner conflict.[39]

Be that as it may, it is plain that the unusual course of the Salem trials also resulted from the peculiar political conditions of the moment. When the initial witchcraft charges surfaced, the Massachusetts colony lacked both a governor and a governing charter. The old authorities had been deposed three years earlier, in the aftermath of England's Glorious Revolution, and Phips was en route to America with the new charter when the Salem magistrates conducted their first hearings. When Phips at last reached Boston, he made only cursory inquiries into the charges of witchcraft before leaving for Maine, where he passed the summer fighting Indians.

Because of Phips' absence, Lieutenant Governor Stoughton presided over the trials and handed down death sentences to nineteen of the convicted prisoners. Stoughton had been trained for the ministry and regularly received advice on how to conduct the trials from Cotton Mather, the spokesman for the Boston ministers.[40] Thus, the Salem cases devolved into the hands of godly reformers who were fully convinced of the devil's terrifying power to bewitch God's faithful servants. One of the leading Boston divines, Deodat Lawson, visited Salem in late March to observe firsthand the seizures of the possessed. He was not disappointed and found himself inspired to deliver a sermon to the local magistrates. Not surprisingly, Reverend Lawson took as his theme the devil's use of witches as instruments for the affliction of his followers. Soon afterward, the Salem magistrates were moved to order a public fast as a demonstration to God of the community's penitence, and in May the General Court of Massachusetts proclaimed a day of fasting throughout the colony. The sense of spiritual impurity and need for purgative repentance that had triggered the first accusations of witchcraft in Reverend Parris's household during February thus was generalized throughout the colony. During a few decisive months in 1692, a small group of godly reformers was able to reassert the covenant mentality of the earliest New England Puritans. For what turned out to be the last time, Puritan divines controlled the legal and political apparatus of the Massachusetts colony. Certain that Satan was loose in their midst, they created a short-lived but crucial consensus in support of witch trials.[41]

The atmosphere at the Salem trials closely resembled the public exorcisms played out among the possessed in French convents. Court hearings took place in a wild environment of convulsive seizures, for the accusers gave visible testimony of their sufferings when confronted by the prisoners. Deodat Lawson's description of a preliminary hearing conducted before the Salem magistrates conveys the sense of drama:

> The Reverend Mr. Hale begun with Prayer, and the Warrant being read, she [i.e., the defendant, Rebecca Nurse, age 71] was required to give answer, Why she afflicted those persons? She pleaded her owne innocency with earnestness. Thomas Putnam's Wife, Abigail Williams and Thomas Putnam's daughter accused her that she appeared to them, and afflicted them in their fits: but some of the other [afflicted] said, that they had not seen her, but knew not that ever she had hurt them; amongst which was Mary Walcut, who was presently after she had so declared bitten, and cryed out of her in the meeting-house; producing [the defendant's] Marks of teeth on her wrist. . . . And [the defendant's] Motions did produce like effect [in the afflicted] as to Biteing, Pinching, Bruising, Tormenting, at their Breasts by her Leaning, and when, bended Back, were as if their Backs was broken. The afflicted persons said, the Black Man whispered to her in the Assembly, and therefore she could not hear what the Magistrates said unto her. They said also that she did then ride by the Meeting-house, behind the Black Man. Thomas Putnam's wife had a grievous Fit, in the time of Examination, to the very great Impairing of her strength, and wasting of her spirits, insomuch as she could hardly move hand, or foot, when she was carryed out. Others also were there grievously afflicted, so that there was once such an hideous scrietch and noise, (which I heard as I walked, at a little distance from the Meeting house,) as did amaze me, and some that were within told me the whole assembly was struck with consternation, and they were afraid, that those that sate next to them, were under the influence of Witchcraft. This woman also was that day committed to Salem Prison.[42]

The constitutional uncertainties of the moment, the chronic Indian raids, and a strong tendency among Puritan preachers of this generation to see in all misfortunes the signs of divine punishment for the community's sins—all contributed to a psychology that made many New Englanders want to see witchcraft behind the bizarre behavior of the afflicted girls. Similar combinations of political instability and spiritual fervor can be detected in European possession and witchcraft episodes.

In the case of Salem, the "spectral evidence" of affliction caused by the spirit or specter of the accused finally was deemed unreliable by Reverend Increase Mather (Cotton's father) and other experts. They persuaded an undoubtedly relieved Governor Phips to halt the trials and free those still in prison.[43] But this was in October, after hundreds had been charged and twenty had died. In the meantime, the fearful spectacle of apparent demonic possession had stirred the latent fears and suspicions harbored by many of the Massachusetts colony's godly reformers. Social tensions were expressed in spiritual terms, a pattern completely appropriate in a society dominated by religious ideology. Not just "the whole assembly" of Lawson's account, but the whole colony for a time seemed "afraid, that those that sate next to them, were under the influence of Witchcraft."

The possessed of Salem were adolescent girls living in a highly restrictive domestic environment that was ripe for interpersonal conflict, depressive states, and delusions. Possession allowed these young women to unconsciously act out forbidden fantasies and to relieve deep guilt feelings in the spotlight of benevolent concern from their superiors. For as long as they remained bewitched, they were not obscure village girls. The attention lavished on them was a great contrast to the repression and indifference they had formerly experienced.[44] Once more, witch trials seem to emerge from the point of contact between popular anxieties and the preoccupations of the elites.

Also, we again confront the theme of women as marginal and powerless members of society who must resort to supernatural methods to achieve status. Small wonder that nearly all the possessed were women and children. Women also played prominent roles in the ecstatic religious sects of seventeenth-century England and France, a feature that surely helped discredit such groups in the eyes of orthodox observers.[45] The propensity of some women to seek interior means of spiritual expression in the era of the Reformation, whether it took the form of mystical elevation or demonic possession, was in part a consequence of the lack of alternate outlets for female religious expression. Since women were barred from official positions in all the mainstream churches, their faith had to be expressed in private, individual ways. A woman could not preach publicly in church, except when she was possessed. Only under such extraordinary circumstances did clerics waive the biblical prohibition against sermons by females, even on occasion to the extent of erecting stages in the churches so that thousands might witness the performances of the possessed. Further, the holy careers pursued by some leading characters in French possession affairs after their cures shows how possession could be the route to a woman's spiritual fulfillment and public recognition.[46]

Even before their cures, the protagonists in convent possession outbreaks were, in effect, presiding over a female subculture. Like members of female possession cults the world over, their religious ecstasy freed them of restrictions placed on them by a male-dominated society. Together with other weak and downtrodden groups, women have been especially susceptible to ecstatic experience. The prestige derived from supposed contact with the spirit world secured a degree of recognition and power otherwise unavailable to them. In general, the underprivileged and the oppressed are most likely to have recourse to the supernatural, because physical reality offers them so few possibilities for advancement. I. M. Lewis observed with regard to female cults of possession in Africa, Asia, and South America that women unconsciously are

> making a special virtue of adversity and affliction, and, often quite literally, capitalizing on their distress. The cult of feminine frailty which, in its aetiolated form, is familiar enough to us from the swooning attacks experienced by Victorian women in similar circumstances, is admirably well adapted to the life situation of those who employ it. By being overcome involuntarily by an arbitrary affliction for which they cannot be held accountable, these possessed women gain attention and consideration and, within variously defined limits, successfully manipulate their husbands and menfolk.[47]

Unlike females in non-Western possession cults, the possessed women of Salem and the French convents expressed their frustrations in ways that ultimately proved to be destructive of social stability. For this reason, such outbreaks of demonic possession could not become the basis for permanent institutions of female cultural expression. In the possession-incited witch trials of the seventeenth century, cues by reform-minded authorities prompted highly suggestible individuals to exhibit symptoms of possession and to lodge accusations of witchcraft. By so doing, the possessed temporarily relieved their frustrations, provided themselves with an enhanced spiritual self-image, and produced an apparent cleansing of society, all by means acceptable to religious and political leaders imbued with the spirit of godly reform. Yet, when these kinds of witchcraft accusations exploded into mass panics, they could prove highly threatening to societal equilibrium.

In the Scandinavian possession cases, children often brought charges against their parents. At Salem this did not happen, but most of the accused women were in the same social situation as the mothers of the afflicted: married or widowed, and over forty. In both places, the great majority of the accusers were teenagers or younger, and the women charged were at least one generation older.[48] Whether the possessed accused their own parents or surrogate authority figures, witchcraft trials brought on by cases of demonic possession had the potential to destroy the most intimate ties—between neighbor and neighbor, child and parent, husband and wife, brother and sister, penitent and confessor. The charges of the possessed could threaten the social order at its roots. When this danger became clear to those in authority, they stopped encouraging such accusations. Very likely it is more than coincidence that a cluster of trials involving demonic possession immediately preceded the sudden end of the witch craze. As the erstwhile witch hunter John Hale wrote in his 1702 account of the Salem trials, "at last it was evidently seen that there must be a stop put, or the Generation of Children of God would fall under . . . condemnation" for witchcraft.[49]

By the time Hale wrote these words, his point had already become clear to most political and judicial authorities in Europe and North America. In a remarkably short time, trials for witchcraft declined in number and then disappeared. Episodes of demonic possession continued, but only rarely did the possessed of the eighteenth century think to blame a witch for their afflictions. Without the special spiritual and political environment fostered by continual witch hunting, those individuals with a gift for interior religious illumination had no occasion to connect their ecstatic insights with a human devil figure or even with the devil himself. Christian mystics, like their predecessors in the Middle Ages, once again could sink into ecstasy without arousing fears, in others and themselves, that behind their apparently benign spiritual communion might lurk the figure of Satan.[50]

The possessed, like the charity refuser and the bereaved parent, were frequent sources of witchcraft accusations. But large numbers of witch suspects were implicated not because of their occupation, social status, or relationship to a demoniac. Instead, they were accused by another witch suspect under torture. The next chapter takes up the political and psychological meaning of the systematic use of torture in witch trials.

6

In the Torture Chamber
Legal Reform and
Psychological Breakdown

Without torture there would have been no witch craze. Certainly, some trials for witchcraft would have occurred in early modern Europe even without the use of torture to elicit confessions. But the immense scale of witch hunting derived in large part from the spread of coercive techniques in criminal law procedure. Even in England and New England, where most forms of torture were forbidden, the authorities' ideas about witches were strongly influenced by continental writers who drew their evidence from confessions extracted by torture. In the same way, those who encouraged suggestible men and women to believe themselves bewitched had become familiar with witchcraft through accounts extracted under threatened or actual torture.

A case study can illustrate the impact of torture on witchcraft prosecution. Among the most wrenching documents to come down to us from the witch trials is the letter of Johannes Junius, a burgomaster in the German city of Bamberg. Junius was arrested on charges of witchcraft in 1628, while the community was in the midst of a large-scale witch panic. He was tortured, confessed, and went to the stake, but before his death Junius managed to compose an account of his imprisonment in a letter to his daughter. The burgomaster described his interrogation:

> I will tell you how it has gone with me. When I was the first time put to the torture, Dr. Braun, Dr. Kötzendorffer, and two strange doctors were there. Then Dr. Braun asks me, "Kinsman, how come you here?" I answer, "Through falsehood, through misfortune." "Hear you," he says, "you are a witch; will you confess voluntarily? If not we'll bring in witnesses and the executioner for you." I said, "I am no witch, I have a pure conscience on the

matter; if there are a thousand witnesses, I am not anxious, but I'll gladly hear the witnesses." Now the chancellor's son was set before me . . . and afterward Hoppfen Elss. She had seen me dance on Haupts-moor. . . . I answered: "I have never renounced God, and will never do it—God graciously keep me from it. I'll rather bear whatever I must." And then came also—God in highest Heaven have mercy—the executioner, and put the thumb-screws on me, both hands bound together, so that the blood ran out at the nails and everywhere, so that for four weeks I could not use my hands, as you can see from the writing. . . . Thereafter they first stripped me, bound my hands behind me, and drew me up in the torture. Then I thought heaven and earth were at an end; eight times did they draw me up and let me fall again, so that I suffered terrible agony.

Despite his suffering, Junius refused to confess. Finally, he was sent back to his cell.

When at last the executioner led me back into the prison, he said to me: "Sir, I beg you, for God's sake confess something, whether it be true or not. Invent something, for you cannot endure the torture which you will be put to, and, even if you bear it all, yet you will not excape, not even if you were an earl, but one torture will follow after another until you say you are a witch. Not before that," he said, "will they let you go, as you may see by all their trials, for one is just like another. . . ."

And so I begged, since I was in wretched plight, to be given one day for thought and a priest. The priest was refused me, but the time for thought was given. Now, my dear child, see in what hazard I stood and still stand. I must say that I am a witch, though I am not, must now renounce God, though I have never done it before. Day and night I was deeply troubled, but at last there came to me a new idea. I would not be anxious, but, since I had been given no priest with whom I could take counsel, I would myself think of something and say it. It were surely better that I just say it with mouth and words, even though I had not really done it; and afterwards I would confess to the priest, and let those answer for it who compel me to do it. . . . And so I made my confession, as follows; but it was all a lie.

Junius went on to summarize his confession, in which he admitted to signing a pact with Satan, attending sabbats, and attempting to kill his children. But this was not enough for his interrogators. They insisted that he denounce others as witches:

Then I had to tell what people I had seen at the witch-sabbat. I said that I had not recognized them. "You old rascal, I must set the executioner at you. Say—was not the Chancellor there?" So I said yes. "Who besides?" I had not recognized anybody. So he said: "Take one street after another; begin at the market, go out on one street and back on the next." I had to name several

persons there. Then came the long street. I knew nobody. Had to name eight
persons there. Then the Zinkenwert—one person more. Then over the upper
bridge to the Georgthor, on both sides. Knew nobody again. Did I know
nobody in the castle—whoever it might be, I should speak without fear. And
thus continuously they asked me on all the streets, though I could not and
would not say more. So they gave me to the executioner, told him to strip me,
shave me all over, and put me to the torture. "The rascal knows one on the
market-place, is with him daily, and yet won't name him." By that they meant
Dietmeyer: so I had to name him too.

From his tragic experience Junius drew the lesson that "whoever comes
into the witch prison must be a witch or be tortured until he invents
something out of his head." He concluded:

> Now, dear child, here you have all my confession, for which I must die.
> And they are sheer lies and made-up things, so help me God. For all this I was
> forced to say through fear of the torture which was threatened beyond what I
> had already endured. For they never leave off with the torture till one
> confesses something; be he never so good, he must be a witch. Nobody
> escapes, though he were an earl. . . .
> Dear child, keep this letter secret so that people do not find it, else I shall
> be tortured most piteously and the jailers will be beheaded. So strictly is it
> forbidden. . . . Dear child, pay this man a dollar. . . . I have taken several
> days to write this: my hands are both lame. I am in a sad plight. . . .
> Good night, for your father Johannes Junius will never see you more. July
> 24, 1628.

And on the margin of the letter he added:

> Dear child, six have confessed against me at once; the Chancellor, his son,
> Neudecker, Zaner, Hoffmaisters Ursel, and Hoppfen Els—all false, through
> compulsion, as they have all told me, and begged me forgiveness in God's
> name before they were executed. They know nothing but good of me. They
> were forced to say it, just as I myself was.[1]

The letter of Burgomaster Junius vividly illustrates the power of torture to break a prisoner's resistance. Just as striking is Junius's account of
the way an initial accusation led to a continuously widening net of suspects,
for each prisoner was forced to blurt out fresh names to the interrogators.
Taking the Junius letter as its text, this chapter explores the political and
psychological meaning of torture in the witch trials.

In entering the torture chamber, we come upon perhaps the most
obscure part of witch hunting's mysterious domain. Torture is the last piece

that remains to be placed in the witch-craze puzzle, but it does not fall neatly into position. Rough as its outlines are, an investigation of torture can bring us close to the specific historical circumstances that produced thousands of confessions to witchcraft. It can also show us the timeless elements of witch hunting still with us today.

The Politics of Torture

To understand the impact of torture, we need to consider the political context of the witch craze. The century after 1560 was probably the most politically unstable Europe had experienced since the invasions of the early Middle Ages. War—among competing rulers, aristocratic factions, and religious confessions—was a normal part of life. Traditional tensions between central authorities and provincial magnates became particularly acute, for religious divisions and economic change created great strains on political institutions.

The striking chronological parallel of political instability and witch hunting suggests that the witch panics may have been one symptom of a generalized and chronic atmosphere of governmental crisis that affected Europe during the most unsettled century of modern times. We have seen in previous chapters that the spiritual tensions of the Reformation era and the social stresses of early modern village life combined to produce an environment favorable to witchcraft accusations. Now it remains to be shown how the course of the witch craze reflected the dominant political realities of the sixteenth and seventeenth centuries.

Legal reform was one of the most important weapons of centralizing rulers in early modern Europe. Since the late 1400s, ambitious princes had been engaged in a continual effort to subject law courts to firmer direction from above. One example of the rulers' attempts to exert control over judicial officials was the promulgation of elaborately detailed written law codes meant to standardize and regularize court procedure. The codes were the legal embodiment of monarchical claims to sovereignty over the array of aristocrats, municipalities, and religious bodies with which medieval rulers had long shared authority. The new statutes challenged the family-centered customs of feud and vendetta that had prevailed for centuries and substituted a new principle, the supremacy of the king's law over all loyalties to clan, region, or order. The sovereignty of the state—as personified in the ruler—was intended to provide a higher level of civil peace than was possible in medieval times.

One of the unanticipated side effects of legal change was the creation of a judicial apparatus and criminal law procedure conducive to large-scale witch hunting. The rulers' new legal codes were mostly drawn from the law of imperial Rome and the church's canon law. In the Middle Ages, these legal traditions were embraced by the papal Inquisition and by Italian city-states because of their favorable implication for central authority. Then, in early modern times, the inquisitorial method (for which the Inquisition was named) became established as the dominant procedure in most European (but not English) secular courts. Under these codes based on Roman and canon law, rulers appointed prosecutor-judges—the two functions were combined in the same individual—for whom the inquisitorial procedure offered many advantages in their efforts to secure guilty verdicts. A prisoner had no right to be informed of the charges against him or of his accuser's identity. Since testimony was taken in private, the defendant was denied the opportunity to confront unfriendly witnesses, much less to cross-examine them. Defense attorneys were usually unknown. Except in England, her North American colonies, and a few other regions on Europe's cultural periphery, witch trials of the sixteenth and seventeenth centuries unfolded in the procedural context of the inquisitorial system. This method, which had first been applied in medieval church courts to the exceptional crime of heresy, now became the norm for all criminal cases.[2]

Because torture used to elicit confessions was a central part of inquisitorial procedure in the later Middle Ages, this feature was adopted by sixteenth- and seventeenth-century legal reformers when they took up inquisitorial methods. Judicial torture (as it was called) became a regular element in criminal procedure. For witch hunting, this was the most important element of legal reform. Judicial torture was administered in graded degrees of severity, culminating in the "third degree," an expression still used to refer to brutal interrogation. Lesser degrees of torture included the use of thumbscrews and instruments for the tearing out of fingernails. More severe varieties entailed stretching a victim on the rack, crushing his legs in the "boot," or—the torture administered to Burgomaster Junius—subjecting a prisoner to the strappado, in which he was bound with weights before being repeatedly dropped to the floor by a pulley. Not as technologically inventive a torture method, but just as effective, was deprivation of sleep for days on end. Often the mere threat of these brutal treatments was enough to gain the desired confession.[3]

Torture is perhaps the most telling symbol of the new controls early modern rulers sought to impose on their subjects. Even before conviction, the prisoner found himself subjected to punishing physical pain. Under the inquisitorial procedure a firm line between guilt and innocence, a hallmark of modern criminal law, was blurred almost beyond recognition.[4] For example, the German imperial law code of 1532, called the *Carolina* after Emperor Charles V, allowed the use of torture whenever there was probable cause to believe a defendant guilty. Probable cause meant one eyewitness—two were enough to convict without a confession—or the presence of circumstantial evidence (for example, if a suspected felon was caught with the weapon and the loot). In the eyes of the law, probable cause implied that the accused was at least semiguilty and thus deserving of torture.

Yet the drafters of the new law codes were well aware of the potential abuses inherent in the employment of judicial torture. Without probable cause no one could be put to torture under the *Carolina*. The contemporary French legal code of Francis I went even further, calling on judges to exhaust all other investigatory means and mandating the approval of a panel of legal advisors before administering torture. Another of the rules generally used to govern the application of judicial torture was the test of *corpus delicti*, a requirement that the judge first determine that a crime had been committed before putting a suspect to the question (the euphemism for administering torture). These restrictions suggest that jurists were concerned to safeguard the innocent suspect against wrongful convictions elicited by coercion.[5]

The application of the law of torture to witchcraft cases offers a fascinating example of the interplay of principles of jurisprudence and deeply felt social pressures. It might seem that the law codes' procedural barriers to the administration of torture would have protected accused witches even more than other suspected criminals. The weapons and rewards of witchcraft were usually less obvious than a dagger or a sack of money. And how could any judge certify that a death, illness, or some other misfortune was the result of witchcraft rather than a natural cause? Ironically, however, these very problems contributed to the widespread application of torture in witchcraft cases. Since maleficent witchcraft was supposedly accomplished by supernatural means, one could hardly expect an eyewitness, circumstantial evidence, or even assurance that criminality was involved; for, as the legal phrase had it, these were deeds whose traces vanished with the act. Thus, the judge's sole recourse was to obtain a confession, and this almost always required torture. Although in ordinary cases torture might be a last resort, in the exceptional crime of witchcraft it was often seen as society's first and only instrument.[6]

The arguments of the *Malleus Maleficarum* on this subject came close to the views of many witch-hunting judges of the late sixteenth and seventeenth centuries. The authors of the *Malleus* accepted torture as a necessity in witch trials if the accused refused to confess freely, which meant in nearly all cases. Over a century later, King James VI spoke for many of his contemporaries when he maintained that only the extreme pain of torture could weaken the devil's strong grip over his servants. As the ruler of Scotland, he applied this maxim in the many witch trials conducted under royal commission during the 1590s.[7]

A terrible fear of witches and their powers eroded the safeguards against wrongful use of torture that judges and legal scholars had erected in the new codes of criminal law. After 1560, rulers and their judicial officials systematically discarded the protections built into the law codes promulgated by their immediate predecessors. Their evasion of recently created legal barriers was symptomatic of the ambivalence, confusion, and sense of helplessness that characterized the authorities' efforts to come to grips with the problem of witchcraft. King James's assertions about the necessity of torture constituted the conventional wisdom of the European judicial elite in the decades around 1600.

Context is crucial if we are to understand these rapid shifts. We need always to remember that the witch craze took place against a background of intense religious conflict. Consciousness of sin was a fundamental characteristic of Catholic and Protestant reformers, and the elites were exhibiting the effects of a dramatic rise in spiritual awareness. Having internalized the values of religious reform, they became acutely sensitive to moral deviation. This was particularly true in areas where rival churches competed for dominance. These often were the same places that experienced a high incidence of witch hunting.

The consensus among the spiritually sensitized political and judicial elites of the late sixteenth and early seventeenth centuries was that witchcraft was an extraordinary menace requiring drastic remedies. These leaders cast the witch in the role of arch-heretic. During the Middle Ages, heresy had been regarded as treason against God. Inquisitorial procedures against heretics were modeled on the imperial Roman law's treatment of lèse-majesté or treason, an exceptional crime requiring the most extreme countermeasures. In Reformation times as well, clerical and lay officials deemed heresy the ultimate crime. To reject God's word was to challenge the authority of rulers, judges, masters of all kinds. To become a heretic was to subvert the principle of hierarchy that held society together, for all social relationships rested on legitimation by divine authority. Religious dissent consequently suggested to the upper classes the worst kinds of political and social disorder. Because witchcraft was classed as a kind of heresy, accused witches in many countries were regarded as guilty of a heinous crime that necessitated exceptionally rigorous prosecution.[8]

In England, the traditions of the common law prohibited most types of torture.[9] Consequently, the witch trials there provide a kind of basal measure of witch hunting. They suggest how witch trials might have been conducted everywhere had torture not been introduced. Although witchcraft was for a time the second most commonly prosecuted crime in the kingdom, as compared with other countries England saw relatively few trials. The best estimate is under one thousand executions for witchcraft, and the actual number may be closer to five hundred. By comparison, Scotland, a Roman-law country with a much smaller population, had over a thousand executions. Further, English courts were unusually lenient. In the country of Essex, only 24 percent of those indicted for witchcraft were executed, a proportion far below the norm for places employing torture. English witch hunts generally involved only one or a very few suspects. As described in an earlier chapter, the English trials stemmed primarily from the psychological dynamics of village social structure, and the crime of witchcraft in England stressed malefice rather than devil worship. Many historians have pointed out that the lurid details of the sabbat are seldom found in English witch cases. Although the sexual element is present in the tales of animal familiars and the witch's tit widely encountered in English trials, without torture the sexual side of witchcraft was considerably muted compared to the standard witch stereotype found in Scotland and on the European continent.

Unlike France, Germany, Scotland, and nearly all other European countries, England emerged from the Middle Ages with a single system of law that applied to the entire kingdom. English rulers had few of the incentives that motivated their continental counterparts to introduce new legal systems as centralizing devices. The common law generally served the English crown's needs well enough. Thus, the Tudor monarchs of the sixteenth century, and even their less prudent Stuart successors, James I and Charles I, undertook only limited innovations of the inquisitorial type. Hostile reaction to the new courts of Star Chamber and High Commission demonstrated just how difficult would be the thorough imposition of foreign legal principles. Except perhaps for Charles I, English rulers never seriously considered such a departure in the law. Instead, they generally found the unitary system of the common law an adequate prop for powerful kingships. The Shakespearean audience shocked by the destructive feuding of Capulets and Montagues could flatter itself that vendettas and private armies of retainers were scourges against which English law and strong monarchy constituted an effective barrier. Spaniards watching Lope de Vega's *The Sheep Well*, or Frenchmen at the first performance of Corneille's *The Cid*—like *Romeo and Juliet*, plays about conflicting claims of love, aristocratic honor, and state law—could not have been nearly so confident of the capacity of their own political and legal institutions to withstand the disorderliness of powerful corporate groups that claimed to be a law unto themselves.

The career of Matthew Hopkins, Witch-Finder General under the Puritans in 1645 and 1646, was an exception to the usual English pattern and underscores the differences between common law and inquisitorial procedure. In the confused circumstances of civil war and disruption of regular justice, Hopkins secured confessions through torture, chiefly by depriving prisoners of sleep for long periods. Unlike nearly all other English witch suspects, his victims admitted to sexual intercourse with Satan and attendance at the sabbat. Hopkins also imitated continental witch hunters by insisting that each confession include lists of accomplices. Thus, a small number of accusations quickly exploded into what was, for England, an unprecedented series of trials. Hopkins hanged seventeen women in Essex in 1645.[10]

Hopkin's exploits are unique in the history of English witchcraft. But in other European countries witch hunters of his sort were all too common. Indisputably, some judges made their careers as professional witch prosecutors. These were men who tortured remorselessly and in some cases executed hundreds. In French-speaking lands, such judges flourished in the years around 1600. Several wrote accounts of their exploits in the form of demonological manuals. These included Henri Boguet, a judge in the Habsburg Franche-Comté of Burgundy; Nicolas Rémy, attorney general of Lorraine; and Pierre de Lancre, the judge of the Parlement of Bordeaux who presided over the Basque witch panic in southwestern France. All three consistently used torture to extract confessions and to implicate new suspects.[11]

These men followed a path first charted in France by the very distinguished lawyer and political theorist, Jean Bodin, one of the greatest thinkers of the late sixteenth century. His treatise on witches, published in 1580 and very popular during its author's lifetime, was one of the first important demonological works to appear in France during the witch craze. Although Bodin was not a judge and thus tried no one, his presence among the theoreticians of witch hunting often has been a painful embarrassment to his admirers. The ferocious tone of Bodin's *Démonomanie* and its credulous acceptance of the witch stereotype seem inconsistent with his liberal views on religious toleration and his brilliant economic insights. But Bodin's opinions on witchcraft stemmed from a deep professional knowledge of the law and were consistent with his general philosophy.[12]

In the late sixteenth century, judges who were exposed to movements for spiritual reform were developing a keen interest in cases of supposed witchcraft. Bodin, Boguet, Rémy, and de Lancre all made clear that their disgust with witchcraft derived primarily from the "superstitious" (that is, heretical) activities attributed to witches. Although much work on this subject remains to be done in the French judicial archives, available evidence suggests that in France the trials spread because witch hunting meshed with the development of the judicial elite's religious sensibilities in the wake of Catholic reform. A sampling of the records of the Parlement of Rouen, for example, shows that the court heard no witchcraft cases at all in 1548–49 or 1576. By 1585–88, however, 3.1 percent of the tribunal's business involved witchcraft, and this percentage more than tripled by 1604–06, when witchcraft represented fully one-tenth of the Parlement's total caseload. At the same time, the court's docket also saw an abrupt rise in cases of incest, adultery, sodomy, and infanticide. Plainly, the sudden appearance and rise to prominence of such crimes against morality points to a broad change in collective judicial attitudes.[13]

The political leadership's concern with witchcraft in French-speaking lands was expressed in edicts that broadened the rights of local courts in witch cases. In 1604 the Habsburg rulers gave local courts expanded authority in the Burgundian Franche-Comté (as well as in the provinces of the Spanish Netherlands), while Boguet was still active. Henceforth, the numerous landlords who retained rights of high justice from feudal days were permitted to try cases of witchcraft, with appeal of the verdicts allowed to the Parlement of Dôle. Witchcraft trials and the severity of punishment increased in the Franche-Comté during the next few years.[14]

Another species of political intervention spurred witch hunting in Lorraine. There Duke Charles III gave his appellate judges at Nancy full authority to review all witchcraft sentences. Although in other places decrees requiring mandatory appeal by high courts moderated the penalties for witchcraft, in Lorraine Nicolas Rémy was one of the duke's appellate judges. He saw it as his duty to travel around the duchy urging local courts, which were usually staffed with nonprofessional judges, to initiate witch trials. Rémy bragged of executing nine hundred witches between 1576 and 1591, a total no doubt swollen by Duke Charles's centralizing measure.[15]

Both in the Franche-Comté and in Lorraine, then, the rulers' innovations in legal procedures served to encourage the spread of witch trials. Similarly, Pierre de Lancre's witch hunt in the Basque country was carried out under the specific authorization of King Henry IV. Without a doubt, Boguet, Rémy, and de Lancre decisively affected the course of events in their regions of operation. But they could not have succeeded in conducting extensive witch hunts without the wide support of other judicial and political notables in French-speaking lands.

Judicial witch finders were especially common in Germany, the scene of at least half of all the witchcraft executions.[16] Many, if not most, of these German trials were presided over not by local judges but by special investigators, who often were learned university doctors trained in Roman law and inquisitorial procedure. Such scholar-investigators were appointed by the German princes. In this way, the rulers removed jurisdiction over witchcraft from local officials. Authority was placed in the hands of professional jurists whose university backgrounds had exposed them to the values of spiritual reform characteristic of the learned elites.

The German princes' use of university jurists as judges in witch trials reflects the efforts of the rulers to standardize and professionalize the administration of justice in their territories. Until the sixteenth century, German local courts had been virtually independent of centralized direction. There were over two thousand such courts in Saxony alone, only a few of which could have had professional judges. Thus, German princes had to overcome a formidable problem if they were to standardize the administration of justice under central authority. The *Carolina*'s solution was to leave the local courts with their lay judges largely intact, but to require that these laymen seek the nonbinding advice of professional jurists in cases involving serious crimes. Later in the sixteenth century, German princes began to decree that in such cases university law faculties *must* review all decisions of the local courts before sentence was carried out, and the opinions of the faculties were to be binding. As a result, professional judges came to exert a controlling influence in many criminal cases, even without the appointment of a special investigator.

These interventions in local justice by the German legal profession meant that the elites' demonological concept of witchcraft and its encouragement of judicial torture could penetrate deeply into German society. The Criminal Constitution of Electoral Saxony, for instance, mandated in 1572 that "if anyone, forgetting his Christian faith, sets up a pact with the devil or has anything to do with him, *regardless of whether he has harmed anyone by magic*, he should be condemned to death by fire." Here the growing preoccupation of the elites with devil worship is manifest, especially when we compare the analogous paragraph of the *Carolina*, promulgated only forty years earlier. The *Carolina* had decreed the death penalty *only* in cases where witchcraft had caused harm to people. From the 1570s on, the Saxon formulation was widely imitated in Germany, and large-scale witch panics became frighteningly common. Saxony was also one of the leaders in establishing the principle of mandatory and binding appellate review by professional jurists, and the Saxon high court, with its great prestige and regular practice of printing its reports for wide circulation, greatly influenced other German judges.

A pattern of increasing ferocity in sixteenth-century witchcraft statutes can also be found outside Germany. The witch had been considered a menace to her neighbors in the early sixteenth century, but later the elites in many countries came to see her in addition as the enemy of God, state, and society. Her crime was now being redefined: it lay in what she was, not primarily in what (if anything) she did.

In the Spanish Netherlands, there was a particularly striking contrast in the decrees on witchcraft issued in Philip II's name in 1570 and 1592. The provincial council of Luxembourg, in applying the king's first criminal ordinance, noted disapprovingly that local judges were torturing and sometimes executing men and women for witchcraft, "some even without any legitimate cause," and were failing to consult the council's jurists. The council's edict went on to specify that torture could be administered only after express permission had been obtained from "men of letters, learned and versed in the law." A suspect who confessed under torture had to confirm her admission the next day, and, if she refused, only the council could authorize renewed torture. Anyone tortured twice could be put to the question again only if new evidence came to light. Twenty-two years later, in 1592, Philip issued a new decree associating witchcraft with heresy and demonic magic. To all authorities, secular and religious, the king addressed a ringing call "requiring, exhorting, admonishing and commanding them to keep all eyes open so as to extirpate this great wickedness." In less than a generation, moderate principles had given way to incendiary language.[17]

A similar progression took place in Scotland, where Roman law procedure was making deep inroads during the sixteenth century. The first Scottish statute against witchcraft was passed in 1563, but trials were infrequent until the 1590s. Then, urged by the General Assembly of the dominant Presbyterian church, King James VI's Privy Council took control of witchcraft prosecutions. Operating under explicit orders to use torture on recalcitrant suspects, the royal commissioners presided over at least three hundred witchcraft cases between 1591 and 1597. This was an indiscriminate national witch-panic carried out under official state auspices. As in other places, these Scottish witch hunts reflected the growing legal powers of centralizing secular rulers.[18]

In the Spanish Netherlands and Scotland, as in Germany, legal changes in the late sixteenth century preceded a dramatic increase in the frequency of witch trials. The same was true in other places, where the adoption of statutes on witchcraft was soon followed by prosecutions. Once the authority of princes and provincial councils was established, centralizing forces that originally had acted as brakes on procedural abuses could, when reversed in course, greatly accelerate the pace of witch hunting.

The Jesuit Friedrich von Spee vividly described how specially appointed investigators who were convinced that devil worship was rampant could use the new inquisitorial rules to convict any and all suspects in German witch trials. His *Cautio Criminalis (Advice to Prosecutors)*, first published in 1631, described the typical cycle of a German witch panic. First, a helpless old woman was subjected to torture until she confessed. Should she admit her guilt after only the first degree of torture, the official transcript would state that she confessed freely, thereby leading any appellate body to believe that the admission was offered without torture. The judge, Spee continued, then suppressed any evidence pointing to the accused's innocence. He forced her to implicate many others, "whose names are frequently put into her mouth by the investigators or suggested by the executioner, or of whom she has heard as suspected or accused. These in turn are forced to accuse others, and these still others, and so it goes on."[19]

Spee's account shows that a century after the promulgation of the *Carolina* many of its provisions for protecting the rights of the accused had become dead letters, at least for witch trials. For example, denunciation by alleged accomplices was considered dubious grounds for torture in the *Carolina* but became accepted evidence in the witch panics. Further, the *Carolina* was eloquent on the judge's responsibility to encourage a suspect who is too intimidated to establish his innocence: "Such exhortation is thus needed because many a person out of simpleness or fright, even when he is quite innocent, does not know he should proceed to exculpate himself."[20] Far from taking to heart this compassionate stricture, many judges resorted to leading the accused with suggestive questions, a practice explicitly prohibited in Charles V's code. When accused by another official of violating the provisions of the *Carolina*, one special investigator of the 1620s responded that the code was antiquated and inadequate for dealing with the witch problem.[21]

By 1600, it was commonplace for judges to use standardized questionnaires in their interrogation of suspected witches, a practice inherited from
the medieval Inquisition and encouraged in the *Malleus Maleficarum*. Many
surviving confessions consist of a list of numbers, each followed by a "yes"
or the equivalent. Quite obviously, these documents betray their origin in
the prepared interrogatories of the questioners. The prosecutor in the
southwestern German territory of Ellwangen was typical. H. C. Erik Midelfort recounts that he interrogated suspects from a prepared list of thirty
questions

> that began by asking if the accused could say the Lord's Prayer, the Ave
> Maria, the Creed, and the Ten Commandments, but then moved on directly
> to the question of who seduced her into witchcraft. How did this seduction
> occur? Why did she give in? Where? What was the devil like? What did he
> promise? What was it like to have sexual relations with him? Why did she not
> break off the relationship when she realized that he was a devil? And so on and
> on. . . . We do not need to theorize [Midelfort concludes] that the witches
> must have had some cult in order to explain their agreement on the most
> minute details. The questions asked supply us with a sufficient answer. By
> constant use of these formulas it was even possible to set the pattern or
> sequence of events in a witch's confession.[22]

Dr. Martin Eschbach, a councillor of the margrave of Baden-Baden,
was an active witch eradicator in the years around 1630, when Spee was
composing his protest against the procedures used in witch trials.
Eschbach's cases were especially notable for their high productivity. The
trials over which he presided yielded an average of fifteen denunciations per
suspect. Only 3 percent of those tried in his court were acquitted, possibly a
record low for all Europe. Such brutality makes one suspect that, if anything, Spee was understating the extent of abuse.[23]

A catalogue of the killings across Germany reinforces this impression.
Over one thousand people were put to death in secular territories of
southwestern Germany, and perhaps another two thousand were executed
in the duchy of Bavaria. The most frightful carnage occurred in the prince-
bishoprics and other ecclesiastical states of central Germany, where more
than three thousand may have died at the stake: 368 from 22 villages in the
Archbishopric-Electorate of Trier between 1587 and 1593, between 300 and
600 in the Bishopric of Bamberg from 1623 to 1633, 274 in the Bishopric of
Eichstätt in the single year 1629, 900 in the Prince-Bishopric of Würzburg
in the 1620s, 133 executed in the lands of the convent of Quedlindbergh on
just one day in 1589, 390 in the ecclesiastical territory of Ellwangen from

1611 to 1618.[24] Even granting that some of these figures may be overesti-
mates, a pattern of ferocious prosecution is very clear.

The princes' mandate to send all serious criminal cases for binding
review by learned jurists was creating a "common law" for Germany that
was greatly conducive to witch trials. Impetus in the same direction came
from the appointment of special investigators, who brought the professional's broad knowledge of legal precedents to the local scene. In both ways,
intervention in local justice by rulers encouraged the spread of witch
panics.[25] But the proliferation of witch panics did not depend exclusively on
direct intervention from above. So great was the respect accorded legal
professionals that even the independent judges of such free imperial cities as
Nördlingen, Offenburg, and Schwäbisch Gmünd closely tailored the procedures followed in municipal witch trials to the patterns they knew
were approved by the university scholars and princely jurists.[26] By direct
and indirect methods, then, legal reforms spurred on the German witch
hunts.

Inquisitorial procedure greatly encouraged this kind of aggressive style
of criminal investigation. By combining the functions of judge and prosecutor, the Roman-canonical legal system placed nearly irresistible temptation
in the hands of eager officials. As a modern legal historian has observed,
"only a judge equipped with superhuman capabilities could keep his de-
cisional function free from . . . the influences of his own instigating and
investigating activities."[27] In the late seventeenth century, an experienced
French judge made the same point in a book attacking the use of torture in
witchcraft trials. Augustin Nicolas stressed that abstract rules of torture
devised by scholarly doctors of law were applied by judges caught up in the
task of trying to convict the prisoner: "In this situation the judge is not
exempt from passion" and may be brought to use excessive force in his zeal
for a confession.[28]

Witch-hunting manuals left so much discretion in judges' hands that an
eager prosecutor could nearly always find some way to justify torture. Henri
Boguet, for example, listed as grounds for torture the accusation of another
witch, association with a known witch, possession of powders or unguents,
and, when accompanied by other indications, "common rumor" of witchcraft. As if this was not enough to keep the torture chambers fully booked,
Boguet also had a group of "light indications" that collectively added up to a
warrant for torture. These included an expression of fear on the prisoner's
face, any use of blasphemous language, the inability to shed tears, and the
bad luck of having a parent who had been convicted of witchcraft. Also on
this list was failure to seek redress if one had been reproached as a witch at

some previous time. If applied rigorously, these criteria could send almost anyone to torture.[29]

The importance of judges' willingness or reluctance to disregard the restrictions on torture laid down in the *Carolina* also can be illustrated by the experience of the French-speaking cantons of Switzerland, still officially subject to the German imperial law at this time. There, as E. William Monter has shown, the percentage of accused witches who were executed varied directly with the scrupulousness of the local judges in adhering to the letter of the law when administering torture. Thus, in the Calvinist territory of Vaud, the suspect was deemed guilty in advance, the strictures of the *Carolina* were ignored in the torture chamber, and 90 percent of the accused went to the stake. In the nearby Catholic canton of Fribourg, however, only one-third of those arrested eventually suffered execution. Of 124 individuals tortured there between 1607 and 1683, 75 underwent the experience without confessing. In Fribourg, as in the nearby republic of Geneva, where only a very low 21 percent of the trials resulted in the death sentence, suspects were not presumed guilty, and the rules of the *Carolina* were observed scrupulously. In general, Switzerland was spared the large-scale panics common in neighboring German lands. Most Swiss trials were either isolated episodes involving one, two, or three accused, or were "small panics" in which at most ten or twelve were arrested.[30]

The Swiss model of relative restraint stands in sharp contrast to the excesses that characterized many witch-hunting outbreaks in Germany. Although the kind of event that triggered a trial was similar everywhere, subsequent developments often diverged markedly. Throughout Europe, the first person accused was usually an old, impoverished woman who fit the standard stereotype of the witch. In German lands, however, such women were far more likely to be tortured into naming their accomplices than were their counterparts in, for example, most jurisdictions of French Switzerland. And German judges typically proceeded to arrest those so named, tortured them to discover still more suspects, arrested and tortured the latter, and so on. It appears that in the German panics little distinction was made between the initial suspect—against whom there was generally stronger evidence in the form of numerous witnesses to her malefice, and who sometimes may even have believed herself to be a witch—and later suspects, against whom the only evidence was an accusation made by a desperate victim of torture. The judges in Swiss Fribourg used milder coercion on those charged only by a confessed witch, and judges in Geneva usually disregarded charges from so dubious a source. But, in the absence of such self-restraint on the part of the authorities, a single accusation triggered a chain reaction in many German communities, and large-scale trials unfolded.[31]

Such was the pattern at Ellwangen, in the German southwest.[32] In 1611, the authorities arrested and jailed Barbara Rüfin, a seventy-year-old villager. She had been accused of witchcraft by her husband, her son, and her daughter-in-law, who testified that Barbara had attempted to poison her son because she disapproved of his marriage. The prisoner was also accused of killing cattle, not surprising in a community that had experienced an unusual number of unexplained animal deaths, as well as baffling human epidemics, in the immediately preceding years. After two weeks' imprisonment, there was such damaging testimony in hand against Rüfin that the examiners commenced torturing. The torture was supervised by a group of town officials appointed by the ecclesiastical prince-provost who governed the territory. Rüfin was twice stretched on the rack in fifteen-minute sessions on April 20. But the old woman refused to confess. She steadfastly maintained her innocence and proclaimed her faith that God would send a sign to clear her. Two days later, after suffering a total of seven torture sessions, Rüfin finally broke down and admitted not only to performing malefice against her son, the crops, and domestic animals, but also to signing a pact and copulating with the devil. She also named several accomplices. The next day, when questioned without torture, she renounced her confession but was immediately tortured again to confirm it. Soon Rüfin was completely confused, alternately admitting and denying everything. After ten more days of this kind of interrogation, the old woman finally confessed everything required of her. Within a week she was executed by the sword, her body burned, and all her belongings confiscated by the government.

The case of Barbara Rüfin presents many of the characteristics of the typical German witch trial. It originated from charges of malefice in a rural environment, accusations made plausible by family rivalries and disease in the community. Rüfin was also forced to confess to devil worship, thereby confirming the judges' stereotypical understanding of witchcraft. An old woman who fit the image of the witch, Rüfin was an ordinary victim. But her trial did not close the case. Like falling dominoes, more and more suspects were arrested, tortured, and forced to name accomplices before being put to death. By 1618, over four hundred people had been executed in Ellwangen. In the midst of the trials, the Jesuit Johann Finck wrote: "I do not see where this case will lead and what effect it will have, for this evil has so taken over, and like the plague has affected so many, that if the magistrates continue their office, in a few years the city will be in miserable ruins."[33] Midelfort, the closest student of the Ellwangen trials, has described the mechanism by which accusations snowballed as follows:

> The Ellwangen officials were occasionally extremely successful in eliciting long lists of persons seen at the sabbath. Weiner Anna, for example, denounced 24 different persons, and the *Schweizerin* 17. A woman called simply Cleva denounced a string of 29 persons, but then revoked several of them. The effect of such lists may well be imagined. In some cases they were used fully 23 years after they were written down: some of the denunciations from 1588 played a role in 1611. In addition, witches very commonly denounced persons in other towns and in completely different jurisdictions. In this way the germ of witch hunting could pass from town to town very much like an epidemic. To assist their neighboring regions, the officials at Ellwangen even assembled a book of persons denounced from regions outside the territory, alphabetically by town.[34]

Plainly, the torture machine was remarkably productive in yielding fresh batches of suspects. But the mechanism often went out of control and could even consume its operators. Michael Dier, one of the judges of the court of Ellwangen, had to witness his wife's execution for witchcraft. When he persisted in publicly proclaiming her innocence, he too was arrested, forced to confess under torture, and duly executed. Other government officials were condemned and their property confiscated. Probably even more shocking to the populace was the conviction of three priests and a church organist.[35]

These incidents from the Ellwangen panic are duplicated in the records of many German trials. Although the first accused was nearly always a helpless individual, the ripple effect produced by indiscriminate torture eventually implicated more well-born people, even those at the top of the community social structure. Teachers, clerics, officials, lawyers, and wealthy merchants were accused and executed in significant numbers. The wide spectrum of victims makes it impossible to suggest any kind of simple social analysis for these large-scale panics. Nor is it easy to capture the motivations of judges who prosecuted influential members of their own communities. Confiscation of the victim's property does not seem to have been an important incentive in most situations. Many places prohibited the practice, and, even where confiscation was the rule, the available evidence indicates that only a small fraction of rich victims' property was taken. In most cases it was the government's treasury and not individual judges that gained by confiscation. In any case, the great majority of victims were poor folk whose resources, even if appropriated in toto, could barely have offset

146 Servants of Satan

the considerable expense of imprisoning, feeding, guarding, trying, and executing a witch. (Imprisonment was not a normal feature of early modern criminal justice.) Jealousy of and grudges held against creditors may have played a role in trials involving the rich, and it is also hard to believe that those in control of the judicial apparatus always resisted the temptation to use it against their personal enemies.[36] Yet no historian has been able to create a model of the large-scale trials that persuasively explains them in terms of German social structure.

This failure suggests that, to a great degree, the German witch panics lacked rational meaning; because of the way torture was used, whatever social utility (in functionalist terms) each panic may have had at its outset was eventually lost as more and more victims were implicated. The dynamics of the trials often gave them a life of their own. One step led inexorably to the next, and, although each step may have had a reasonable basis, the total process was often irrational in its random destructiveness. The German panics are the clearest example of witch hunts gone out of everyone's control. In those trials the combination of popular fears, elite suspicions, and procedural abuses produced monumentally destructive results.

Such carnage stemmed not from some defect in the German character but from a series of contributing circumstances that were uniquely intense in many German states. Religious antagonisms were especially strong and deep-seated. Spiritual anxiety and political shocks accompanied pervasive legal reform, which removed judicial control from local officials and transferred it to the authors and interpreters of the new law codes. The inquisitorial method was articulated throughout German society as princes required local officials to regularly consult with professional jurists and to imitate their techniques.

Germany was the extreme in a pattern discernible all across Europe. Wherever intense spiritual reform efforts coincided with the introduction of inquisitorial procedure, witch trials flourished. Scotland experienced the simultaneous imposition of Presbyterian Calvinism and Roman-canonical legal procedure; witch panics there approximated the German trials in scope and intensity. In the Spanish Netherlands, the introduction of a new criminal code by the foreign ruler Philip II in the 1590s, along with the simultaneous onset of Jesuit religious reform, greatly accelerated the pace of accusations and trials. In French Switzerland, where witch panics were relatively small and infrequent, religious conflict was pervasive, but the local Swiss courts were probably less subject to control from professional university jurists and centralizing rulers than were their German equivalents. In France itself, legal reform had mostly come earlier, before the era of the witch trials. Although there were many witch trials in France, especially during the era of civil-religious wars in the late sixteenth century, in most parts of the country snowballing panics were exceptional, and the pace of prosecution seems to have declined after 1600. Witch trials in Sweden and Finland began only after 1650, when Scandinavian university law faculties came under the influence of German juridical principles. Often these law schools took the lead in witchcraft prosecutions and introduced into Scandinavia the previously unknown practice of judicial torture. England, where changes in religious practice came about largely under state direction and where there was almost no inquisitorial procedure, had comparatively few trials. In Spain the result was similar: there the Protestant challenge hardly penetrated, and the Catholic kings' newly founded Spanish Inquisition applied its rigorous methods to Jews and Moslems but virtually ignored witches. Central and southern Italy experienced neither major legal innovations nor significant religious conflict in this period. These areas were spared trials for witchcraft. In short, the differing impact of challenges to spiritual values and legal traditions appears to have created a spectrum of political stresses. At the upper end of the range, where challenges were simultaneous and profound, the strains on elite institutions were greatest and witch trials proliferated.[37]

Thus, the relationship between political centralization and witch hunting turns out to be more complicated than might have been expected. Early in the sixteenth century, centralizing monarchs promulgated law codes that legitimated torture but also restricted judges' authority to use it. After 1560, these restrictions were severely eroded in many places, due in part to the interventions of judges and princely councillors imbued with the missionary impulses of spiritual reform and the absolutist impulses of state sovereignty. These authorities used the judicial mechanisms established by their predecessors to expand the grounds for torture and to impose professional judges and academic jurisprudence on criminal procedure. In this way they created the witch panics.

The Psychology of Torture

In the history of Western civilization, judicial authorities have sometimes widely approved the use of torture, on occasion totally forbidden it, and most often tacitly accepted its presence. Except for the twentieth century, no period has been more receptive to the physical coercion of suspects than was the era of the witch trials. But, unlike contemporary dictatorships, which try to hide the evidence of their horrors behind prison walls or in remote concentration camps, early modern authorities usually did not disguise their use of force. Although judges sometimes played down the role of torture when they reported confessions, there were few challenges to the principle of coercion by the state. At no other time in medieval or modern history were. the rights of the authorities over the physical persons of subjects so universally acknowledged. Political explanations of this nearly unique receptivity to torture can take us only part way toward an understanding of the phenomenon. The psychology of torture also must be examined.

Consider the case of Rebekka Lemp, imprisoned on charges of witchcraft at the Lutheran free imperial city of Nördlingen in 1590. Letters Rebekka wrote to her husband Peter, an important civic official in charge of collecting indirect taxes, were preserved in the records of her trial. These letters enable us to follow Rebekka through the various stages of the judicial proceedings. The first letter was sent soon after her arrest:

> My beloved treasure, have no fear. If a thousand people accuse me, I am still innocent—or let all the devils come and tear me apart. And if they interrogate me under torture, I could confess nothing, even if they tear me into a thousand pieces. . . . If I am guilty, then may God never let me appear before his face for all eternity. If they don't believe me, God almighty will watch over me and send them a sign. For if I am abandoned in my need, then there is no God in heaven.[38]

It is clear that the Lemps were a devoted couple. Peter made an impassioned statement to the council of judges, pointing out Rebekka's piety and her devotion as a wife and mother of six children. But the council ignored him and ordered Rebekka to be tortured. This interrogation produced a confession, retracted in another letter to Peter:

> O my chosen treasure, must I thus be torn in all innocence from you? That will cry out to God for all time. They force one, they make one talk; they have tortured me. I am as innocent as God in heaven. If I knew as much as one iota of these things, then I would deserve that God should deny me paradise. . . . Father, send me something so that I die, otherwise I will break down under torture.[39]

Aware at last that there was no longer any hope, Rebekka sent her remaining jewelry home and with it these instructions: "Wear the ring in memory of me. Divide the necklace into six pieces and have our children wear them on their hands for the rest of their lives."[40] Shortly afterward the authorities ordered that Rebekka Lemp be burned at the stake. Lest one conclude that she fell victim to enemies of her tax collector husband, it should be noted by way of postscript that Peter Lemp's career continued to prosper after his wife's death. Eventually he became a member of the same town council that had condemned her.

Another surviving letter from a condemned witch to her husband comes from Ellwangen in 1614. Magdalena Weixler, wife of the chapter scribe Georg, wrote shortly before her execution: "I know that my innocence will come to light, even if I do not live to see it. I would not be concerned that I must die, if it were not for my poor children; but if it must be so, may God give me the grace that I may endure it with patience."[41]

Weixler's case was especially horrible because her jailer had tricked her into turning over her jewelry and granting him sexual favors in return for a false promise to spare her from torture. Soon afterward, the jailer was caught and tried for bribery and breaking the secrecy of court proceedings. His trial revealed widespread rape of imprisoned women and the existence of an extortion racket whereby guards sold names to torture victims who desperately needed people to accuse of complicity in witchcraft. Such corruption among jailers must have been common when prisons themselves were a kind of torture, especially for those too poor to buy food and warm clothing from the turnkey.[42]

These letters, like the one by Burgomaster Junius quoted at the beginning of this chapter, offer dramatic testimony to the degradations visited on those charged with witchcraft. Perhaps, then, it is difficult to regard the judges who inflicted such tortures as anything but greedy and power-hungry individuals. Historians have sometimes characterized such prosecutors as men eager to destroy the lives of their victims for selfish goals. Often, too, witch hunters have been charged with hypocrisy, because the trial transcripts record their constant religious appeals to prisoners to confess, repent, and save their souls from eternal damnation. But greed and hypocrisy seem insufficient explanations for so widespread a pattern of behavior. No doubt some of the prosecutors stood to gain from their victims' deaths or consciously cloaked their unholy ambitions in religious language. Such a line of interpretation, however, must confront the insuperable problem of explaining why throughout Europe the judicial elite as a body seems suddenly to have turned so avaricious and duplicitous.[43]

Far more plausible is an understanding that takes at face value the spiritual concern expressed by the witch hunters. Etienne Delcambre, the most careful scholar of witch trials in the duchy of Lorraine, concluded after reading hundreds of trial dossiers that the average judge was neither avaricious nor hypocritical.[44] In this independent territory near the Franco-German cultural frontier, Delcambre found prosecutors with an apparently sincere concern for the spiritual welfare of their prisoners. These judges were usually nonprofessionals drawn from the same peasant origins as most of their victims. They continually exhorted suspects to think of the welfare of their souls. Typical was one interrogator's plea to a woman who had already made a first confession to "try especially hard to recall any other deeds which she had done by this witchcraft, to declare them truly tomorrow morning, in order to discharge her poor soul of such a great and enormous sin, so that after a good confession in court and full repentance of her faults, our God will be more inclined to have grace and mercy upon her."[45] The interrogators often reminded accused witches of the brevity of this earthly life and the horrors of hell, sometimes expanding this theme into lengthy sermons addressed to their prisoners. They reminded suspects that those who died unconfessed were doomed to hell. Plainly, this was an effective prosecutorial tactic and may well have succeeded in inducing reluctant prisoners to confess. But many such statements of solicitude came after confession and thus seem to have been motivated by genuine concern.

In taking on the priestly roles of sermonizer and confessor, the judges of Lorraine—and no doubt those in other places as well—were giving witness to the growing influence of spiritual values even at lower levels of lay society. When one finds peasant judges using the vocabulary of godly reform, it seems reasonable to argue for the acculturating impact of Christianization. Delcambre was convinced that the judges were motivated "by a real sentiment of Christian charity and an authentic apostolic urge."[46] Their exhortations to have faith in the efficacy of prayer and their consolation of those about to go to the stake were the acts of sincere men moved by a deeply held religious ideology.

Comparable in this respect to the interrogators in the Stalinist purge trials of the 1930s, such judges were able to justify the most terrible kinds of violence in the name of a supposed higher good, whose ideological foundations they accepted completely. Like their predecessors in the papal Inquisition of medieval times, the lay magistrates who presided over most of the witch trials believed that heresy against God was the worst possible offense, that extraordinary measures were necessary to save society from the effects of such heresy, and that the fate of the soul after death meant a great deal more than the fate of the body in this world. Thus, the judicial remedies adopted by the witch hunters were entirely consistent with and appropriate to their ideological stance. The trials conformed very well with the underlying assumptions of secular and spiritual authorities.

In the judges' insistence on confession can be detected the deeper meaning of an enhanced stress on social control in the early modern period. It was not enough for the accused to be guilty under the law. The prisoner had to be conscious of his guilt and acknowledge this consciousness by confessing. In Scotland, the few executions of witches without confession were regarded by the judiciary as incomplete successes. Like modern militant ideologues, the judges in the witch trials were not satisfied with mere outward conformity to social norms. They insisted that wrongdoers give witness to their internalization of the required values. By confessing to the crime of witchcraft, the accused could be considered by her judges to have recognized her guilt. By giving voice to her repentance, she seemed to accept the victory of the authorities over her mind. As in modern political trials, a confession to crime was the last step in ideological reeducation.[47]

A psychology of erotic violence, which earlier was suggested as a foundation for the fantasy of the witches' sabbat and examination of female suspects for the devil's mark, offers another framework for interpreting the growing incidence of torture during the age of the witch trials. Torture was not applied only to accused witches in the sixteenth and seventeenth centuries. It became a normal feature of criminal investigation of all types in most continental jurisdictions. The increased employment of torture surely was one way the early modern state asserted its control over the populace. But coercion appealed not only to officials but also to people at other social levels. This period also saw the rise to routine use of elaborate tortures at well-attended public executions. What Michel Foucault called "the spectacle of the scaffold" was fascinating in its horror. The popularity of outdoor hangings, decapitations, and drawing-and-quarterings, often accompanied by excruciating preliminary punishments, suggests the subliminal ties binding together state and society through the attractions of torture.[48]

To Philippe Ariès, early modern culture's fascination with physical violence, agonizing suffering, and painful death represent a subtle but profound shift in consciousness: "Death is no longer a peaceful event. . . . Nor is death any longer a moment of moral and psychological concentration, as it was in the *artes moriendi*. Death has become inseparable from violence and pain. . . . These violent scenes excited spectators and aroused primitive forces whose sexual nature seems obvious today."[49] It is always dangerous to read social realities into works of artistic imagination. But the many violent scenes of torture depicted in vivid baroque paintings found their counterparts in the lives of thousands of Europeans during the age of the witch hunts. Whether art was the model for imitation or reflected the law's greater tolerance of torture is an unanswerable and probably fruitless question. The important point is that both art and the legal system reveal the deep fascination of early modern society with a sensibility of sexuality and pain that eventually would be labeled sadistic.

When Bernini tried to capture in stone the mystical ecstasies of St. Theresa of Avila and Ludovica Albertini, he showed them as voluptuous beauties swooning in a helpless rapture suggestive of both agony and orgasm. St. Theresa's own description of her sensations at the moment of mystical union speaks of the "surpassing . . . sweetness of . . . excessive pain," and of being repeatedly pierced in the area of the intestines with a fire-tipped spear held by an angel.[50] The combination of violence, eros, and religious excitement was achieved not only by the individual mystic in the sixteenth and seventeenth centuries. It was also one of the unconscious emotional bases of an evangelically inspired society, many of whose most prominent members likewise yearned for a sense of union with the divine. Torture, as will soon be explained, was viewed as a way of communicating with God. Thus torturers—and perhaps a good number of their victims as well—interpreted in spiritual terms what the modern temper is more inclined to see as unconscious impulses of love and death.

One central problem still remains in this attempt to understand the psychological interrelationships of judges and their victims: Why was it not realized that confessions extorted by torture were not reliable evidence? Possibly the strangest feature of the witch trials was the near-universal acceptance of coerced admissions as genuine. Friedrich von Spee and others eventually came to suspect such testimony, but throughout the greater part of the witch hunting era the use of confessions elicited by torture went nearly unquestioned.

According to our modern way of thinking, acceptance of torture as the means of eliciting admissions points to the sheer unscrupulousness of the authorities. But there is abundant evidence that neither the judges nor the accused regarded torture in this way. Instead, torture was almost universally considered a kind of test, an ordeal through which the suspect would definitively establish her guilt or innocence. Rebekka Lemp was certain that if she was tortured, "God almighty will watch over me and send them a sign" of her innocence. Barbara Rüfin, too, had faith that God would miraculously protect her from the pain so that by withstanding torture her blamelessness would be made manifest. These cases were far from unique. Delcambre found that in Lorraine "most men were convinced that Providence intervened to succor the innocent person and to prevent him, despite his sufferings, from succumbing through false confessions of witchcraft."[51] Because of this commonly held belief in God's protection of the innocent, it may not have occurred to most judges that those who confessed under torture might simply have been making up crimes in order to spare themselves further pain.

Torture was considered an almost infallible way of establishing truth in the era of witch hunts. It still retained psychological connections with the old medieval ordeal. Judicial torture had originated in the Middle Ages as an extension of the judicial combats, oath-swearing, and other tests employed to establish guilt or innocence in medieval courts. During the early Middle Ages, the accused could clear himself of felony charges by invoking divine assistance. If he were a nobleman, he or a representative would do battle against his accuser. In theory, God decided the outcome and gave the victory to the rightful party. Those of lower social classes, untrained in arms, underwent another kind of test, the judicial ordeal. This took several forms. Typical was the ordeal by fire, which required the accused to grasp a red-hot iron for a few moments. When the bandages were removed several days later, the presence or absence of a scar served as evidence for his guilt or innocence.

Sophisticated people of the High Middle Ages increasingly perceived these remnants of Germanic tribal law as crude, and in 1215 the Fourth Lateran Council, under the leadership of Pope Innocent III, formally decreed the abolition of the ordeal. Yet in the seventeenth century accused witches in England, New England, and Germany were still regularly subjected to the ordeal by water, and learned judges were still protesting its use. "Swimming the witch" meant tossing her, bound hand and foot, into a stream. Guilt was revealed if she floated, for it was thought that pure water would not receive an unjust person. Witnesses stood ready to fish out the half-drowned woman who successfully completed the ordeal, whereas a suspect who failed the test often went directly from the water to the fire.[52]

The conviction that God was acting everywhere in the world at each moment—a view shared by people of all social and cultural levels—underlay this concept of torture as ordeal. Participants in witch trials did not picture the world as an impersonal machine operating according to mathematical laws of nature. Instead, they regarded the cosmos as personal and moral. Thus, they believed, God would perform a miracle rather than permit an innocent man to confess falsely under pain of torture. This reasoning often led accused witches to accept torture willingly, even to request it, in the belief that through God's protection such a test would clear them. In Scotland, where the search for the devil's mark was the most common type of ordeal, suspects and their relatives actually suggested that their innocence be established by taking them to a "brodder" or "jobber," popular names for professional witch-prickers.[53]

Under torture, prisoners in Lorraine invoked heavenly assistance by calling out the names of Jesus and the saints. When they nevertheless felt unbearable pain, they almost always confessed. Only 10 percent of the Lorraine torture victims withstood the agony and persisted in their denials. Most confessed only after the milder, preliminary tortures. No doubt many such admissions reflected the prisoner's conclusion that she might as well give up and at least spare herself further pain. But Delcambre proposed that many confessions stemmed from the honest belief of suggestible suspects in their own guilt when they saw that God did not protect them from the pain of torture. The shattering experience of entering the torture chamber only to discover that God was withholding his protection from suffering did not cause prisoners to give up their faith in divine providence, for to abandon this belief was to sacrifice the only available way to make sense of reality. Instead, the accused had to abandon the picture of herself as an upright Christian.[54]

This interpretation can help explain the comparative rarity of prisoners who retracted their confessions after torture. It also makes understandable the frequent expressions of gratitude made by suspects to their accusers once their trials had been concluded and execution decreed. Of course, allowances must be made for the desire of prisoners to have their death sentences commuted by well-disposed judges. No doubt many also were aware that retraction of a confession would simply prompt renewed torture. Still, Delcambre's careful reading of the sources convinced him that many of the confessed witches in Lorraine came to believe firmly in their guilt after failing the ordeals of thumbscrews, rack, or strappado. Often they admitted to more serious crimes but steadfastly denied lesser ones, as in the case of a woman who confessed to killing people while she vigorously refuted charges of harming cows.[55]

Such individuals probably imagined that they possessed demonic powers. Perhaps they attached a cause-and-effect relationship to their malevolent thoughts about a neighbor and the neighbor's subsequent death. It is also possible that a woman's sexual activities outside marriage were being reinterpreted in her confessions to copulation with the devil. The torture was to her a test of the suspicions she privately harbored about herself. When the resultant pain confirmed the victim's predisposition to see herself as an evildoer, she confessed, but only to crimes she was convinced she had committed.

Thus, there is reason to believe that a considerable number of such confessions were "genuine," in the sense that the unexpected pain of torture destroyed the prisoner's fragile sense of justification in God's sight. In a society preoccupied with sin and guilt, the self-esteem of many individuals must have been a very delicate commodity, especially among the poor and downtrodden who comprised most witch suspects. Recently evangelized peasants very likely were predisposed to doubt themselves, as was suggested previously in discussing the transformation in self-image of the *benandanti*. The stress-filled situation of imprisonment and torture made suspects receptive to suggestions of criminal offense. Relatively few prisoners had enough confidence and insight to keep their psychological bearings under the strain of imprisonment and torture. Burgomaster Junius of Bamberg might retain the detachment to perceive and report the necessity of a consciously false confession, but most witch suspects lacked the learning and the self-esteem possessed by a community leader.

Confessions elicited by torture, then, do not represent exclusively elite views. The image of the witch as Satan's servant had been effectively inculcated into popular consciousness, and the stereotyped formulations of the confessions reveal the deep impression such a picture of witchcraft had on ordinary folk. As Christina Larner observed with regard to the Scottish trials, "Witch confessions represent an agreed story between the witch and inquisitor in which the witch drew, through hallucination or imagination, on a common store of myth, fantasy, and nightmare to respond to the inquisitor's questions."[56]

In modern cases it has been shown many times that the power of suggestion, when applied in a stressful situation to a subject inclined to self-doubt, can produce freely given confessions, even false ones. Belief in the validity of the method of interrogation is the key psychological element. In the contemporary world, where faith in the machine has largely supplanted faith in God, the lie detector test can be viewed as a rough equivalent of the ordeal-by-torture employed in the witch trials. Criminologists now know that the polygraph is not an especially accurate device, because the connections between lying, conflict, emotion, and bodily responses are imprecise and variable.[57] Yet the lie detector is very effective in eliciting information from subjects who believe in it. As an instrument of social control it works in much the same manner as did the torture chamber. Both kinds of ordeals can prompt a subject to suspend his critical faculties in the face of apparently irrefutable evidence deriving from the test.

A striking recent example of this process is the case of Peter Reilly, the Connecticut teenager accused of murdering his mother in 1973. After the shock of discovering her bloody body on the floor of her bedroom, Peter immediately was arrested and held incommunicado by the state police for two nights, during which time he was subjected to over twenty-five hours of interrogation. He was allowed just a few hours of sleep, and ate only an occasional sandwich. Finally his interrogators led Peter to ask for a lie detector test the results of which, the operator told him, indicated that he had killed his mother and then blanked out all memory of the event. The police, who throughout presented themselves as Peter's friends and confidants, then reconstructed the crime for him. In his bewildered state, he probably believed the confession they induced him to sign. Although friendly counselors soon brought Peter to see that his statement was false, it was admitted as evidence by the trial judge and provided the main grounds for the jury's guilty verdict. Only after two years and much publicity was Peter finally cleared. For anyone curious about the ability of authority figures to lead a suggestible and frightened prisoner to a false confession, the transcripts of the interrogations of Peter Reilly, particularly under the lie detector, are most revealing.[58] These documents bear an extraordinary resemblance to many witch-trial accounts.

Some of Peter Reilly's predecessors in the New England courts underwent quite similar stresses during the Salem trials of 1692. On one occasion, six Andover women were brought to the town meeting house, where several possessed girls publicly accused them of bewitchment. Apparently sympathetic town fathers and the prisoners' own husbands and other relatives immediately urged the shocked and disoriented women to confess and throw themselves on the mercy of the court. After many hours of persistent questioning, during which the women were denied sleep and forced to stand for long periods, they finally admitted to witchcraft. As one of them later recounted, "she thought verily her life would have gone from her," and, under protracted interrogation (by her brother, among others) "became so terrifyed in her mind that she own'd at length to anything that they propounded to her." And this under the relatively mild procedure of the English common law![59]

Another modern example bearing on the witch trials is the thought reform or brainwashing practiced in Chinese prisons after the Communist victory. As was the case for many witch hunts, "it was the combination of *external force or coercion* with an appeal to *inner enthusiasm through evangelistic exhortation* which gave thought reform its emotional scope and power."[60] The evaluation is Robert Jay Lifton's, based on his extensive interviews with numerous former prisoners shortly after their expulsion from China. The experiences of those who underwent thought reform are strongly reminiscent of testimonies cited earlier in this chapter. Dr. Charles Vincent recounted his feeling in the initial stages of his imprisonment, when he was undergoing continual torture:

> You are annihilated . . . exhausted . . . you can't control yourself, or remember what you said two minutes before. You feel that all is lost . . . From that moment, the judge is the real master of you. You accept anything he says. When he asks how many "intelligences" you gave to that person, you just put out a number in order to satisfy him. If he says, "Only those?" you say, "No, there are more." If he says, "One hundred," you say, "One hundred. . . ." You do whatever they want. You don't pay any more attention to your life or your handcuffed arms. You can't distinguish right from left. You just wonder when you will be shot—and begin to hope for the end of all this.[61]

At a similar stage Father Francis Luca also was led to the point of surrender:

> It is as I have been told. They will have their false confession. But I don't want to make a false confession. Maybe there is a way to say something that is not totally untrue to satisfy them—but what? . . . I've said the truth. They don't want the truth. I've only one way to escape: to guess what they really want.[62]

Many prisoners eventually experienced delusions and could no longer accurately distinguish fantasy from reality. Very few were able to resist thought reform successfully, because the interrogators combined physical force with assaults on the psyche of the prisoner.[63] Lifton described in detail the attack on identity that enabled the authorities to rechannel a prisoner's sense of guilt in the desired direction. The individuals who were most susceptible to this treatment were those who had been raised in a rigid framework of moral absolutes and were predisposed to feel guilty about their past behavior. Already suffering from a low sense of self-esteem and perceiving themselves in all-or-nothing, black-or-white moral terms, these prisoners became apparent converts to the Chinese ideology and, after their release, experienced prolonged difficulty in shaking the effects of thought reform. To such prisoners, wrote Lifton, confession in prison had provided a kind of catharsis, ridding them of guilt feelings.[64]

The Chinese communist system of group control in prison went far beyond anything consciously attempted by the judges of early modern Europe. But modern philosophies of ideological totalism are not completely unlike the doctrines of religious renewal of the Reformation era. A demand for purity and extensive control over the milieu were characteristic of both religious and political authorities at that time, though their efforts in these directions were often mitigated by countervailing concepts of human dignity and individual freedom as well as by technological limitations. No doubt it would be highly misleading to characterize the richly ambiguous attitudes of sixteenth- and seventeenth-century religious reformers and political leaders in terms of modern totalitarian ideologies. Yet Lifton's penetrating analysis of modern ideologues could apply to many of the witch hunters:

> Ideological totalists do not pursue this approach *solely* for the purpose of maintaining a sense of power over others. Rather they are impelled by a special kind of mystique which not only justifies such manipulations, but makes them mandatory. Included in this mystique is a sense of "higher purpose. . . ." By thus becoming the instruments of their own mystique, they create a mystical aura around the manipulating institutions—the Party, the Government, the Organization. They are the agents "chosen" (by history, by God, or by some other supernatural force) to carry out the "mystical imperative," the pursuit of which must supersede all considerations of decency or of immediate human welfare. . . . This same mystical imperative produces the apparent extremes of idealism and cynicism which occur in connection with the manipulations of any totalist environment: even those actions which seem cynical in the extreme can be seen as having ultimate relationship to the "higher purpose."[65]

Mao's exhortation to "carry out various effective measures to transform the various evil ideological conceptions in the minds of the people so that they may be educated and reformed into new people"[66] resembles the goals of religious reformers in the sixteenth and seventeenth centuries. No matter how dissimilar the content of the communist and early modern Christian philosophies, they have in common a world-view that fosters pervasive preoccupation with deviance and profound consciousness of the need to control dissidents by any and all means.

Lucien Febvre, one of the most astute and influential modern French historians, counseled students of the witch hunts to remember that the mind of one age does not necessarily operate according to the same rules as another's.[67] His wise observation is borne out by this examination of the supernatural underpinnings of the psychology at work in witch trial procedures. Yet, when we see the same patterns of action—minus supernatural justifications—in contemporary experience, it is appropriate to ask if the so-called modern mentality is really very different after all or if our ideological age simply applies different names and a different rationale to the same psychological dynamics that were at work among the ideologues of the witch hunts.

7

An End to Witch Hunting

In a span of one or two generations, witchcraft went from a source of obsessive dread to a matter of apparent indifference. Witch trials rapidly declined in the late seventeenth century. Except in Eastern Europe, where the decline was somewhat delayed, trials had practically disappeared by 1700. Witchcraft cases, formerly classed among the most heinous crimes, vanished from the statute books and the criminal courts. Within half a century after the Salem trials, it was no more possible to bring a charge of witchcraft in nearly all Western courts than it is today.

What caused these dramatic changes? Any attempt to answer this question must confront certain built-in difficulties. As in all efforts to explain nonevents—in this case, the absence of continued witch trials—the problem is in finding relevant evidence. In general, historians find negative questions difficult. The tools of historical research seem inadequate to establish why something did not occur. Scholars admit as much when they call the decline of the trials the most baffling aspect of the witch craze.[1] Much of the evidence for the decline of witchcraft is indirect or circumstantial, and the consequently tentative conclusions must be understood in light of their problematic derivation.

For a negative assertion it might be appropriate to proceed via negations. It is possible to state with a fair degree of reliability that some things did *not* lead to the end of witch hunting. These can be grouped under the general heading of social improvement. If one starts with the assumption that witchcraft accusations reflect the miseries endured by ordinary people in everyday life, it follows that a decline in accusations would ensue from a reduction in such misery. As Keith Thomas has pointed out, however, there is nothing in the externals of European life to suggest the easing of general economic conditions in the late seventeenth century, the period that saw the most abrupt decline in witch hunting. Basic conditions of life for most people remained unchanged. Disease and famine persisted even as witch trials decreased. Although the seventeenth century was the age of scientific revolution, the big breakthroughs in applied science that brought vast improvements in medicine and technology were almost entirely absent until after 1800. Improved nutrition, a somewhat lengthened average life span, and a general, if slight, increase in the standards of living of some urban and rural sectors were part of the eighteenth-century social scene. But these changes occurred only slowly and were far from uniform. The end of the witch craze, however, came relatively quickly and by 1750 was universal throughout Western civilization.

These chronological discrepancies make it very difficult to argue persuasively that witch trials stopped because ordinary people were no longer as anxious and fearful as they had previously been about an oppressive physical environment. European villagers no doubt continued to experience anxiety about such fundamentals as birth, death, disease, and the weather during the late seventeenth and eighteenth centuries. These villagers also continued to see witchcraft behind many misfortunes. After all, the only change we are certain about occurred in the area of witch *trials*, not witch beliefs. The authorities, that is, stopped bringing charges of witchcraft to formal trial; in so doing they were likely turning away ordinary folk who continued to accuse their neighbors, as in bygone days. Although the sources are mostly silent on this matter, there are some scattered references to extralegal vigilante actions against accused witches in the eighteenth century. Such episodes may have stemmed from the refusal of state officials to take seriously popular suspicions of witchcraft. And, as recently as the late nineteenth century, rural folklore retained the kind of "mad beliefs" described by Eugen Weber in his *Peasants into Frenchmen*.[2]

In this regard, an intriguing hint comes from an account of a witch trial *manqué* in Alsace around 1716. In the village of Heiligenstein, near Barr, the town cooper was startled early one morning to find the local carpenter unconscious in his garret. The cooper suspected that the carpenter had broken in to rob him, and his fears were not allayed by the carpenter's claim that he had no idea of how he had arrived in the cooper's shop. Taken before the magistrates of Barr, one of whom is the source for this account, the carpenter told of stumbling on a strange predawn gathering in a clearing outside of town. There, brightly illuminated in the night, was a scene of riotous revelry, complete with dancing and a sumptuous feast. The carpenter found these attractions irresistible, but after joining in for a few minutes he blacked out and, next thing he knew, awoke in the cooper's garret. The story turned from bizarre to tragic when the carpenter named two women of Barr whom he had recognized in the woods. Immediately these women hanged themselves in their houses. The magistrates, fearing the scandal that might result from a full investigation, decided to consider the women mad and the carpenter a victim of hallucinations. As a result, the matter was hushed up and no judicial proceeding ensued.[3]

The Heiligenstein carpenter's strange tale is the sort that might have inspired earlier authorities to open a formal inquiry into witchcraft. But, like their contemporaries throughout Western Europe, the judges of the early eighteenth century were most reluctant to entertain witchcraft charges. In Alsace and elsewhere, whatever the reasons for the end of witch trials, they must be sought among the elite classes. We simply do not know enough about the beliefs and practices of ordinary people to make credible any assertions about their altered psychological state in the era of declining witch hunts. The corollary of this negative conclusion may be helpful, however. For, if changes in the consciousness of the elites can be identified, such changes can be a sufficient explanation for the end of witch trials. This would not work the other way around. Even if the populace had suddenly given up all ideas about witchcraft, the authorities' control of the political and judicial apparatus would have enabled them to persist in trying witches had they desired to do so. Just as the impetus for the witch craze—as distinct from witch beliefs—came mainly from above, so too the initial reasons for the decline must be traced to the elite classes.

In explaining the decline of witch hunting, then, we can say very little about the views or behavior of the popular classes. The methodological tool employed in previous chapters of this book—understanding the dynamics of witch trials through the interplay of elite and popular cultures—cannot be used when trial records dwindle and disappear. In the absence of sources reflecting popular values on the subject of witchcraft, we must reconstruct the decline of witch trials exclusively from elite sources. Thus, the present chapter stands apart from the rest of this book in subject matter and method. We are dealing here with a different set of problems, one that requires separate full-length treatment for adequate discussion. All that is attempted here is an epilogue sketching out some of the areas worthy of consideration in future research on the decline of witch hunting.

Although strong patterns of continuity marked European social and economic life as the age of witch hunting ended, the life of the mind was being transformed by the rise of science. The seventeenth century was the great turning point in the intellectual history of Western civilization. The scientific advances that began with Copernicus and culminated in Newton constitute one of the few so-called revolutionary movements for which the term truly is appropriate.

Three major changes were brought about by scientific thinking. First, of course, was the content of the new astronomy and the new physics: the heliocentric universe, elliptically orbiting planets, and the laws of motion. These theories overturned age-old Western images of the cosmos and man's place in the scheme of things. They revealed the universe as a self-regulating system in which direct and constant divine intervention was unnecessary. Second was the precise mathematical language that was the code science used to formulate nature's secrets. The triumph of mathematical reasoning challenged the overwhelmingly verbal bias of the learning of past times and substituted a new model for the most efficient pursuit of knowledge. Yet another element of the new scientific method involved a third great change, the stress on experiment and direct observation, together with their corollary of skepticism about received opinions. Henceforth, it was not enough simply to cite the authorities of the past to settle a disputed point; some empirical technique was deemed the best proof, even (or especially) if Aristotle had spoken on the subject. After all, if Ptolemy and other ancient writers had been mistaken about the heavens, there was no reason to regard any authority as immune from error. By modifying the picture Europeans had of the universe and changing their mode of learned expression and their attitude toward their predecessors, seventeenth-century science had the effect of transforming nearly everything connected with intellectual life.

The impact of scientific thinking on the end of witch trials has been studied most systematically for France. There the royal high courts, the parlements, took the lead in suppressing witchcraft prosecutions. The role of the Parlement of Paris, which was a supreme court for nearly half the kingdom, was especially important. From the 1620s—and by one scholar's account even a generation earlier—the judges of the Paris parlement consistently reduced penalties and threw out witchcraft convictions decreed in lower courts. After 1624, the Paris magistrates required that all death sentences for witchcraft be brought to the parlement for review, and the high court proceeded to punish inferior magistrates who insisted on summary justice in cases of witchcraft. After 1640, some of the other French parlements began to exhibit similar skepticism about witch convictions in outlying provinces of France. Matters came to a head in the 1670s. First Louis XIV's chief domestic minister, Colbert, challenged the conviction of several prisoners condemned for witchcraft by the Parlement of Rouen. Then came the so-called affair of the poisons, a notorious scandal implicating a number of the king's courtiers in allegations of murder and black masses. These unpleasantries, combined with the longstanding doubts of many judges, prompted the Sun King to declare in 1682 that witchcraft had no reality other than as a type of fraud. Although scattered witch trials cropped up into the eighteenth century, Louis XIV's edict marked the real end of the age of the witch hunts in France.[4]

In his thorough study of the subject, Robert Mandrou suggested that the cessation of witchcraft trials in France was symptomatic of a "crisis of consciousness" on the part of the judicial elite.[5] First in Paris and later in the provincial centers, the wealthy aristocratic judges of the parlements came under the influence of new ways of thinking inspired by science and Cartesian philosophy. Through exposure to public discussions and printed works, and eventually in the advanced schools their fathers sent them to, generations of judges learned the content and method of scientific inquiry. The lessons thus acquired were reflected in their conduct of legal business, and the effects were especially obvious in witchcraft cases.

When considering these changes in elite mentality, it is important to recognize just what objections the educated judiciary of the French parlements had in the cases they reviewed on appeal. They did not challenge the reality of witchcraft itself. Neither in France nor anywhere else did those seventeenth-century judges who ended witch hunting profess that there were no witches. Like Newton and other scientists of the time, judges apparently continued to accept supernatural magic as theoretically plausible.[6] Instead, the judges questioned the methods used to identify witches in individual cases. Examinations for the devil's mark, accounts of the sabbat, spectral evidence of possession, the association of a curse with subsequent disaster—in short, the basic stock in trade of witch prosecutors for a century—were subjected to intense scrutiny. Together with many of their counterparts elsewhere in Europe, the French parlementaires came to insist on uncoerced confessions or the firsthand testimony of at least two trustworthy witnesses as grounds for conviction. Such judicial demands did nothing more than apply to cases of witchcraft the same criteria for conviction used in judging other offenses.[7] When judges stopped seeing witchcraft as an exceptional crime requiring extraordinary remedies, they were well on their way to ending witch hunts altogether.

The participation of the Parisian judges in debates about the nature of possession was especially crucial in shaping their views of witchcraft. The critique of witch trial procedure was greatly aided by the rise of demonic possession episodes in witchcraft cases of the seventeenth century. Other kinds of witchcraft might be hard to investigate, but anyone could observe the behavior of the possessed and draw his own conclusions. The celebrated French convent cases of the seventeenth century, with their open exorcisms and wide publicity, provoked much comment. Some observers believed the phenomenon supernatural, others declared the proceedings a hoax, and a third opinion was that this was a medical matter, not a theological one. Although no clear consensus emerged, the very existence of a public debate was significant in itself.

Although there were a few scattered episodes of supposed demonic possession in France during the late seventeenth and early eighteenth centuries, none of them led to executions for witchcraft. For example, the Cadière-Girard affair of the 1730s in Toulon is in many ways reminiscent of the episodes at Aix and Loudun a hundred years earlier. But, as B. Robert Kreiser has noted in his recent piece on this affair, the important difference is that, in the "devils of Toulon" episode, the accused priest died in his bed, not at the stake.[8]

Thus, although late seventeenth- and early eighteenth-century judges did not explicitly reject witchcraft as a concept, the implicit message of their reforms was that this was an area of no interest to the law. In earlier times, centralized judicial direction emerged as one of the most powerful accelerating forces in the witch craze. Learned judges had encouraged witch hunting, imposed demonological views of witchcraft, and fostered the indiscriminate use of torture. But, by the mid-seventeenth century, the engine of high justice was reversing course. Now professional judges increasingly used their power as a brake on witchcraft proceedings.

The new judicial tendency to view things in a critical light was a turn of mind greatly encouraged by the new scientific philosophy. It is fair to say that scientific thinking helped tip the balance against witch trial procedures and contributed greatly to their abandonment. There were numerous precedents for a more critical attitude toward witch trials, however, even from the height of the craze. Writers of the seventeenth century who argued against witch-hunting methods often echoed sixteenth-century critics on many points. Throughout the witch craze there had been an undercurrent of protest, and this stream fed into later, more influential dissension. Criticism of witch trials was far from a novelty, but earlier critics had great difficulty in persuading their audiences. A glance at two of the most thoroughgoing of the early critics, Reginald Scot and Michael de Montaigne, can clarify the relative strengths of sixteenth-century (and later) skeptics.

Scot, a self-taught English country gentleman, wrote the most consistently skeptical critique of witch trials to appear in the late sixteenth century. He used philological arguments to undermine the oft-cited biblical justifications for witch trials and proceeded to offer an entirely naturalistic interpretation of events conventionally attributed to supernatural witch-

craft. To Scot, the whole idea of witchcraft seemed a vast misunder-
standing.[9] Montaigne was somewhat more circumspect in expressing his
doubts about witch trials, but the great French essayist also found accusations against witches generally implausible. In his succinct and brilliant
piece, "Of Cripples," Montaigne summarized his reservations about the
abilities of a crippled human reason to comprehend the supernatural,
remarked that the accused witches of his acquaintance appeared more in
need of medical than judicial attention, and produced one of his most
devastating aphorisms in concluding that "after all, it is putting a very high
price on one's conjectures to have a man roasted alive because of them."[10]
     In their lifetimes, the cautionary counsel of Scot and Montaigne was
brushed aside. Suggestions that the Bible might not mean what it appeared
to say and that men could not really understand why things happened were
completely out of tune with the dominant themes of the age. An ideological
era in which true believers of various persuasions occupied most positions
of leadership could not fathom the historical relativism implicit in Scot's
critique of biblical sources or the sense of detachment that underlay Montaigne's careful prudence. Indeed, scriptural and other authorities of the
past comprised the foundations of all knowledge and theories of social
organization. The skepticism of Scot or Montaigne could only attack intellectual traditions and cast doubt on the institutions built on them; it did not
offer anything with which to replace the rubble. This was the dilemma of all
skeptical thinkers in the sixteenth century. Not surprisingly, confronted
with the prospect of intellectual and institutional ruin, the learned elites
instinctively shied away from such threatening challenges. Scot and Montaigne were both outsiders, the one an autodidact gentleman-farmer,
the other self-exiled to a reclusive life in his tower-study. Neither could
speak to or for the organized intellectual disciplines of their day. Thus,
mainstream traditions of medicine, theology, philosophy, and law all ignored them.[11]
     A hundred years later, the world was greatly changed. The triumph of
scientific reasoning had made the critical spirit more acceptable. Questioning of ancient authority, very dangerous in the sixteenth century, was
becoming a conventional part of all branches of intellectual activity, even
Bible studies.[12] People more confident of their ability to understand universal laws and of their potential power to control nature no longer needed the
psychological security that came from unqualified acceptance of past authority.
     As educated Europeans gained confidence in their capacity to deal with
the natural, the terrain of the supernatural shrank for them. There can be

little doubt that the new scientific definitions of the reasonable—that which could be established by mathematical and empirical methods—eventually made the idea of witchcraft seem implausible, even ridiculous, to most educated people. Cyrano de Bergerac, the Cartesian Oratorian Nicholas de Malebranche, the Protestant pastor Balthasar Bekker, and many other writers expressed the late seventeenth century's new orientation when they sought to explain witch beliefs in naturalistic terms.[13] Here was the beginning of a disenchantment of the world; literally so, as the witch's maleficent chantings lost their demonic psychological overtones and became merely mechanical movements of vocal chords and air.

Similar naturalistic interpretations of witchcraft had fared less well earlier, when physicians like Richard Napier and Robert Burton habitually mixed religious and magical views into their medical expertise on witchcraft. For example, the Dutch physician Johann Weyer was roundly denounced in the 1580s for his assertion that the great majority of so-called witches were deluded old women suffering from melancholia, or what we would call depression. Weyer's most effective critic, Jean Bodin, pointed out the inconsistencies of Weyer's theses when compared with received medical opinion.[14] But, a century later, Malebranche propounded a psychological explanation of witch beliefs that was squarely in the tradition of Weyer's medical analysis. Malebranche's views proved influential, whereas Weyer's rather similar opinions had not. What had changed was not so much the substance of the debate as the intellectual climate in which the discussion took place. By the late seventeenth century, educated people were far more open to naturalistic explanations of events than their grandfathers had been. In a world acknowledged to operate in accord with mechanical laws, Malebranche's rather crude ideas about images engraved on suggestible minds found a receptive audience.

Conversely, the assumptions of earlier generations about divine intervention in everyday affairs gradually faded from elite consciousness. An example is the questioning of the validity of the ordeal of torture. In the seventeenth century, observers began to raise general objections to the use of torture. Such commentators as the German Jesuit Friedrich von Spee and the Burgundian judge Augustin Nicolas wrote of the abuses inherent in the application of torture to witch suspects and other criminals.[15] These writers derived their opinions from firsthand trial experience, but their conclusions were greatly reinforced by the triumph of the scientific worldview. It no longer seemed imperative to see the hand of God behind each prisoner's actions. Once torture was no longer regarded as an ordeal in which divine providence would declare guilt or innocence, it rapidly lost credibility in witchcraft investigations. Thus, doubts about the validity of coerced confessions, almost unthinkable in Weyer's day, became quite plausible when the elites accepted science's redefinition of the universe as an impersonal mechanism.

In short, science provided a new frame of reference in which old ideas were articulated more persuasively. Scientific change, however, is not in itself a satisfying explanation for the end of witch hunting. Without engaging in fruitless chicken-and-egg debates about science's impact on or derivation from social forces, we may fairly ask why seventeenth-century authorities took to heart science's implicit objections to witch prosecution. The sheer intellectual power of scientific arguments may well have contributed to the end of witch trials, but there can be no doubt that these arguments also fit very well the emergent political and ideological patterns of the late seventeenth century.

Many historians have sensed a general calming of European political affairs after the disruptions of the crisis-ridden century from 1560 to 1660. Clearly, few leaders of the late seventeenth century wished to perpetuate the unhappy legacy of chronic instability and generalized upheaval. Leaders were motivated primarily by a determination to alter the institutional arrangements that had led to structural political weakness and civil warfare. The political melees of the age of crisis gave way to a more stable environment controlled by better organized governments. Endemic civil war and depradations by private armies ceased to be the leading features of European political life. These changes accompanied a growing awareness among the elites of the destructive social potential inherent in religious ideologies. An emerging consensus on this matter permitted rulers to restrict the independence and authority of church institutions. Many princes even came to accept religious pluralism among their subjects. No longer did it seem crucial for all to worship in the same church, because secularized theories of natural right were becoming the new way of legitimating authority.

A dramatic falling-off ensued in preoccupation with the afterlife and with religious matters in general. By the mid-eighteenth century in France, a great decline had begun in contributions willed to religious establishments to ensure the repose of the soul of the deceased. "Dechristianization" was beginning, after the high tide of Christian social influence in the age of religious reform.[16] Even before this, an environment perceived by the elites as less threatening no longer seemed to require a personification of evil in satanic shape. The passing of the fervent age of religious ideology reduced the preoccupation of the elites with conspiratorial heresy and thus made much less plausible the stereotype of the witches' sabbat and related imagery. Late-seventeenth-century theologians rediscovered the ancient Christian tradition that emphasized Christ's power over the devil, a point of view that had never gone completely underground and had helped to moderate witch prosecutions in some places even at the height of the craze. With Satan now seen as safely confined to hell, his actions were no longer deemed the cause of misfortune in this world. And some thinkers even wondered if hell itself might be only a metaphor.[17]

As the upper classes began to perceive the political world as somewhat less confused and unpredictable than it previously had seemed, their dread of demonic forces receded. Although Europeans of the late seventeenth century may not have actually had much more practical control over their environment than had their grandparents, the elites were coming to believe that they did—or soon would—and this perception worked a decisive change in witch hunting. Above all, Europe's intellectual and political leaders now developed an optimistic outlook about life and society. In conquering their fears or, in Peter Gay's phrase, in recovering the "nerve" previously exhibited by humanists and other optimistic forebears in the Western tradition, the European elites were freeing themselves from their preoccupation with satanic evil.[18]

The end of witch hunting, therefore, reflects a change not only in scientific views but also in the broader climate of the age. As dogmatically held religious ideologies ceased to be the main axis of orientation for elite identity and political action, new secular views took the place of religion. In this switch of psychological direction lies a key to explaining the rapid rise of science in seventeenth-century cultural consciousness. Science quickly became the basis of an upper-class cultural style. Whereas the gentleman of 1600 might have sought above all to embody religious values in his way of life, his grandchildren were far more likely to spend their time dabbling in scientific experimentation and collecting exotic natural specimens. To a considerable degree, the focus for the self-image of lay elites shifted from the religious to the secular over the course of the seventeenth century. In sum, the contours of Europe's ideological scenery underwent drastic changes in the late seventeenth century. Political and intellectual leaders combined to sweep away the ideology that had fostered witch hunting since 1560. The union of a new political ideology and scientific method produced successful challenges to witch hunts all over Western Europe by 1700.

Probably the earliest instance of an effective attack on witch hunting came, however, from what would appear to be a most unlikely source. In 1611, Father Alonso de Salazar, a judge of the Spanish Inquisition, produced a report containing decisive and devastating objections to witch trials. The occasion was a witch panic in the Basque country of northern Spain. Accounts of witches' sabbats had spread from the French side of the border, where numerous witch trials had been instigated by the jurist and demonologist Pierre de Lancre two years earlier. Salazar decided to test the reality of these accounts. He ordered his assistants to take confessed witches to the scene of the supposed sabbat one by one, secretly, and in daylight. The confessed witches, many of whom were children, were asked to specify exactly where the devil sat, where they had eaten and danced, how long it took to travel to the sabbat, whether they traveled alone or in groups, how they got in and out of the house, whether they heard clocks or bells in the vicinity of the meeting place, and, to quote Salazar's questionnaire, "any other circumstances which might serve to clarify the problem and provide us with sure proofs of these things."[19] The confessed witches contradicted each other in answering nearly all these questions. Salazar wrote that the results of his experiment had convinced him that there was not to be "found a single proof nor even the slightest indication from which to infer that one act of witchcraft has actually taken place."[20]

Salazar had also experimented with alleged hallucinatory ointments said to be used by witches. When he fed them to animals they turned out to be harmless substances.[21] The inquisitor's empirical methods led him to conclude that all the accusations and confessions had resulted from what we would call mass suggestion, especially on the impressionable minds of the young. Here, as elsewhere, the end of witch hunting may well have been hastened by the doubts authorities began to have about children's tales, which were a major ingredient in many seventeenth-century witchcraft outbreaks.[22]

Salazar's reports succeeded in snuffing out the Basque panic. Even more significantly, no one in Spain was executed for witchcraft afterward. The inquisitor's investigations were regarded by most of his judicial colleagues in Spain as convincing proof of the unreliability of witch accusations and confessions. In a country with a judicial machinery as centralized as the Spanish Inquisition, such demonstrations had lasting impact, especially because witchcraft prosecutions never were an important political tool in Spain. Witchcraft executions had been rare events in Spanish history. Instead of burning witches, the authorities had vigorously pursued nonconforming Jews and Muslims. These persecutions were part of the Christian rulers' successful effort to transform Spain from a pluralistic, multiracial society into a uniformly Catholic community.

Judaism had been illegal in Spain since 1492, when the large and distinguished Spanish Jewish population was forced to choose between conversion and exile. Of the Jews who remained, some continued to practice their ancestral faith in private. Because they had nominally converted to Catholicism, however, the secret Jews were considered heretics and thus suitable targets for the Inquisition. As for the conquered Moriscos, thousands of Spanish Muslims were forced to adopt Christianity in the 1520s. Until 1609, when all Moriscos were forcibly expelled from the country, those caught observing the commandments of Islam were subject to trial for heresy by the Inquisition. Given the presence of these despised minorities, Spain's spiritually motivated elites neglected massive witch hunting. Without a tradition of witch trials, it was possible for Spanish judicial officials to subject the conventional wisdom about witches to systematic testing, long before science made such experimental methods commonplace.[23]

The Spanish authorities' relative lack of interest in witches suggests the strong role of political considerations, as opposed to purely intellectual ones, in the perpetuation and cessation of witch trials. Elsewhere, concern with witches rose and declined in phase with the authorities' preoccupation with heretics, for the crime of witchcraft was usually defined as a kind of heresy. In Spain, however, there was no significant threat of Christian heresy during the era of the witch craze. Instead, with numerous lapsed converts of non-Christian origins at hand, the political and psychological bases of scapegoating readily lent themselves to persecutions of Jewish and Muslim nonbelievers. Because of medieval Spain's exceptional history of conflict with the non-Christian infidel, not the Christian heretic, the ideological foundations of witch hunting were comparatively weak in Spain. Thus, the unique traditions of Spanish Christianity apparently made the Inquisition's judges receptive to the early challenge launched by Salazar's impressive experiments.

Seemingly, then, the end of witch hunting did not stem from changes in popular culture. But the witch trials' cessation appears to reflect changes in attitudes *toward* popular culture on the part of the elites. The rise of witchcraft in elite consciousness is widely agreed to have coincided with the authorities' growing preoccupation with popular heresy. Accordingly, the challenge to witch-trial procedures generally had to await a decline in preoccupation with heresy and related forms of dissent. Such a falling-off finally took hold throughout Western Europe by the late seventeenth century.

Clearly, the general decline of fear among the European ruling classes at this time removed the need to engage in traditional kinds of massive and systematic scapegoating. Consider, for example, the marked toning down of previously fervent efforts to reform popular culture. Religiously grounded antipathies toward rural traditions, which had produced zealous missionary efforts aimed at the reform of villagers' behavior, now gave way to less highly colored views of peasant life. Except for the exertions of evangelical groups like the English Methodists (among whom witch beliefs were revived in the eighteenth century), the vigorous suppression of popular habits was replaced by a less dramatic, slower process of acculturation after 1650. State authorities replaced religious figures as the main representatives of elite reforming efforts in rural Europe, and the vocabulary of reform consequently took on a secular cast increasingly free of supernatural associations. Loyalty to kings supplanted devotion to God as the primary goal of reformers, who were far more likely to be royal bureaucrats than men of the cloth. Government officials continued to denounce popular superstitions, but these secular reformers now classed belief in witchcraft as a superstitious error.[24]

Once the authorities abandoned an attitude of missionary zeal in their dealings with ordinary folk, they began to notice the negative potential inherent in witch hunting. Experience always had been a good teacher, one that brought to a close numerous local witch panics. In many cases, the end of a large witch hunt came when the authorities realized how disastrous such episodes could be for social stability. German witch panics often stopped when high-born members of society were implicated.[25] Moreover, a frightening outbreak frequently provided immunity to witch hunting for a generation or more, as the town fathers avoided any step that might trigger another mass panic. But it was a long time before such locally drawn lessons could be generalized, given the strength of witch-hunting traditions. So, at first, immunity required direct exposure to the disease.

After 1640, however, local judges in Scotland, Alsace, southwestern Germany, and northern France—and, further research likely will show, in many other places—regularly allowed the victims of witch accusations to sue their accusers for slander.[26] These local judges were in effect reviving the ancient principle of accusatory legal procedure that held a complainant liable if he was unable to sustain his charge. As the spirit of religious reform ceased to be the prime focus for these local magistrates, it became possible for them to return to legal traditions that had been ignored by their predecessors during the witch craze. When citizens found complainants fined for falsely accusing their neighbors, the incentive for subsequent charges must have been reduced considerably.

Although prosecutions for witchcraft declined, so, it seems, did trials for such moral offenses as incest, sodomy, adultery, and infanticide. These sins had been criminalized when the witch-hunting era commenced, and evidence suggests that they all disappeared from judicial consciousness at about the same time.[27] In the eighteenth century, rulers and judges directed most of their attention to crimes against property, instead of concerning themselves with the "victimless" crimes that had preoccupied judges in the age of religious reform. Capital offenses multiplied, but, in an ever more materialistic society, the poor man's theft of a loaf of bread, not an adulterous relationship, was more likely to bring him to the scaffold.

The obsessive fear of women also seems to have receded as a widespread cultural feature during the era of witch hunting's decline.[28] The traditional Christian view of woman as temptress and source of evil, a stereotype that religious reformers brought to the forefront of elite consciousness in the late sixteenth and seventeenth centuries, had fueled the misogyny that underlay witch hunting. From the late seventeenth century, however, this view competed with new images. An elevated picture of female abilities and a heightened appreciation of supposedly feminine qualities were apparent in some circles before 1700. In England, where such matters have been investigated most systematically, changes in ideals of family life gave ties of affection between spouses an unprecedented place in marriage. Men even began to admit an interest in their roles as husbands and fathers. These transformations in attitudes actually seem to have made for improvement in the lives led by many women, at least among the upper classes.

In the process, fear of female sexual appetites, the threatening force that buttressed traditional Western misogyny, generally began to fade from the mentality of the elites. Two contradictory views about women's sexuality emerged in the eighteenth century. The first accepted the libido of women, as well as that of men, as a natural and morally neutral human characteristic. A novel ideal of receptivity toward sexual pleasure made eighteenth-century upper-class society much more open and less repressive in sexual matters than had been the case in the 1500s and 1600s. Christian moralists even began to revise their views on original sin to take into account the new moral standards of the elites. A second cultural ideal about women began to emerge in the mid-eighteenth century and gained considerable influence after 1770, as the brief era of sexual permissiveness waned. This was the concept of the asexual female, whose immunity to base sensuality qualified her for an exalted role as man's superior and model of perfection. The new image of ideal womanhood was that of a woman who remained, emotionally, a perpetual virgin, regardless of the physical reality. The high price of this change was the denial of woman's sexuality. As females rose in esteem, their sexual side was suppressed. Elevated to an uncomfortable pedestal after centuries in the gutter, women might hope to reap the mixed rewards of the revered goddess. Yet, whatever misfortunes either of these eighteenth-century female ideals might have entailed, the stereotype of witchcraft no longer fit the new models of women. A rapid disintegration of the ancient image of woman as witch is one of the most impressive instances of dramatic cultural change in the era of the witch trials' decline.

Practical experience with destructive, uncontrollable witch panics taught judges direct lessons about the negative potential of witch hunting. Science provided a powerful tool for criticizing expert demonologists of the past and traditional ideas about the kingdom of Satan. Practice and theory both reflect a profound political and ideological change. The European elites simply lost interest in persecuting heretics of all kinds. Religious dissenters, ordinary folk who engaged in previously forbidden forms of sexual behavior, or women practicing black magic—none of these inter-related, stereotypical nonconformists engaged the consciousness of the authorities any longer.

By 1700, most educated people believed witchcraft to be a dubious concept encountered most often in the folk beliefs of the ignorant. Long before the heyday of the philosophies, skeptical writers on witchcraft attributed such beliefs to the lower classes. For instance, Laurent Bordelon, in his satirical *L'Histoire des imaginations extravagantes de M. Oufle*, first published in 1710, remarked that "the Common People attribute to Devils a prodigious Number of Feats, which undoubtedly they would not ascribe to them if they were better acquainted with the Power of Nature."[29] Similarly, the physician Francois de Saint-André, in his *Lettres au sujet de la magie, des maléfices et des sorciers* of 1725, brought his medical expertise to bear on the question of the supposedly magical origins of impotence. Citing psychological and physiological explanations for a condition long associated with witchcraft, Saint-André dismissed the belief that a witch can "tie the knot" to cast a spell of sexual malfunction. Significantly, he attributed this false belief to the "people."[30]

But the irony, as we have seen, is that during the witch craze a preoccupation with the satanic and the specifically sexual elements of witchcraft had been the concern of the elites, not ordinary folk. There was little diabolism, for example, in the popular literature of the *bibliothèque bleue* in the seventeenth and eighteenth centuries. Popular almanacs of the period paid considerable attention to such areas of the occult as astrology and divination, but dealt hardly at all with the demonic. Here we have good evidence for the failure of elite preoccupation with Satan to filter down into lower cultural levels. Yet, after 1650, skeptical opinion among the elites simply assumed that diabolism was a popular superstition. Cyrano saw beliefs in the witches' sabbat as a hallmark of the ignorant country bumpkin; Malebranche thought that tales of witchcraft flourished in isolated pastoral environments. Few of their learned contemporaries appeared to imagine that the numerous witch trials of the preceding era were in large part instigated from above by reformers who read devil worship into folk culture.

Thus, both during the witch craze and in its eighteenth-century aftermath, popular culture was held at fault by elite opinion. While witch hunting flourished, the authorities saw the peasants as mired in superstition, by which they meant false religious opinions, not irrational beliefs. Superstition to them implied heresy, and heresy suggested witchcraft. Later, as the definition of superstition changed to denote irrationality, the skeptical voices of elite opinion blamed popular culture for ostensibly continuing to profess witchcraft ideas that had been pretty much abandoned by the learned. In both cases, the populace was condemned for refusing to accept the conventional wisdom of educated men, who earlier had contended that the devil lay behind all malefice and later explained misfortune by natural causes.

Meanwhile, as elite orthodoxies changed dramatically, the available evidence suggests that the core of popular beliefs remained pretty much intact. Popular acceptance of the possibility of supernatural causation, both benign and malign, predated the era of witch hunting and persisted long after the authorities lost interest in fomenting witch panics. In fact, the absence of long-term impact on popular culture by the elites' diabolical preoccupations is most striking. Diabolism came in with the witch trials and vanished almost without a trace when the elites stopped promoting the idea of sabbats and attendant fantasies. Recent scholarship (for example, that of Peter Burke and Carlo Ginzburg) has drawn our attention to changes in popular attitudes and behavior under the acculturating impact of early modern interventions from above. One lesson of the witchcraft evidence, however, is that we should pay more attention to the inner strengths, powers of resistance, and general resilience inherent in popular beliefs, which maintain their hold in the face of all the fickle shifts in elite consciousness.

By the first years of the eighteenth century, discussion of witchcraft was pretty much dead. Isolated trials still occurred and occasionally provoked some pamphleteering, but the general attitude on the subject was typified by Joseph Addison's dispassionate, almost bored comment of 1711 in his very widely read and influential periodical, *The Spectator*:

> There are some opinions in which a man should stand neuter, without engaging his assent to one side or the other. Such a hovering faith as this, which refuses to settle upon any determination, is absolutely necessary in a mind that is careful to avoid errors and prepossessions. When the arguments press equally on both sides on matters that are indifferent to us, the safest method is to give ourselves up to neither . . . I believe in general that there is, and has been such a thing as witchcraft; but at the same time can give no credit to any particular instance of it.[31]

The key phrase in this passage is "on matters that are indifferent to us." To the men of Addison's day, witchcraft might or might not exist, but the entire issue was becoming an abstraction of no real consequence.

Addison's determination to avoid "errors and prepossessions" exemplifies the cool, detached, secularized rationality highly valued in scientific thinking. The adoption of this cultural style by the social elite that *The Spectator*'s authors both mirrored and molded shows how greatly values had changed since the ideological days of competing religious dogmas, when neutrality was considered suspect, detachment could be advocated safely only from the security of Montaigne's tower, and no one regarded witchcraft as a matter of indifference. The ideology of this enlightened, materialistic, and practical age had no place for the old-fashioned idea of the witch. Works on occult and magical subjects represent an infinitesimal proportion of the books published in eighteenth-century Europe.[32] Witchcraft was a subject that just disappeared from the collective mentality of the elites. In this new climate, the hunting of witches simply died of disinterest.

The world of the early modern witch hunters has long since disappeared, but the psychology that was the underpinning for the witch trials remains. No doubt Addison and his optimistic contemporaries would be astonished and profoundly disheartened by the large-scale revival of scapegoating and ideological fervor in the modern world. Although the psychology of fear receded temporarily during the eighteenth century, it has returned with unprecedented force in our mass movements of nationalism and revolution. Contemporary ideologies are mostly secular in nature, and modern nonconformists generally are denounced as enemies of the state or the people, not enemies of God. Racism, as in modern antisemitic movements, and class rivalries, found among authoritarian regimes of the left and right, have become the vehicles for today's equivalents of the witch trials. The underlying dynamics do not appear much changed, however. As adults we say we have outgrown our terror of witches. Yet it seems inescapably clear that the primordial fears are always intact, ready to yield their bitter fruits whenever the anxieties of individual men and women are channeled by their leaders along paths of destruction.

Notes

Introduction

1. A collection of essays providing an anthropological survey of witchcraft beliefs around the world is Max Marwick, ed., *Witchcraft and Sorcery* (Baltimore, 1970). The essay by Philip Mayer is particularly helpful in explaining the intellectual and psychological foundations of witch beliefs; Mayer, "Witches," in Marwick, *Witchcraft and Sorcery*, pp. 45–64.

2. *New York Times*, March 31, 1976. See chap. 1 n. 9.

3. The most complete statistical compilations of documented witchcraft cases appear in E. William Monter, *Witchcraft in France and Switzerland: The Borderlands in the Reformation* (Ithaca, 1976), pp. 119–20; and Hugh V. MacLachlan and J. K. Swales, "Lord Hale, Witches, and Rape," *British Journal of Law and Society* 5 (1978): 225.

4. See Lucien Febvre, "Witchcraft: Nonsense or a Mental Revolution?" in Febvre, *A New Kind of History and Other Essays*, ed. Peter Burke (New York, 1973), pp. 189–91. This essay was first published in 1948.

1. The Witchcraft Enigma

1. On these historians, see Jeffry B. Russell, *Witchcraft in the Middle Ages* (Ithaca, 1972), pp. 30–34.

2. Norman Cohn, *Europe's Inner Demons* (London, 1975), pp. 126–46; and Richard Kieckhefer, *European Witch Trials: Their Foundations in Popular and Learned Culture, 1300–1500* (Berkeley, 1976), pp. 16–18.

3. Cohn, *Demons*, pp. 99–125; see also Russell, *Witchcraft*, pp. 36–37.

4. Most prominently, Arno Runeberg, *Witches, Demons, and Fertility* (Helsinki, 1947); and Elliot Rose, *A Razor for a Goat* (Toronto, 1962).

5. Jules Michelet, *Satanism and Witchcraft* (1863; reprint ed., New York, 1939). See also Russell, *Witchcraft*; and Emmanuel Le Roy Ladurie, *Les Paysans de Languedoc* (Paris, 1966), pp. 407–13. Le Roy Ladurie's work is translated in E. William Monter, ed., *European Witchcraft* (New York, 1969), pp. 164–72.

6. Montague Summers, a contemporary of Margaret Murray, used this kind of argument to assert not only the reality of devil worship but also the reality of the devil. See, for example, the introduction to his translation of the *Malleus Maleficarum* (London, 1928), pp. xi–xvi; cf. Cohn, *Demons*, pp. 120–21. Jeffry B. Russell has lately exhibited similar tendencies; see Russell, *The Devil: Perceptions of Evil from Antiquity to Primitive Christianity* (Ithaca, 1977), pp. 258–60, and *Satan: The Early Christian Tradition* (Ithaca, 1981), pp. 11–12, 219–30.

7. Bernard Barnett, "Witchcraft, Psychopathology, and Hallucinations," *British Journal of Psychiatry* 3 (1965): 439–45; and Michael J. Harner, "The Role of Hallucinogenic Plants in European Witchcraft," in his *Hallucinogens and Shamanism* (New York, 1973), pp. 125–50.

8. Gustav Henningsen, *The Witches' Advocate* (Reno, 1980), pp. 4–6, 295–301,

391, and references cited therein; and Julio Caro Baroja, *The World of the Witches*, trans. O. N. V. Glindinning (Chicago, 1955), pp. 180–89. Cf. Carlo Ginzburg, *The Night Battles: Witchcraft and Agrarian Cults in the Sixteenth and Seventeenth Centuries* (Baltimore, 1983), pp. 17–18.

9. Linnda R. Caporael, "Ergotism: The Satan Loosed in Salem?" *Science* 192 (1976), pp. 21–26; cf. the critique by Nicholas P. Spanos and Jack Gottlieb, "Ergotism and the Salem Village Witch Trials," *Science* 194 (1976), pp. 1390–94. See also Cohn, *Demons*, pp. 119–20; and Christina Larner, *Enemies of God: The Witch-Hunt in Scotland* (Baltimore, 1981), p. 220.

10. An effective criticism of the psychiatric interpretation of witch trials is Nicholas P. Spanos, "Witchcraft in Histories of Psychiatry: A Critical Analysis and an Alternative Conceptualization," *Psychological Bulletin* 85 (1978): 417–39. Similar conclusions are reached by Thomas J. Schoeneman, "The Role of Mental Illness in the European Witch Hunts of the Sixteenth and Seventeenth Centuries: An Assessment," *Journal of the History of the Behavioral Sciences* 18 (1977): 337–51. See also Thomas S. Szasz, *The Manufacture of Madness* (New York, 1970), pp. 68–81.

11. Modern scholarship on this subject begins with E. E. Evans-Pritchard, *Witchcraft, Oracles, and Magic among the Azande* (Oxford, 1937). An overview of anthropological findings is provided in Marwick, *Witchcraft and Sorcery*. An attempted synthesis is Mary Douglas's introduction to her collection, *Witchcraft Confessions and Accusations* (London, 1970), pp. xiii–xxvi.

12. See Keith Thomas, *Religion and the Decline of Magic* (New York, 1971), pp. 3–21, 78–96, 469–77, and *passim*.

13. Philippe Ariès, *The Hour of Our Death*, trans. Helen Weaver (New York, 1981), p. 605.

14. Thomas, *Religion*, pp. 25–173.

15. See Alan Macfarlane, *Witchcraft in Tudor and Stuart England* (London, 1970), pp. 194–95.

16. Thomas, *Religion*, pp. 177–252; Macfarlane, *Witchcraft in Tudor and Stuart England*, pp. 115–34; Etienne Delcambre, *Le Concept de la sorcellerie dans le duché de Lorraine au XVIe et au XVIIe siècles* (Nancy, 1951), 3:27–124, 163–203; William A. Christian, Jr., *Local Religion in Sixteenth-Century Spain* (Princeton, 1981), pp. 28–30; Henningsen, *Advocate*, p. 303; Russell Zguta, "Witchcraft and Medicine in Pre-Petrine Russia," *Russian Review* 37 (1978): 438–48; and Larner, *Enemies*, pp. 138–43. See also Jerome D. Frank, *Persuasion and Healing* (Baltimore, 1973), pp. 46–77, 136–64.

17. Aline Rousselle, "From Sanctuary to Miracle Worker: Healing in Fourth-Century Gaul," in *Ritual, Religion, and the Sacred: Selections from the Annales*, eds. Robert Forster and Orest Ranum (Baltimore, 1982), pp. 95–127; P. A. Sigal, "Miracles et guérisons au XIIe siècle," *Annales: Economies, Sociétés, Civilisations* 24 (1969): 1522–39; Christian, *Local Religion*, pp. 92–105; and Delcambre, *Concept*, pp. 11–25, 125–61.

18. Marc Bloch, *The Royal Touch: Sacred Monarchy and Scrofula in France and England*, trans. J. E. Anderson (London, 1973); see also Thomas, *Religion*, pp. 192–204.

19. Christian, *Local Religion*, p. 102.

20. Quoted by Brian Easlea, *Witch Hunting, Magic, and the New Philosophy: An Introduction to Debates of the Scientific Revolution* (Atlantic Highlands, N.J., 1980), p. 1.

21. Stephen A. Cappanari et al., "Voodoo in the General Hospital: A Case of Hexing and Regional Enteritis," *Journal of the American Medical Association* 232 (1975): 938–40, and bibliography cited therein. See also I. M. Lewis, *Ecstatic*

Religion (Baltimore, 1971), pp. 66–99; Thomas, *Religion*, pp. 177–211, 502–12; and Herbert Rappaport and Margaret Rappaport, "The Integration of Scientific and Traditional Healing: A Proposed Model," *American Psychologist* 36 (1981): 774–81. Henri Ellenberger surveys the varieties of nonscientific psychotherapy in *The Discovery of the Unconscious* (New York, 1970), pp. 3–52.
22. Thomas, *Religion*, pp. 51–77, 469–501. For details, see chap. 5.
23. Cohn, *Demons*; Kieckhefer, *Witch Trials*; Larner, *Enemies*; Robert Muchembled et. al., *Prophètes and sorciers dans les Pays-Bas, XVIe–XVIIIe siècles* (Paris, 1978); Robert Muchembled, *Culture populaire et culture des élites dans la France moderne* (Paris, 1978), *Les Derniers bûchers* (Paris, 1981), and "The Witches of the Cambrésis: The Acculturation of the Rural World in the Sixteenth and Seventeenth Centuries," in James Obelkevich, ed., *Religion and the People, 800–1700* (Chapel Hill, 1979), pp. 221–76.
24. John Boswell, *Christianity, Social Tolerance, and Homosexuality: Gay People in Western Europe from the Beginning of the Christian Era to the Fourteenth Century* (Chicago, 1980), p. 38.
25. Marc Bloch, *Land and Work in Medieval Europe*, trans. J. E. Anderson (Berkeley, 1967), p. 48.

2. Medieval Witches

1. Lynn White, Jr., "Death and the Devil," in Robert S. Kinsman, ed., *The Darker Vision of the Renaissance* (Berkeley, 1974), pp. 25–46. See also Boswell, *Christianity*, pp. 269ff.
2. See Philippe Ariès, *Western Attitudes toward Death from the Middle Ages to the Present*, trans. Patricia M. Ranum (Baltimore, 1974), pp. 26–52.
3. See the chapter on "Demonic Aliens" in Salo Wittmayer Baron, *A Social and Religious History of the Jews*, 2d ed. (New York, 1967), 12: 122–91; also White, "Death," pp. 42–43; and Leon Poliakov, *The History of Anti-Semitism* (New York, 1974), 1:41–95.
4. Boswell, *Christianity*, pp. 269–302, esp. 292.
5. See Gordon Leff, *Heresy in the Later Middle Ages* (Manchester, 1967), 2:445–85; Cohn, *Demons*, pp. 32–42; Jeffry B. Russell, *Dissent and Reform in the Early Middle Ages* (Berkeley, 1965), pp. 205–15.
6. On these themes, see Austin P. Evans, "Hunting Subversion in the Middle Ages," *Speculum* 33 (1958):1–22.
7. Cohn, *Demons*, pp. 16–31, 54–59.
8. The following discussion is drawn from Cohn, *Demons*, pp. 60–74; and Peter Brown, "Sorcery, Demons, and the Rise of Christianity from Late Antiquity into the Middle Ages," in Douglas, *Witchcraft Confessions*, pp. 17–45.
9. Rousselle, "Sanctuary," p. 122.
10. Cohn, *Demons*, pp. 70, 71–74. See also Russell, *Witchcraft*, pp. 116–20.
11. On the Inquisition, the classic work is Henry Charles Lea, *A History of the Inquisition in the Middle Ages*, 3 vols. (New York, 1888). A good survey is G. G. Coulton, *Inquisition and Liberty* (London, 1938). A recent summary is provided in Leff, *Heresy*.
12. A fine overview is in Cohn, *Demons*, pp. 75–98. A recent full-length study is Malcolm Barber's judicious account, *The Trial of the Templars* (Cambridge, 1978).
13. Barber, *Trial of the Templars*, p. 181.
14. A convenient collection of essays is available in William Bowsky, ed., *The Black Death: A Turning Point in History?* (New York, 1971).

180

Notes

15. Thomas, *Religion*, p. 8. See also Carlo Cipolla, *Faith, Reason, and the Plague in Seventeenth-Century Tuscany*, trans. Muriel Kittel (Ithaca, 1979), pp. 6–9; and Thomas F. Sheppard, *Lourmarin in the Eighteenth Century* (Baltimore, 1971), pp. 116–27.

16. On tarantism, see Lewis, *Ecstatic Religion*, pp. 41–43, 89–101. A brief introduction to the flagellants is provided in Philip Ziegler, *The Black Death* (London, 1969), pp. 86–97. Norman Cohn places them in the context of late medieval apocalyptic movements (*The Pursuit of the Millennium*, rev. ed. [New York, 1970]; pp. 127–47). See also Leff, *Heresy*, pp. 485–493.

17. Ziegler, *Black Death*, pp. 97–109; Baron, *Jews*, 12:122–91; Poliakov, *Anti-Semitism*, pp. 101–55. Cf. Venetia Newall, "The Jew as Witch Figure," in Newall, ed., *The Witch Figure* (London, 1973), pp. 95–124.

18. Thomas, *Religion*, pp. 559–60.

19. Ariès summarized his views in *Western Attitudes*, chaps. 1 and 2; a fuller statement is in his *The Hour of Our Death*, pts 1 and 2. See also Kathleen Cohen, *Metamorphosis of a Death Symbol: The Transi Tomb in the Late Middle Ages and the Renaissance* (Berkeley, 1973), esp. pp. 1–10.

20. *Hamlet*, act 3, sc. 1; Ariès, *Western Attitudes*, pp. 44–45; and *Romeo and Juliet*, act 4, sc 5. See also Jan Huizinga, *The Waning of the Middle Ages* (Garden City, N.Y., 1954), chap. 11.

21. Quoted by Marina Warner, *Alone of All Her Sex: The Myth and Cult of the Virgin Mary* (New York, 1976), pp. 318–19.

22. Ariès, *Hour*, pp. 109 (quotation), 106–10.

23. See ibid., pp. 95–110; D. D. R. Owen, *The Vision of Hell: Infernal Journeys in Medieval French Literature* (Edinburgh, 1970); Jean Delumeau, *La Peur en occident, XIVᵉ–XVIIᵉ siècles* (Paris, 1978), chap. 7; and Thomas, *Religion*, chap. 3.

24. Cohn, *Demons*, p. 156; and *Corpus Juris Civilis*, codex 9, title 18.

25. Donald J. Wilcox, *In Search of God and Self: Renaissance and Reformation Thought* (Boston, 1975), p. 116. Wilcox's discussion of Renaissance magic is most helpful.

26. A thorough introduction to these matters is D. P. Walker, *Spiritual and Demonic Magic from Ficino to Campanella* (London, 1958).

27. On astrology, see Thomas, *Religion*, pp. 283–385. For the alchemical tradition, very valuable is Betty Jo Teeter Dobbs, *The Foundations of Newton's Alchemy* (Cambridge, 1975), pp. 25–92.

28. The classic work on this subject is Frances A. Yates, *Giordano Bruno and the Hermetic Tradition* (Chicago, 1964). See also Wayne Shumaker, *The Occult Sciences in the Renaissance* (Berkeley, 1972), pp. 201–51.

29. Quoted by Brian Copenhaver, *Symphorien Champier and the Reception of the Occult Tradition in France* (The Hague, 1978), p. 37.

30. See Edward Peters, *The Magician, the Witch, and the Law* (Philadelphia, 1978), pp. 116ff.

31. E. M. Butler, *Ritual Magic* (Cambridge, 1949); Cohn, *Demons*, pp. 165–73; Kieckhefer, *Witch Trials*, pp. 6–7, 34–35, 69–71; Russell, *Witchcraft*, pp. 5–13; and Gene A. Brucker, "Sorcery in Early Renaissance Florence," *Studies in the Renaissance* 10 (1963): 7–24.

32. Charles Edward Hopkin, *The Share of Thomas Aquinas in the Growth of the Witchcraft Delusion* (Philadelphia, 1940), pp. 174–84; Cohn, *Demons*, pp. 174–79. An excerpt from Aquinas's *Summa contra Gentiles* appears in Alan C. Kors and Edward Peters, eds., *Witchcraft in Europe, 1100–1700: A Documentary History* (Philadelphia, 1972), 53–62.

33. Kieckhefer, *Witch Trials*, pp. 13–18, 111; Cohn, *Demons*, pp. 75–98, 180–204; and Russell, *Witchcraft*, 189–93.

34. William R. Jones, "The Political Uses of Sorcery in Medieval Europe," *The Historian* 34 (1972): 670–82.

35. Kieckhefer, *Witch Trials*, pp. 115–16.

36. Ibid., pp. 20, 117; and Cohn, *Demons*, pp. 197–204.

37. Cohn, *Demons*, pp. 204–05; and Kieckhefer, *Witch Trials*, pp. 20, 117.

38. Cohn, *Demons*, pp. 126–46; and Kieckhefer, *Witch Trials*, pp. 16–19.

39. Kieckhefer, *Witch Trials*, pp. 88–102; and Cohn, *Demons*, pp. 239–55. Cf. Brucker, "Sorcery," pp. 21ff.

40. Cohn, *Demons*, pp. 160–63, 254–55; Peter Brown, "Society and the Supernatural: A Medieval Change," *Daedalus*, Spring 1975, pp. 135–40; John H. Langbein, *Prosecuting Crime in the Renaissance* (Cambridge, Mass., 1974), pp. 130–39, and *Torture and the Law of Proof: Europe and England in the Ancien Régime* (Chicago, 1977), pp. 3–16. See also chap. 6.

41. On the Canon Episcopi, see Russell, *Witchcraft*, pp. 75–80; Cohn, *Demons*, pp. 210–12; and Kieckhefer, *Witch Trials*, pp. 38–39.

42. Cohn, *Demons*, pp. 227ff. See also chap. 3.

43. Kieckhefer, *Witch Trials*, pp. 88–102; and Cohn, *Demons*, pp. 239–55.

44. Kieckhefer, *Witch Trials*, pp. 11, 115–47.

45. Cohn, *Demons*, pp. 222–30. The word "voodoo" does not derive from *vauderie*, but is based on a West African root.

46. Quoted by Marina Warner, *Joan of Arc: The Image of Female Heroism* (New York, 1981), 110–11.

47. *Henry VI, Part One*, act I, sc 5.

48. Warner, *Joan*, pp. 96–116.

49. Ibid., p. 97; Jones, "Political Uses," pp. 682–87.

50. Lea, *Inquisition*, 3:519–34; and Cohn, *Demons*, pp. 230–32.

51. Philip Mayer, "Witches," p. 52.

52. The most convenient edition is Montague Summer's translation, first published in London in 1928. Extensive excerpts are in Kors and Peters, *Witchcraft*, pp. 113–89.

53. This aspect of the *Malleus*'s appeal is emphasized in Sydney Anglo, "Evident Authority and Authoritative Evidence: The *Malleus Maleficarum*," in Anglo, *The Damned Art: Essays in the Literature of Witchcraft* (London, 1977), pp. 1–31.

54. On differences between Protestant and Catholic interpretations of witchcraft, see H. C. Erik Midelfort, "Witchcraft and Religion in Sixteenth-Century Germany: The Formation and Consequences of an Orthodoxy," *Archiv für Reformationsgeschichte* 62 (1971): 266–78; and Monter, *Witchcraft in France and Switzerland*, pp. 105–09.

55. Kieckhefer, *Witch Trials*, pp. 10–26, 106–47; and H. C. Erik Midelfort, *Witch Hunting in Southwestern Germany, 1562–1684* (Stanford, 1972), pp. 199–230.

56. See the printing history in Summers's edition, pp. xvii–xviii; cf. Monter, *European Witchcraft*, pp. 59–60.

57. See the list of demonological works compiled by Rossell Hope Robbins, *The Encyclopedia of Witchcraft and Demonology* (New York, 1959), pp. 145–47.

58. Ibid., pp. 123–26. See Midelfort, *Witch Hunting*, pp. 67–84.

59. Cf. Elizabeth L. Eisenstein, *The Printing Press as an Agent of Change* (Cambridge, 1979), 1:433–39.

3. *Sexual Politics and Religious Reform*
in the Witch Craze

1. See Introduction, n. 3.

2. Kieckhefer, *Witch Trials*, p. 96; Macfarlane, *Witchcraft in Tudor and Stuart England*, p. 160; and John P. Demos, *Entertaining Satan: Witchcraft and the Culture of Early New England* (New York, 1982), pp. 60–64.

3. Pierre de Lancre, *Tableau de l'inconstance des mauvais anges et démons* (Paris, 1612) pp. 65–168, 193–234; cf. Margaret M. McGowan, "Pierre de Lancre's *Tableau de l'inconstance des mauvais anges et démons*: The Sabbat Sensationalized," in Anglo, *The Damned Art*, pp. 182–201.

4. Peters, *Magician*, p. 174; Russell, *Witchcraft*, pp. 237–38, 243; Midelfort, *Witch Hunting*, p. 24; Peter Burke, "Witchcraft and Magic in Renaissance Italy: Gianfrancesco Pico and His Strix," in Anglo, *The Damned Art*, pp. 39, 47; McGowan, "Pierre de Lancre's *Tableau*," in Anglo, *The Damned Art*, pp. 187, 192, 199; and John L. Teall, "Witchcraft and Calvinism in Elizabethan England: Divine Power and Human Agency," *Journal of the History of Ideas* 23 (1962): 26–27.

5. Macfarlane, *Witchcraft in Tudor and Stuart England*, p. 137; Wallace Notestein, *The History of English Witchcraft* (New York, 1968), pp. 204–06; McGowan, "Pierre de Lancre's *Tableau*," p. 185; Monter, *Witchcraft in France and Switzerland*, pp. 157–65; Russell, *Witchcraft*, pp. 242–43; Larner, *Enemies*, pp. 110–12, 172, 200–01; and Sanford J. Fox, *Science and Justice: The Massachusetts Witchcraft Trials* (Baltimore, 1968), pp. 77–79. In the contemporary sources, see Henri Boguet, *An Examen of Witches* (n.p., 1929), chap. 44. Boguet was first published as *Discours des sorciers* (Lyons, 1602). See also Francesco Maria Guazzo, *Compendium Maleficarum*, trans. and ed. Montague Summers (New York, 1974), book 1, chap. 6. Guazzo's work was first published in Milan in 1608.

6. Monter, *Witchcraft in France and Switzerland*, pp. 62–65; cf. Boguet, *Examen*, chap. 44.

7. Michael Dalton, *The Country Justice* (London, 1618), cited in Herbert Leventhal, *In the Shadow of the Enlightenment: Occultism and Renaissance Science in Eighteenth-Century America* (New York, 1972), p. 82; and Monter, *Witchcraft in France and Switzerland*, p. 161.

8. Quoted by Paul Boyer and Stephen Nissenbaum, *Salem Possessed: The Social Origins of Witchcraft* (Cambridge, Mass., 1974), p. 13. See also Demos, *Entertaining Satan*, pp. 180–81.

9. Stuart Clark, "Inversion, Misrule, and the Meaning of Witchcraft," *Past and Present*, no. 87 (1980), pp. 98-127. See also on this subject, Henry Charles Lea, *Materials toward a History of Witchcraft* (Philadelphia, 1939), 3:1205; and Baroja, *World*, pp. 168–69.

10. Midelfort, *Witch Hunting*, pp. 22–24, and "Heartland of the Witchcraze: Central and Northern Europe," *History Today*, February 1981, pp. 29–30.

11. Muchembled, "Witches," p. 261; Larner, *Enemies*, pp. 107–112, 145–46, 66–72, 107–12; and Boguet, *Examen*, chap. 61.

12. Kieckhefer, *Witch Trials*, p. 96; Monter, *Witchcraft in France and Switzerland*, pp. 119–20; and Larner, *Enemies*, p. 149.

13. On these themes, see Jean Delumeau, *Catholicism between Luther and Voltaire*, trans. Jeremy Moiser (New York, 1977), chaps. 3 and 4; Peter Burke, *Popular Culture in Early Modern Europe* (New York, 1978), chaps. 7 and 8; and Muchembled, *Culture populaire*, chaps. 4–6.

14. Luther, "Commentary on St. Paul's Epistle to the Galatians," in Kors and

Peters, *Witchcraft in Europe*, p. 200; Calvin, "Institutes of the Christian Religion," in Kors and Peters, *Witchcraft in Europe*, pp. 202–12; and Thomas, *Religion*, p. 476. Cf. Monter, *Witchcraft in France and Switzerland*, pp. 31–32.

15. Thomas, *Religion*, p. 471.

16. Ibid., p. 472.

17. Jean Delumeau, *Catholicism*, pp. 162–74; and Christian, *Local Religion*, p. 161. See also Delumeau, *Peur*, pp. 233–53.

18. David Nicholls, "The Devil in Renaissance France," *History Today*, November 1980, p. 29.

19. Warner, *Alone*, pp. 323–29. On these themes, see Mikhail Bakhtin, *Rabelais and His World*, trans. Helene Iswolsky (Cambridge, Mass., 1968), *passim*.

20. Larner, *Enemies*, pp. 147–48.

21. The following discussion is drawn from Ginzburg, *The Night Battles*, *passim*.

22. Macfarlane, *Witchcraft in Tudor and Stuart England*, p. 120.

23. See Delcambre, *Concept*, vol. 3, esp. pp. 205–19; and Larner, *Enemies*, p. 171.

24. Sarah D. Pomeroy, *Goddesses, Whores, Wives, and Slaves: Women in Classical Antiquity* (New York, 1975); Russell, *Witchcraft*, pp. 283–84; Warner, *Alone*, pp. 50–78, 234–35, 306; Ian Maclean, *The Renaissance Notion of Women* (Cambridge, 1980), p. 23; and Lionel Rothkrug, "Religious Practices and Collective Perceptions: Hidden Homologies in the Renaissance and Reformation," *Historical Reflections* 7 (1980):82–83.

25. See John T. Noonan, Jr., *Contraception: A History of Its Treatment by the Catholic Theologians and Canonists* (Cambridge, Mass., 1965), pp. 107–39, 171–99; Thomas N. Tentler, *Sin and Confession on the Eve of the Reformation* (Princeton, 1977), pp. 162–232; and Lawrence Stone, *The Family, Sex, and Marriage in England, 1500–1800* (New York, 1977) pp. 102–09, 195–206.

26. J. N. D. Kelly, *Jerome: His Life, Writings, and Controversies* (New York, 1975), pp. 20–21, 50–52, 101–04, 295; Friedrich Heer, *The Medieval World*, trans. Janet Sondheimer (London, 1962), p. 265; and Easlea, *Witch Hunting, Magic, and the New Philosophy*, p. 34.

27. Part I, questions VI and XI of the *Malleus Maleficarum*, reprinted in Kors and Peters, *Witchcraft in Europe*, pp. 114–27.

28. Nicolas Rémy, *Demonolatry*, ed. Montague Summers (New York, 1974), book 1, chap. 15 (first published Lyon, 1595); James I, *Demonology* (London, 1603), book 2, chap. 5; and Boguet, *Examen*, chap. 13.

29. François Rabelais, *The Histories of Gargantua and Pantagruel*, trans. John M. Cohen (Baltimore, 1955), book 3, chap. 32. See also Vern L. Bullough, *The Subordinate Sex: A History of Attitudes toward Women* (Urbana, 1973), chaps. 1–9; Ruth Kelso, *Doctrine for the Lady of the Renaissance* (Urbana, 1956), esp. pp. 5–37; and the perceptive comments of William J. Bouwsma, "Christian Adulthood," *Daedalus*, Spring 1976, pp. 77–79.

30. Thomas, *Religion*, pp. 568–69; Maclean, *Renaissance*, pp. 28–46; and Carolyn C. Lougee, *Le Paradis des Femmes: Women, Salons, and Social Stratification in Seventeenth-Century France* (Princeton, 1976), pp. 11–30.

31. Delumeau, *Peur*, pp. 323–40; and Maclean, *Renaissance*, pp. 26, 85.

32. See Monter, *Witchcraft in France and Switzerland*, pp. 121–24.

33. Stone, *Family*, pp. 102–05, 195–206.

34. Natalie Zemon Davis, *Society and Culture in Early Modern France* (Stanford, 1975), pp. 124–51; Clark, "Inversion," pp. 98–127; and Midelfort, *Witch Hunting*, pp. 183–84.

35. Baroja, *World*, pp. 156–60; and McGowan, "Pierre de Lancre's *Tableau*," pp. 182–201.

36. See Keith Thomas, "Women and the Civil War Sects," in Trevor Aston, ed., *Crisis in Europe, 1560–1660* (London, 1965), pp. 317–40.

37. Marie Sylvie Dupont-Bouchat, "La répression de la sorcellerie dans le duché de Luxembourg aux XVIe et XVIIe siècles," in Muchembled, *Prophètes et sorciers*, pp. 66–67, 78–86.

38. On Daneau, see Olivier Fatio, "Lambert Daneau," in Jill Raitt, ed., *Shapers of Religious Traditions in Germany, Switzerland, and Poland, 1560–1660* (New Haven, 1981), pp. 105–20.

39. Rémy, *Demonolatry*, book 3, chap. 1; cf. Lucien Dintzer, *Nicolas Rémy et son oeuvre démonologique* (Lyon, 1936), pp. 17–22, 83–95; and Jean Bodin, *De la démonomanie des sorciers* (Paris, 1580), book 2, chap. 4. See also chap. 6, n. 11 and 12.

40. Delumeau, *Peur*, pp. 341–44; Maclean, *Renaissance*, pp. 24–25; and Monter, *Witchcraft in France and Switzerland*, pp. 122–23.

41. Ariès, *Hour*, pp. 369–81, 391–95; Stone, *Family*, pp. 163–65, 439–40; George Lincoln Burr, ed., *Narratives of the Witchcraft Cases, 1648–1706* (New York, 1914), p. 325; and M. Wynn Thomas, "Cotton Mather's *Wonders of the Invisible World:* Some Metamorphoses of Salem Witchcraft," in Anglo, *The Damned Art*, p. 206.

42. Ariès, *Hour*, p. 370. See the treatments by Hans Baldung Grien and Nikolaus Deutsch, in *Hans Baldung Grien: Prints and Drawings* (n.p., 1981), pp. 10, 35.

43. The following discussion is drawn from Alan Shestack, "An Introduction to Hans Baldung Grien," in *Hans Baldung Grien*, pp. 4–5; Charles W. Talbot, "Baldung and the Female Nude," ibid., pp. 19–37; Linda C. Hults, "Baldung and the Reformation," ibid., pp. 40, 51–58; catalog commentaries, ibid., pp. 114–23, 171–77, 243–49, 264–75; and Robert A. Koch, *Hans Baldung Grien: Eve, the Serpent, and Death* (Ottawa, 1974), pp. 12–16, 22–24. Cf. Dale Hoak, "Witch Hunting and Women in the Art of the Renaissance," *History Today*, February 1981, pp. 22–26.

44. On handkerchiefs and forks, see Norbert Elias, *The Civilizing Process: The History of Manners*, trans. Edmund Jephcott (New York, 1978); on corridors, Mark Girouard, *Life in the English Country House* (New Haven, 1978); and Jean-Louis Flandrin, *Families in Past Times*, trans. Richard Southern (New York, 1979), pp. 93–101.

45. Stone, *Family*, pp. 161–78; Winthrop D. Jordan, *White Over Black: American Attitudes toward the Negro, 1550–1812* (Chapel Hill, 1968), pp. 150–63; Colin A. Palmer, *Slaves of the White God: Blacks in Mexico, 1570–1660* (Cambridge, Mass., 1976), pp. 145–66.

46. Muchembled, "Witches," pp. 232, 238–41; Midelfort, *Witch Hunting*, pp. 182–83; Warner, *Joan of Arc*, pp. 1–15, 96ff.; Dupont-Bouchat, "Répression," p. 142; and Jean-Louis Flandrin, "Contraception, Marriage, and Sexual Relations in the Christian West," in Robert Forster and Orest Ranum, eds., *Biology of Man in History: Essays from the Annales* (Baltimore, 1975), p. 37.

47. Kieckhefer, *Witch Trials*, p. 96; cf. Larner, *Enemies*, p. 149.

48. Cf. Stone, *Family*, pp. 90, 501–07.

49. Muchembled, "Witches," pp. 265–67.

50. Warner, *Alone*, p. 234.

51. Emmanuel Le Roy Ladurie, *Montaillou*, trans. Barbara Bray (New York, 1978), chaps. 8–12; and Delumeau, *Peur*, p. 324.

52. Flandrin, *Families*, pp. 180–85.

53. Burke, *Popular Culture*, pp. 211–12.

54. Larner, *Enemies*, p. 68; Jonathan Dewald, *The Formation of a Provincial Nobility: The Magistrates of the Parlement of Rouen, 1499–1610* (Princeton, 1980), pp. 318–22; Monter, *Witchcraft in France and Switzerland*, pp. 135–36, 197–98; Dupont-Bouchat, "Répression," pp. 141–44; Christopher R. Friedrichs, *Urban Society in an Age of War: Nördlingen, 1580–1720* (Princeton, 1979), pp. 199–206; E. William Monter "La sodomie à l'époque moderne en Suisse romande," *Annales: Economies, Sociétés, Civilisations* 29 (1974): 1023–33; Jean-Louis Flandrin, "Repression and Change in the Sexual Life of Young People in Medieval and Early Modern Times," in Robert Wheaton and Tamara K. Hareven, eds., *Family and Sexuality in French History* (Philadelphia, 1980), p. 35; Bruce Lenman and Geoffrey Parker, "The State, the Community and the Criminal Law in Early Modern Europe," in V. A. C. Gatrell *et al.*, *Crime and the Law* (London, 1980), p. 37.

55. Stone, *Family*, pp. 523, 607–14; and Keith Thomas, "The Puritans and Adultery: The Act of 1650 Reconsidered," in Donald Pennington and Keith Thomas, eds., *Puritans and Revolutionaries: Essays in Seventeenth-Century History Presented to Christopher Hill* (Oxford, 1978), pp. 257–82.

56. Cf. Larner, *Enemies*, p. 149; and Monter, *Witchcraft in France and Switzerland*, pp. 165–66.

57. Burke, *Popular Culture*, pp. 178–204; Davis, *Society*, pp. 147–50; and Emmanuel Le Roy Ladurie, *Carnival in Romans*, trans. Mary Feeney (New York, 1979). See also Muchembled, *Culture populaire*, p. 256; John Bossy, "The Counter-Reformation and the People of Catholic Europe," *Past and Present* 47 (1970): 51–70; and Philip Benedict, "The Catholic Response to Protestantism: Church Activity and Popular Piety in Rouen, 1560–1600," in Obelkevich, *Religion and the People*, p. 174.

58. Larner, *Enemies*, p. 153.

59. Rémy, *Demonolatry*, book I, chap. 16.

60. Burke, *Popular Culture*, p. 217; and Christian, *Local Religion*, pp. 161–63.

61. Davis, *Society*, pp. 97–124, 152–89.

62. Carlo Ginzburg, *The Cheese and the Worms*, trans. John Tedeschi and Anne Tedeschi (Baltimore, 1980), p. xxv.

63. Burke, *Popular Culture*, pp. 207–43; Denis Richet, "Aspects socio-culturels des conflits religieux à Paris dans la seconde moitié du XVIᵉ siècle," *Annales: Economies, Sociétés, Civilisations* 32 (1977): 783; and Timothy Tackett, *Priest and Parish in Eighteenth-Century France* (Princeton, 1976), pp. 202–14.

64. See Monter, *Witchcraft in France and Switzerland*, pp. 142–66, 191–93. On the relatively mild fear of the devil in popular literature, see Robert Mandrou, *De la culture populaire au XVIIᵉ et XVIIIᵉ siècles: La Bibliothèque bleue de Troyes* (Paris, 1964), p. 73.

65. Henningsen, *Advocate*, esp. p. 390, and "The Greatest Witch-Trial of Them All: Navarre, 1609–1614," *History Today*, November 1980, pp. 36–39. Cf. Larner, *Enemies*, p. 144.

66. Cf. E. William Monter, "Pedestal and Stake: Courtly Love and Witchcraft," in Renate Bridenthal and Claudia Koonz, eds., *Becoming Visible: Women in European History* (Boston, 1977), pp. 129–35; Monter, *Witchcraft in France and Switzerland*, pp. 17, 197–98; Clarke Garrett, "Women and Witches: Patterns of Analysis," *Signs* 3 (1977): 461–70; and Thomas, *Religion*, pp. 568–69.

67. In addition to the above citations, see, for France, Richet, "Aspects socio-culturels," pp. 778–83; and Robert J. Harding, "Revolutions and Reform in the Holy League: Angers, Rennes, Nantes," *Journal of Modern History* 53 (1981): 379–416. On Eastern Europe, see R. J. W. Evans, *The Making of the Habsburg*

Monarchy (Oxford, 1979), pp. 400–17; and Russell Zguta, "Witchcraft Trials in Seventeenth-Century Russia," *American Historical Review* 82 (1977): 1187–1207.

4. Classic Witches

1. Cf. Natalie Zemon Davis, "Some Tasks and Themes in the Study of Popular Religion," in Charles Trinkaus and Heiko A. Oberman, eds., *The Pursuit of Holiness in Late Medieval and Renaissance Religion* (Leiden, 1974), pp. 307–36; and Ginzburg, *Cheese*, esp. p. xii.

2. Friedrich von Spee, *Cautio Criminalis* (Rinteln, 1631), in Robbins, *Encyclopedia*, p. 481.

3. See Thomas, *Religion*, pp. 502–12.

4. Thomas, *Religion*, pp. 554 (quotation), 535–69; and Macfarlane, *Witchcraft in Tudor and Stuart England*, esp. pp. 92–99, 158.

5. Monter, *Witchcraft in France and Switzerland*, pp. 124–26, 140; Antero Heikinnen, *Paholaisen Liittolaiset* (Helsinki, 1969), p. 390; and Larner, *Enemies*, pp. 96–98, 124–25.

6. Cf. Larner, *Enemies*, pp. 94–95.

7. On this subject, see Macfarlane, *Witchcraft in Tudor and Stuart England*, pp. 200–06; and Thomas, *Religion*, pp. 78–112, 502–12, 535–46.

8. Paul Slack, "Mortality Crises and Epidemics, 1485–1610," in Charles Webster, ed., *Health, Medicine, and Mortality in the Sixteenth Century* (Cambridge, 1979), esp. p. 57. See also Pierre Goubert, "The French Peasantry of the Seventeenth Century: A Regional Example," in Trevor Aston, ed., *Crisis in Europe, 1560–1660* (London, 1965), pp. 141–65.

9. Marfarlane, *Witchcraft in Tudor and Stuart England*, pp. 150–51; Delumeau, *Peur*, p. 360.

10. The main arguments on the Weber thesis are conveniently compiled in Robert W. Green, ed., *Protestantism, Capitalism, and Social Science: The Weber Thesis Controversy*, 2d ed. (Boston, 1973); see also S. N. Eisenstadt, ed., *The Protestant Ethic and Modernization* (New York, 1968).

11. Alan Macfarlane, *The Origins of English Individualism* (Cambridge, 1979), pp. 1–2, 59; see also the critique by Christina Larner, "*Crimen Exceptum?* The Crime of Witchcraft in Europe," in Gatrell *et al.*, *Crime and the Law*, pp. 61–63.

12. Thomas, *Religion*, pp. 469–501, in addition to sections cited above.

13. Ibid., pp. 435–63.

14. Cohn, *Demons*, pp. 160–63.

15. Theodore K. Rabb, *The Struggle for Stability in Early Modern Europe* (New York, 1975), p. 84.

16. Ibid., p. 87.

17. Muchembled, "Witches," pp. 259–61.

18. Cf. H. R. Trevor-Roper, *The European Witch-Craze of the Sixteenth and Seventeenth Centuries and Other Essays* (New York, 1969), pp. 101–15. A less successful effort is Michael Barkun, *Disaster and the Millennium* (New York, 1974). See also Raoul Naroll, "A Tentative Index of Cultural Stress," *International Journal of Social Psychiatry* 5 (1959):107–16.

19. Monter, *Witchcraft in France and Switzerland*, p. 123; Midelfort, *Witch Hunting*, p. 126.

20. Midelfort, *Witch Hunting*, p. 121.

21. John Hajnal, "European Marriage Patterns in Perspective," in D. V. Glass and D. E. C. Eversley, eds., *Population and History* (Chicago, 1965), pp. 101–43; Midelfort, *Witch Hunting*, p. 184; Pierre Goubert, *Cent mille provinciaux au XVIIe*

siècle: Beauvais et la Beauvaisis de 1600 à 1730 (Paris, 1968), p. 38; and Jonathan L. Pearl, "Witchcraft in New France in the Seventeenth Century: The Social Aspect," *Historical Reflections* 4 (1977): 191–205.

22. Midelfort, *Witch Hunting*, pp. 172, 187; Peter Clark, "The Alehouse and the Alternative Society," in Pennington and Thomas, *Puritans and Revolutionaries*, pp. 65–67; and Etienne Delcambre, "The Psychology of Lorraine Witchcraft Suspects," in Monter, *European Witchcraft*, p. 105.

23. Cf. Jane B. Donegan, *Women and Men Midwives: Medicine, Morality, and Misogyny in Early America* (Westport, Conn., 1978), p. 19; Thomas, *Religion*, pp. 12–13; and Larner, *Enemies*, p. 101.

24. Flandrin, *Families*, p. 217; Thomas R. Forbes, "The Changing Face of Death in London," in Webster, *Health*, p. 139; Stone, *Family*, pp. 66–82; and "Study Finds 1 in 10 Babies Worldwide Die Before 1st Birthday," *Washington Post*, December 13, 1981, p. A16.

25. Many examples of religious rituals and beliefs associated with the desire for healthy children and the fear of deformed babies are given in Thomas, *Religion*, pp. 25–50, 89–96.

26. On midwives in general, see Donegan, *Women and Men Midwives*; Thomas R. Forbes, "Midwifery and Witchcraft," *Journal of the History of Medicine* 17 (1962): 264–83, and in his *The Midwife and the Witch* (New Haven, 1966), pp. 139–55; Thomas G. Benedek, "The Changing Relationship between Midwives and Physicians during the Renaissance," *Bulletin of the History of Medicine* 51 (1977): 550–64; and Davis, *Society*, pp. 217, 258–64. On the reputation of executioners, see Lenman and Parker, "State, Community, and Criminal Law," in Gatrell *et al.*, *Crime and the Law*, p. 13.

27. Notestein, *History*, p. 41; and Thomas, *Religion*, p. 548; cf. Macfarlane, *Witchcraft in Tudor and Stuart England*, p. 180.

28. Fernando de Rojas, *La Celestina*, trans. L. B. Simpson (Berkeley, 1955), p. 82.

29. Cohn, *Demons*, chap. 1; Russell, *Witchcraft*, pp. 239–40; *Malleus Maleficarum*, pt. 1, chap. 11, and pt. 2, question 1, chap. 13; Bodin, *Démonomanie*, book 4, chap. 6; and Boguet, *Examen*, chap. 31.

30. Friedrich Wilhelm Siegel, *Die Hexenverfolgung in Köln* (Bonn, 1959), pp. 92–93, 152–53. See also Larner, *Enemies*, p. 89.

31. Donegan, *Women and Men Midwives*, p. 91; Frederick C. Drake, "Witchcraft in the American Colonies," *American Quarterly* 20 (1968):6698; Carol V. R. George, "Anne Hutchinson and the Revolution Which Never Happened," in George, ed., *"Remember the Ladies": New Perspectives on Women in American History* (Syracuse, 1975), pp. 24–27; and Demos, *Entertaining Satan*, pp. 80–84.

32. Larner, *Enemies*, pp. 146, 97–98, and *"Crimen Exceptum?"* in Gatrell *et al.*, *Crime and the Law*, pp. 70–71; and Boyer and Nissenbaum, *Salem*, pp. 204–09.

33. See Emily Coleman, "Infanticide in the Early Middle Ages," in Susan Mosher Stuard, ed., *Women in Medieval Society* (Philadelphia, 1976), pp. 47–70; and Lloyd DeMause, ed., *The History of Childhood* (New York, 1974), pp. 26–31.

34. Dewald, *Formation*, p. 318; see also Stone, *Family*, pp. 473–74; Peter C. Hoffer and N. E. H. Hull, *Murdering Mothers: Infanticide in England and New England, 1558–1803* (New York, 1981), pp. 3–64; R. Trexler, "Infanticide in Florence," *History of Childhood Quarterly* 1 (1973):98–116; R. W. Malcolmson, "Infanticide in the Eighteenth Century," in J. S. Cockburn, ed., *Crime in England, 1550–1800* (London, 1977), pp. 187–209; and articles by M. J. Tucker, Elizabeth Wirth Marvick, and John F. Walzer in DeMause, *History of Childhood*, pp. 244–45, 282–85, 352–53.

35. Jonathan Dewald, "The Perfect Magistrate: Parlementaires and Crime in Sixteenth-Century Rouen," *Archiv für Reformationsgeschichte* 67 (1976):297; Bodin, *Démonomanie* (Paris, 1584) folios 187–88.

36. Benedek, "Changing Relationship," pp. 550–58; Forbes, "Midwifery," p. 278, *Midwife and Witch*, pp. 139–55; Donegan, *Women and Men Midwives*, pp. 11–13; and G. L. Kittredge, *Witchcraft in Old and New England* (Cambridge, Mass., 1929), pp. 114–15.

37. Forbes, "Midwifery," p. 269; Thomas, *Religion*, p. 188; and Ginzburg, *Night Battles*, pp. 15–16.

38. George T. Matthews, ed., *News and Rumor in Renaissance Europe: The Fugger Newsletters* (New York, 1959), pp. 140 (quotation), 137–43.

39. Larner, *Enemies*, pp. 103–04, 120–25; and Demos, *Entertaining Satan*, pp. 58–59, 138.

40. See Milton Mayer, *They Thought They Were Free: The Germans, 1933–1945* (Chicago, 1955); cf. Trevor-Roper, *European Witch-Craze*, pp. 110–14.

41. Dupont-Bouchat, "Répression," pp. 57–58. See also Muchembled, "Witches," p. 263.

42. Cf. Larner, *Enemies*, p. 100.

43. See ibid., p. 144. Cf. the somewhat exaggerated evaluation of Marvin Harris, *Cows, Pigs, Wars, and Witches: The Riddles of Culture* (New York, 1974), pp. 239–40.

5. Classic Accusers

1. Russell, *Satan*, pp. 230, 237–39; and Cohn, *Demons*, pp. 68–74.

2. The foregoing account follows Febvre, "Witchcraft," pp. 187–88.

3. Etienne Delcambre and J. Lhermitte, *Un Cas énigmatique de possession diabolique en Lorraine au XVIIe siècle: Elisabeth de Ranfaing, l'énergumène de Nancy* (Nancy, 1955). Cf. Robert Mandrou, *Magistrats et sorciers en France au XVIIe siècle* (Paris, 1968), pp. 246–51.

4. Lewis, *Ecstatic Religion*, passim.

5. See Ronald A. Knox, *Enthusiasm* (New York, 1950), esp. chaps. 5 and 6.

6. See Max Weber, *Economy and Society*, ed. Guenther Roth and Claus Wittich (New York, 1968), esp. pt. 2, chap. 14; and S. N. Eisenstadt, ed., *Max Weber on Charisma and Institution Building* (Chicago, 1968). On the heretical association of the Franciscans, see Cohn, *Pursuit*, pp. 158ff.

7. See Knox, *Enthusiasm*, pp. 244ff.

8. Warner, *Joan*, esp. pp. 77–96; and Boyer and Nissenbaum, *Salem*, pp. 25–30, 215–16. See also B. Robert Kreiser, *Miracles, Convulsions, and Ecclesiastical Politics in Early Eighteenth-Century Paris* (Princeton, 1978).

9. George H. Williams, *The Radical Reformation* (Philadelphia, 1962); Henry Kamen, *The Spanish Inquisition* (New York, 1965), pp. 78ff.; and Knox, *Enthusiasm*, chaps. 7–14.

10. Drake, "Witchcraft," pp. 695–725; and Boyer and Nissenbaum, *Salem*, pp. 103ff.

11. John B. Wolf, *Louis XIV* (New York, 1968), pp. 379–401; and Orest Ranum, "Courtesy, Absolutism, and the Rise of the French State, 1630–1660," *Journal of Modern History* 52 (1980):426–51.

12. Christopher Hill, *The World Turned Upside Down: Radical Ideas during the English Revolution* (New York, 1973); Hillel Schwartz, *The French Prophets* (Berkeley, 1980); Margaret C. Jacob, *The Newtonians and the English Revolution, 1689–*

1720 (Ithaca, 1976), pp. 264–70; Knox, *Enthusiasm*, chap. 15; and Michael Mac-Donald, *Mystical Bedlam: Madness, Anxiety, and Healing in Seventeenth-Century England* (Cambridge, 1981), pp. 217–31. For a discussion of the large literature on this subject, see Michael Heyd, "The Reaction to Enthusiasm in the Seventeenth Century: Towards an Integrative Approach," *Journal of Modern History* 53 (1981): 258–63.

13. Foxe is cited in Thomas, *Religion*, pp. 481–82.

14. Ibid., p. 474. See also MacDonald, *Mystical Bedlam*, pp. 198–205. Mac-Donald's full analysis of the casebooks of Richard Napier (uncle of the physician referred to by Thomas) makes clear that hundreds of the patients of a single doctor complained of possession or victimization by witchcraft.

15. Thomas, *Religion*, pp. 477–92.

16. Ibid., pp. 51–55, 74–76; Lewis, *Ecstatic Religion*, pp. 57–60; and D. P. Walker, *Unclean Spirits: Possession and Exorcism in France and England in the Late Sixteenth and Early Seventeenth Centuries* (Philadelphia, 1981), pp. 22, 33–43.

17. Walker, *Unclean Spirits*, pp. 33–43; and Mandrou, *Magistrats*, pp. 163–79.

18. On the Aix episode, see Mandrou, *Magistrats*, pp. 198–210, 226–45.

19. Robbins, *Encyclopedia*, p. 21.

20. Ibid., p. 24.

21. Mandrou, *Magistrats*, pp. 209–10; and Walker, *Unclean Spirits*, pp. 75–76.

22. Quoted in T. K. Oesterreich, *Possession, Demoniacal and Other* (London, 1930), pp. 88, 89. On this episode, see the somewhat fictionalized account by Aldous Huxley, *The Devils of Loudun* (New York, 1952); and Mandrou, *Magistrats*, pp. 210–19, 226–45.

23. On Auxonne, see Mandrou, *Magistrats*, pp. 404–23; cf. ibid., pp. 219–26, 251–60. On witchcraft cases involving demonic possession in nearby regions of France and French Switzerland, see Monter, *Witchcraft in France and Switzerland*, pp. 59–60, 71–72, 138–41; and François Bavoux, *Hantises et diableries dans la terre abbatiale de Luxeil* (Monaco, 1956).

24. Cf. Walker, *Unclean Spirits*, p. 16.

25. Gregory Zilboorg, *A History of Medical Psychology* (New York, 1941), p. 173.

26. See Lewis, *Ecstatic Religion*, p. 45. On the use of the term "hysteria" in discussions of possession, see Spanos, "Witchcraft," pp. 424–25; and Kreiser, *Miracles*, pp. 257ff.

27. Sigmund Freud, "A Seventeenth-Century Demonological Neurosis," in J. Strachey et al., eds., *Complete Psychological Works* (New York, 1953–74), 19:72.

28. Michelet, *Satanism*, pp. 190–91; and Michel Foucault, *The History of Sexuality*, trans. Robert Hurley (New York, 1978), pp. 20–22.

29. Cf. Lewis, *Ecstatic Religion*, pp. 57–60.

30. Bengt Ankarloo, *Trolldomsprocesserna i Sverige* (Stockholm, 1971), pp. 324–39. On the role of children in outbreaks of possession, see Schwartz, *Prophets*, pp. 31–32, 229–31.

31. Boyer and Nissenbaum, *Salem*, pp. 1–2; Chadwick Hansen, *Witchcraft and Salem* (New York, 1969), chaps. 2 and 3; Ernest Caulfield, "Pediatric Aspects of the Salem Witchcraft Tragedy," *American Journal of Diseases of Children* 65 (1943): 798–801. Some of the recent scholarship on Salem is conveniently assembled in Marc Mappen, ed., *Witches and Historians: Interpretations of Salem* (Huntington, N.Y., 1980).

32. Burr, *Narrative*, pp. 23, 25, 133, 342, 412.

33. Ibid., pp. 153–55, 342, 414.

34. Boyer and Nissenbaum, *Salem*, pp. 3, 7–8, 193–94.
35. Drake, "Witchcraft," pp. 697.
36. Cotton Mather, "Memorable Providences, Relating to Witchcraft and Possession," in Burr, *Narratives*, pp. 99–131.
37. Boyer and Nissenbaum, *Salem*, pp. 170, 153–78.
38. Ibid., pp. 30–36, 80–109.
39. Ibid., pp. 181–209.
40. Burr, *Narratives*, pp. 193–95.
41. Ibid., pp. 158n, 160; and Boyer and Nissenbaum, *Salem*, p. 6.
42. Burr, *Narratives*, pp. 158–59.
43. Boyer and Nissenbaum, *Salem*, pp. 9–21.
44. Caulfield, "Pediatric Aspects," pp. 788–802; and John Demos, "Underlying Themes in the Witchcraft of Seventeenth-Century New England," *American Historical Review* 75 (1970): 1311–26.
45. Keith Thomas, "Women and the Civil War Sects," in Aston, *Crisis*, pp. 317–40; Lewis, *Ecstatic Religion*, p. 87; Thomas, *Religion*, pp. 135–38; and Schwartz, *Prophets*, pp. 32–33, 134–46, 229–31.
46. Maclean, *Renaissance*, p. 21; Thomas, "Women," in Aston, *Crisis*, pp. 318–19; and Walker, *Unclean Spirits*, pp. 77–78.
47. Lewis, *Ecstatic Religion*, pp. 85–86.
48. See Demos, "Underlying Themes," pp. 1315–16; and Ankarloo, *Trolldomsprocesserna*, pp. 337–38.
49. Burr, *Narratives*, p. 422.
50. See Jean-Pierre Peter, "Disease and the Sick at the End of the Old Regime," in Robert Forster and Orest Ranum, eds., *Biology of Man in History* (Baltimore, 1975), p. 117; and Kreiser, *Miracles*, pp. 140–80.

6. In the Torture Chamber

1. First printed by George Lincoln Burr, ed., *Translations and Reprints from the Original Sources of European History* (Philadelphia, 1896) 3:23–28; reprinted in Monter, *European Witchcraft*, pp. 82–88.
2. See chap. 2, n. 11 and 40; Peters, *Magician*, pp. 189–92; Wolfgang Kunkel, "The Reception of Roman Law in Germany: An Interpretation," in Gerald Strauss, ed., *Pre-Reformation Germany* (New York, 1972), pp. 263–81; Georg Dahm, "On the Reception of Roman and Italian Law in Germany," ibid., pp. 282–315; and Lenman and Parker, "State, Community, and Criminal Law," in Gatrell *et al.*, *Crime and the Law*, pp. 23–34.
3. Langbein, *Torture*, pp. 18–26.
4. Michel Foucault, *Discipline and Punish: The Birth of the Prison*, trans. Alan Sheridan (New York, 1978), pp. 32–42.
5. On the *Carolina* and the contemporary French criminal code, see Langbein, *Prosecuting Crime*, pp. 155–58, 171–86, 239–41, and *Torture*, pp. 3–16.
6. Langbein, *Torture*, pp. 13–14.
7. *Malleus Maleficarum*, pt. 3, questions 13–16; and Larner, *Enemies*, pp. 70, 108.
8. Lenman and Parker, "State, Community, and Criminal Law," pp. 14–15; and Larner, *"Crimen Exceptum?"* pp. 49ff.
9. On the following, see Thomas, *Religion*, pp. 436–63; Macfarlane, *Witchcraft in Tudor and Stuart England*, pp. 28–65; Christina Larner, "Witch Beliefs and Witch-Hunting in England and Scotland," *History Today*, February 1981, p. 33; and *Enemies*, p. 65.

10. Macfarlane, *Witchcraft in Tudor and Stuart England*, pp. 135–44; and Notestein, *History*, p. 195.

11. On Boguet, see Monter, *Witchcraft in France and Switzerland*, esp. pp. 69–74. On Rémy, see Christian Pfister, "Nicolas Rémy et la sorcellerie en Lorraine à la fin du XVIᵉ siècle," *Revue historique* 93 (1907): 225–39, and 94 (1907):28–44; and Dintzer, *Rémy*. On de Lancre, see chap. 3, n. 3 and 35.

12. Febvre, "Witchcraft," p. 189; E. William Monter, "Inflation and Witchcraft: The Case of Jean Bodin," in T. K. Rabb and J. E. Siegel, eds., *Action and Conviction in Early Modern Europe* (Princeton, 1969), pp. 371–89; Sydney Anglo, "Melancholia and Witchcraft: The Debate between Wier, Bodin, and Scot," in *Folie et déraison à la Renaissance* (Brussels, 1976), pp. 218–22. On Bodin's religious views, see Marion Leathers Daniel Kuntz's introduction to her edition of Jean Bodin, *Colloquium of the Seven Secrets of the Sublime* (Princeton, 1975), esp. pp. xxix–xlvi; and Christopher Baxter, "Jean Bodin's *De la Démonomanie des Sorciers*: The Logic of Persecution," in Anglo, *The Damned Art*, pp. 76–105.

13. Dewald, *Formation*, p. 318; chap. 3, n. 54.

14. Monter, *Witchcraft in France and Switzerland*, pp. 72–73.

15. Pfister, "Rémy," pp. 228–33.

16. The following discussion is drawn from Langbein, *Prosecuting Crime*, pp. 198–202; John P. Dawson, *A History of Lay Judges* (Cambridge, Mass., 1960), pp. 109–15; John P. Dawson, *The Oracles of the Law* (Ann Arbor, 1968), pp. 192–213, 260–62; Midelfort, *Witch Hunting*, pp. 22–24, 69; Midelfort, "Heartland," pp. 29–30; and Gerhard Schormann, *Hexenprozesse in Nordwestdeutschland* (Hildesheim, 1977), pp. 19–44.

17. Dupont-Bouchat, "Répression," pp. 87–91.

18. Larner, *Enemies*, pp. 69–72.

19. A translation of Spee's concluding chapter can be found in Robbins, *Encyclopedia*, pp. 481–84.

20. *Carolina*, article 47, in Langbein, *Prosecuting Crime*, p. 183.

21. See Lois Oliphant Gibbons, "A Seventeenth-Century Humanitarian: Hermann Loher," in *Persecution and Liberty: Essays in Honor of George Lincoln Burr* (New York, 1931), pp. 341–42.

22. Midelfort, *Witch Hunting*, p. 105. Cf. Kieckhefer, *Witch Trials*, pp. 90–92.

23. Midelfort, *Witch Hunting*, p. 133.

24. Midelfort, "Heartland," p. 28; cf. Larner, "*Crimen Exceptum?*" in Gatrell et al., *Crime and the Law*, p. 52.

25. Dawson, *Oracles*, p. 261.

26. Midelfort, *Witch Hunting*, pp. 112–20, 126–31; and Friedrichs, *Urban Society*, pp. 206–14.

27. Quoted by Langbein, *Torture*, p. 8.

28. Ibid., p. 148.

29. Boguet, *Examen*, appendix, articles 27–42.

30. Monter, *Witchcraft in France and Switzerland*, pp. 48–51, 105–07.

31. Cf. Monter, *Witchcraft in France and Switzerland*, pp. 88–114.

32. See Midelfort, *Witch Hunting*, pp. 98–112.

33. Ibid., p. 104. Cf. H. C. Erik Midelfort, "Witch Hunting and the Domino Theory," in Obelkevich, *Religion and the People*, pp. 277–87.

34. Midelfort, *Witch Hunting*, p. 106.

35. Ibid., pp. 104–05, 109–10.

36. Ibid., pp. 164–78.

37. In addition to works cited earlier in this chapter, see Heikinnen, *Paho-*

laisen, pp. 374–94; Ankarloo, *Trolldomsprocesserna*, pp. 324–39; and Kamen, *Spanish Inquisition*, pp. 200–09.

38. Freidrichs, *Urban Society*, pp. 212–13.

39. Ibid., p. 213.

40. Ibid.

41. Midelfort, *Witch Hunting*, p. 109.

42. Ibid., pp. 107–08.

43. See ibid., pp. 164–78.

44. Etienne Delcambre, "Les Procès de sorcellerie en Lorraine: Psychologie des juges," in *Tijdschrift voor Rechtsgeschiedenis* 21 (1953):389–419; portions appear as "Witchcraft Trials in Lorraine: The Psychology of the Judges," in Monter, *European Witchcraft*, pp. 89–95.

45. Monter, *European Witchcraft*, p. 90.

46. Ibid., p. 91.

47. Larner, *Enemies*, p. 184.

48. Foucault, *Discipline*, pp. 32–69.

49. Ariès, *Hour*, pp. 370–72.

50. *The Life of St. Theresa of Avila, Including the Relations of Her Spiritual State, Written by Herself*, trans. David Lewis (Westminster, Md., 1962), pp. 225–26; see Margaret Lewis Furse, *Mysticism: Window on a World View* (Nashville, 1977), pp. 112–24. Cf. Ariès, *Hour*, p. 377.

51. Etienne Delcambre, "The Psychology of Lorraine Witchcraft Suspects," in Monter, *European Witchcraft*, pp. 95–109, trans. of "La Psychologie des inculpés lorrains de sorcellerie," *Revue historique de droit français et étranger* (1954): 383–403, 508–26.

52. Langbein, *Torture*, p. 7; Cohn, *Demons*, pp. 160–63, 254–55; Brown, "Society and the Supernatural," pp. 135–40; Langbein, *Prosecuting Crime*, pp. 130–39; John W. Baldwin, "The Intellectual Preparation for the Canon of 1215 against Ordeals," *Speculum* 36 (1961): 613–36; Schormann, *Hexenprozesse*, pp. 118–24; Boguet, *Examen*, appendix, article 15; and Russell Zguta, "The Ordeal by Water (Swimming of Witches) in the East Slavic World," *Slavic Review* 36 (1977): 220–30.

53. Macfarlane, *Witchcraft in Tudor and Stuart England*, p. 141; and Larner, "Witch Beliefs," p. 24.

54. Delcambre, "Psychology of Suspects," p. 97.

55. Ibid., pp. 99–102.

56. Larner, *Enemies*, pp. 136.

57. See David Thoreson Lykken, *A Tremor in the Blood: Uses and Abuses of the Lie Detector* (New York, 1981), esp. pp. 63–82; and Spanos, "Witchcraft," p. 428.

58. Joan Barthel, *A Death in Canaan* (New York, 1976), pp. 39–131; cf. Lykken, *Tremor*, pp. 209–11.

59. Burr, *Narratives*, p. 377; cf. ibid., pp. 181, 189, 363.

60. Robert Jay Lifton, *Thought Reform and the Psychology of Totalism: A Study of "Brainwashing" in China* (New York, 1961), p. 13 (italics in original).

61. Ibid., p. 23.

62. Ibid., p. 41.

63. On the ability of some individuals to withstand pain in laboratory settings, see Spanos, "Witchcraft," p. 434.

64. Lifton, *Thought Reform*, p. 426; see also ibid., pp. 126–31.

65. Ibid., p. 422.

66. Ibid., p. 14.

67. Febvre, "Witchcraft," p. 191.

7. An End to Witch Hunting

1. See Thomas, *Religion*, p. 570; and Monter, *Witchcraft in France and Switzerland*, p. 37. A stimulating general discussion of the decline of witch hunting is Trevor-Roper, *European Witch-Craze*, pp. 168–192. See also Baroja, *World*, pp. 201–15; Mandrou, *Magistrats, passim.*; Macfarlane, *Witchcraft in Tudor and Stuart England*, pp. 200–07; Thomas, *Religion*, pp. 570–83, 640–68; Keith Thomas, "An Anthropology of Religion and Magic, II," *Journal of Interdisciplinary History* 6 (1975): 91–109; Monter, *Witchcraft in France and Switzerland*, pp. 37–41, 61–66, 67–87; Midelfort, *Witch Hunting*, pp. 81–84, 121–63; Larner, *Enemies*, pp. 175–91; Easlea, *Witch Hunting, Magic, and the New Philosophy*, pp. 196–222; and Joseph Klaits, "Witchcraft Trials and Absolute Monarchy in Alsace," in Richard M. Golden, ed., *Church, State, and Society under the Bourbon Kings of France* (Lawrence, Kans., 1982), pp. 148–72.

2. Thomas, *Religion*, pp. 580–83; Monter, *Witchcraft in France and Switzerland*, pp. 191–92; Larner, *Enemies*, p. 78; and Eugen Weber, *Peasants into Frenchmen* (Stanford, 1976), chap. 2.

3. Augustin Calmet, *The Phantom World* (London, 1850), pp. 134–35; first published Paris, 1746.

4. Mandrou, *Magistrats*, pp. 323–486. Cf. Soman, "Procès," pp. 790–815, and "Parlement of Paris," pp. 31–44.

5. See Mandrou's conclusions in his *Magistrats*, pp. 548–64; and excerpts in Monter, *European Witchcraft*, pp. 127–43.

6. See Dobbs, *Foundations*, pp. 25–92.

7. On similar developments in Scotland, see Larner, *Enemies*, pp. 175–91.

8. Mandrou, *Magistrats*, pp. 263–312; and B. Robert Kreiser, "The Devils of Toulon: Demonic Possession and Religious Politics in Eighteenth-Century France," in Golden, *Church, State, and Society*, pp. 173–221. See also Oskar Diethelm, "The Medical Teaching of Demonology in the Seventeenth and Eighteenth Centuries," *Journal of the History of the Behavioral Sciences* 6 (1970): 3–15.

9. Sydney Anglo, "Reginald Scot's *Discoverie of Witchcraft*: Scepticism and Sadduceeism," in Anglo, *The Damned Art*, pp. 106–39, and "Melancholia," in *Folie et déraison*, pp. 218–22.

10. *The Complete Works of Montaigne*, trans. Donald M. Frame (Stanford, 1957), p. 790. See also Alan Boase, "Montaigne et les sorciers: Une mise au point," in *Culture et politique en France à l'époque de l'humanisme et de la Renaissance* (Turin, 1974), pp. 375–86.

11. See E. William Monter, "Law, Medicine, and the Acceptance of Witchcraft, 1560–1580," in Monter, *European Witchcraft*, pp. 55–71. For another explanation of the skeptics' failure, see Leland L. Estes, "Reginald Scot and his *Discoverie of Witchcraft*: Religion and Science in the Opposition to the European Witch Craze," *Church History* 52 (1983): 444–56. The tradition of skeptical dissent about witch trials is stressed in Jonathan L. Pearl, "French Catholic Demonologists and Their Enemies in the Late Sixteenth and Early Seventeenth Centuries," *Church History* 52 (1983): 457–67.

12. See Paul Hazard, *The European Mind, 1680–1715*, trans. J. Lewis May (Cleveland, 1974).

13. Excerpts from Cyrano and Malebranche on witchcraft are in Monter, *European Witchcraft*, pp. 113–26; excerpts from Bekker can be found in Kors and Peters, *Witchcraft in Europe*, pp. 369–77.

14. MacDonald, *Mystical Bedlam*, pp. 208–17; Christopher Baxter, "Johann Weyer's *De Praestigus Daemonum*: Unsystematic Psychopathology," in Anglo, *The*

Damned Art, pp. 53–75, "Jean Bodin's *De la Démonomanie*," ibid., pp. 76–105; and Anglo, "Melancholia," in *Folie et déraison*, pp. 209–18. A fresh and suggestive analysis is provided by Leland L. Estes, "The Medical Origins of the European Witch Craze: A Hypothesis," *Journal of Social History* 17 (1983): 271–84.

15. Midelfort, *Witch Hunting*, pp. 28–29; Mandrou, *Magistrats*, p. 484; and Larner, *Enemies*, pp. 76, 108–09. On the general abandonment of judicial torture in the late seventeenth and eighteenth centuries, see Langbein, *Torture*.

16. See Michel Vovelle, *Piété baroque et déchristianisation au XVIIIᵉ siècle* (Paris, 1973).

17. For the views of Cyrano and Malebranche on Satan's powerlessness in this world, see Monter, *European Witchcraft*, pp. 118, 126. See Midelfort, *Witch Hunting*, pp. 34–56, and, on Lutheran providential theory, "Were There Really Witches?" in Robert Kingdon, ed., *Transition and Revolution: Problems and Issues of European Renaissance and Reformation History* (Minneapolis, 1974), pp. 189–233. A description of the infernal debates is in D. P. Walker, *The Decline of Hell: Seventeenth-Century Discussions of Eternal Torment* (Chicago, 1964).

18. Peter Gay, *The Enlightenment: An Interpretation* (New York, 1966–69), 2:3–55.

19. Henningsen, *Advocate*, p. 296.

20. Ibid., p. 304. See also Henningsen, "Greatest Witch Trial," pp. 36–39; and Baroja, *World*, pp. 180–89.

21. See chap. 1, n. 10.

22. See also Midelfort, *Witch Hunting*, pp. 140–41; and Monter, *Witchcraft in France and Switzerland*, pp. 127, 139, 196.

23. Bartolome Bennassar, *L'Inquisition espagnole, XVᵉ-XIXᵉ siècles* (Paris, 1979), esp. the graph on p. 23. Bennassar shows the relative insignificance of witchcraft prosecutions by the Inquisition of Toledo; cf. the comments of Geoffrey Parker, "Some Recent Works on the History of the Inquisition in Spain and Italy," *Journal of Modern History* 54 (1982): 519ff. See also Kamen, *Spanish Inquisition*, pp. 22–56, 109–20, 202–209; Henningsen, *Advocate*, pp. 22–23, 388–89; Trevor-Roper, *European Witch-Craze*, pp. 108–13; and Monter, *Witchcraft in France and Switzerland*, pp. 119–20.

24. Burke, *Popular Culture*, pp. 234–43, 270–81; and J. M. Goulemot, "Démons, merveilles et philosophie à l'âge classique," *Annales: Economies, Sociétés, Civilisations* 35 (1980): 1223–50.

25. Midelfort, *Witch Hunting*, pp. 121–63.

26. Ibid., pp. 81–82; Larner, *Enemies*, pp. 76–77, 116–17; Klaits, "Absolute Monarchy," in Golden, *Church, State, and Society*, pp. 158–59; and Mandrou, *Magistrats*, pp. 493–96.

27. Soman, "Procès," pp. 790–815, and "Parlement of Paris," pp. 31–44; and Hoffer and Hull, *Murdering Mothers*, pp. 65ff.

28. The following discussion is drawn from Lougee, *Paradis*, pp. 11–55; Ian Maclean, *Woman Triumphant: Feminism in French Literature, 1610–1652* (Oxford, 1977), esp. chaps. 1–3.; Thomas, *Religion*, p. 569; and, above all, Stone, *Family*, pp. 325–404, 483–545.

29. Quoted in the English translation, Laurent Bordelon, *History of the Ridiculous Extravagances of Monsieur Oufle*, (London, 1711), p. 202.

30. François de Saint-André, *Lettres au sujet de la magie, des maléfices et des sorciers* (Paris, 1725), pp. 109–40; cf. Emmanuel Le Roy Ladurie, "The Aiguillete: Castration by Magic," in Le Roy Ladurie, *The Mind and Method of the Historian*, trans. Sian Reynolds and Ben Reynolds (Chicago, 1981)., pp. 84–96.

31. *The Spectator*, no. 117, July 14, 1711, quoted by Phyllis J. Guskin, "The Context of Witchcraft: The Case of Jane Wenham (1712)," *Eighteenth Century Studies* 15 (1981): 58.

32. Kay S. Wilkins, "Attitudes to Witchcraft and Demonic Possession in France during the Eighteenth Century," *Journal of European Studies* 3 (1973): 359–60. On the decline of the occult tradition in colonial North America, see Jon Butler, "Magic, Astrology, and the Early American Religious Heritage, 1600–1760," *American Historical Review* 84 (1979): 317–46. On the revival of the occult in the late eighteenth century, see Robert Darnton, *Mesmerism and the End of the Enlightenment in France* (Cambridge, Mass., 1968); and Nicholas P. Spanos and Jack Gottlieb, "Demonic Possession, Mesmerism, and Hysteria: A Social Psychological Perspective on Their Historical Interrelations," *Journal of Abnormal Psychology* 88 (1979): 527–46.

Bibliography

Anglo, Sydney. "Evident Authority and Authoritative Evidence: The *Malleus Maleficarum.*" In Anglo, *The Damned Art.*

Anglo, Sydney. "Melancholia and Witchcraft: The Debate between Wier, Bodin, and Scot." In *Folie et déraison à la Renaissance.*

Anglo, Sydney. "Reginald Scot's *Discoverie of Witchcraft*: Scepticism and Sadduceeism." in Anglo, *The Damned Art.*

Anglo, Sydney, ed. *The Damned Art: Essays in the Literature of Witchcraft.* London, 1977.

Ankarloo, Bengt. *Trolldomsprocesserna i Sverige.* Stockholm, 1971.

Ariès, Philippe. *The Hour of our Death.* Translated by Helen Weaver. New York, 1981.

Ariès, Philippe. *Western Attitudes toward Death from the Middle Ages to the Present.* Translated by Patricia M. Ranum. Baltimore, 1974.

Aston, Trevor, ed. *Crisis in Europe, 1560–1660.* London, 1965.

Bakhtin, Mikhail. *Rabelais and His World.* Translated by Helene Iswolsky. Cambridge, Mass., 1968.

Baldwin, John W. "The Intellectual Preparation for the Canon of 1215 against Ordeals." *Speculum* 36 (1961): 613–36.

Barber, Malcolm. *The Trial of the Templars.* Cambridge, 1978.

Barkun, Michael. *Disaster and the Millennium.* New York, 1974.

Barnett, Bernard. "Witchcraft, Psychopathology, and Hallucinations." *British Journal of Psychiatry* 3 (1965): 439–45.

Baroja, Julio Caro. *The World of the Witches.* Translated by O. N. V. Glindinning. Chicago, 1955.

Baron, Salo Wittmayer. *A Social and Religious History of the Jews.* 18 vols. New York, 1952–1983.

Barthel, Joan. *A Death in Canaan.* New York, 1976.

Bavoux, François. *Hantises et diableries dans la terre abbatiale de Luxeil.* Monaco, 1956.

Baxter, Christopher. "Jean Bodin's *De la démonomanie des sorciers*: The Logic of Persecution." In Anglo, *The Damned Art.*

Baxter, Christopher. "Johann Weyer's *De Praestigus Daemonum*: Unsystematic Psychopathology." In Anglo, *The Damned Art.*

Benedek, Thomas G. "The Changing Relationship between Midwives and Physicians during the Renaissance." *Bulletin of the History of Medicine* 51 (1977): 550–64.

Benedict, Philip. "The Catholic Response to Protestantism: Church Activity and Popular Piety in Rouen, 1560–1600." In Obelkevich, *Religion and the People, 800–1700.*

Bennassar, Bartolome. *L'Inquisition espagnole, XVᵉ–XIXᵉ siècles.* Paris, 1979.

Bloch, Marc. *Land and Work in Medieval Europe.* Translated by J. E. Anderson. Berkeley, 1967.

Bloch, Marc. *The Royal Touch: Sacred Monarchy and Scrofula in France and England*. Translated by J. E. Anderson. London, 1973.

Boase, Alan. "Montaigne et les sorciers: Une mise au point." In *Culture et politique en France à l'époque de l'humanisme et de la Renaissance*." Turin, 1974.

Bodin, Jean. *Colloquium of the Seven about Secrets of the Sublime*. Edited and trans. by Marion Leathers Daniel Kuntz. Princeton, 1975.

Bodin, Jean. *De la démonomanie des sorciers*. Paris, 1580.   •

Boguet, Henri. *An Examen of Witches*. N.p., 1929.

Bordelon, Laurent. *History of the Ridiculous Extravagances of Monsieur Oufle*. London, 1711.

Bossy, John. "The Counter-Reformation and the People of Catholic Europe." *Past and Present* 47 (1970): 51–70.

Boswell, John. *Christianity, Social Tolerance, and Homosexuality: Gay People in Western Europe from the Beginning of the Christian Era to the Fourteenth Century*. Chicago, 1980.

Bouwsma, William J. "Christian Adulthood." *Daedalus*, Spring 1976, pp. 77–92.

Bowsky, William, ed. *The Black Death: A Turning Point in History?* New York, 1971.

Boyer, Paul, and Nissenbaum, Stephen. *Salem Possessed: The Social Origins of Witchcraft*. Cambridge, Mass., 1974.

Bridenthal, Renate, and Koonz, Claudia, eds. *Becoming Visible: Women in European History*. Boston, 1977.

Brown, Peter. "Society and the Supernatural: A Medieval Change." *Daedalus*, Spring 1975, pp. 135–40.

Brown, Peter. "Sorcery, Demons, and the Rise of Christianity from Late Antiquity into the Middle Ages." In Douglas, *Witchcraft Confessions and Accusations*.

Brucker, Gene A. "Sorcery in Early Renaissance Florence." *Studies in the Renaissance* 10 (1963): 7–24.

Bullough, Vern L. *The Subordinate Sex: A History of Attitudes toward Women*. Urbana, 1973.

Burke, Peter. *Popular Culture in Early Modern Europe*. New York, 1978.

Burke, Peter. "Witchcraft and Magic in Renaissance Italy: Gianfrancesco Pico and His Strix." In Anglo, *The Damned Art*.

Burr, George Lincoln, ed. *Narratives of the Witchcraft Cases, 1648–1706*. New York, 1914.

Burr, George Lincoln, ed. *Translations and Reprints from the Original Sources of European History*. Philadelphia, 1896.

Butler, E. M. *Ritual Magic*. Cambridge, 1949.

Butler, Jon. "Magic, Astrology, and the Early American Religious Heritage, 1600–1760." *American Historical Review* 84 (1979): 317–46.

Calmet, Augustin. *The Phantom World*. London, 1850.

Caporael, Linnda R. "Ergotism: The Satan Loosed in Salem?" *Science* 192 (1976), pp. 21–26.

Cappanari, Stephen A. *et al.* "Voodoo in the General Hospital: A Case of Hexing and Regional Enteritis." *Journal of the American Medical Association* 232 (1975): 938–40.

Caulfield, Ernest. "Pediatric Aspects of the Salem Witchcraft Tragedy." *American Journal of Diseases of Children* 65 (1943): 798–801.

Christian, William A., Jr. *Local Religion in Sixteenth-Century Spain*. Princeton, 1981.

Cipolla, Carlo. *Faith, Reason, and the Plague in Seventeenth-Century Tuscany*. Translated by Muriel Kittel. Ithaca, 1979.

Clark, Peter. "The Alehouse and the Alternative Society." In Pennington and Thomas, *Puritans and Revolutionaries*.

Clark, Stuart. "Inversion, Misrule, and the Meaning of Witchcraft." *Past and Present*, no. 87 (1980), pp. 98–127.

Cockburn, J. S., ed. *Crime in England, 1550–1800*. London, 1977.

Cohen, Kathleen. *Metamorphosis of a Death Symbol: The Transi Tomb in the Late Middle Ages and the Renaissance*. Berkeley, 1973.

Cohn, Norman. *Europe's Inner Demons*. London, 1975.

Cohn, Norman. *The Pursuit of the Millennium*. Rev. ed. New York, 1970.

Coleman, Emily. "Infanticide in the Early Middle Ages." In Stuard, *Women in Medieval Society*.

Copenhaver, Brian. *Symphorien Champier and the Reception of the Occult Tradition in France*. The Hague, 1978.

Coulton, G. G. *Inquisition and Liberty*. London, 1938.

Culture et politique en France à l'époque de l'humanisme et de la Renaissance. Turin, 1974.

Dahm, Georg. "On the Reception of Roman and Italian Law in Germany." In Strauss, *Pre-Reformation Germany*.

Darnton, Robert. *Mesmerism and the End of the Enlightenment in France*. Cambridge, Mass., 1968.

Davis, Natalie Zemon. *Society and Culture in Early Modern France*. Stanford, 1975.

Davis, Natalie Zemon. "Some Tasks and Themes in the Study of Popular Religion." In Trinkaus and Oberman, *The Pursuit of Holiness in Late Medieval and Renaissance Religion*.

Dawson, John P. *A History of Lay Judges*. Cambridge, Mass., 1960.

Dawson, John P. *The Oracles of the Law*. Ann Arbor, 1968.

De Lancre, Pierre. *Tableau de l'inconstance des mauvais anges et démons*. Paris, 1612.

Delcambre, Etienne. "La Psychologie des inculpés lorrains de sorcellerie." *Revue historique de droit français et étranger* (1954): 383–403, 508–26.

Delcambre, Etienne. *Le Concept de la sorcellerie dans le duché de Lorraine au XVIᵉ et au XVIIᵉ siècles*. 3 vols. Nancy, 1951.

Delcambre, Etienne. "Les Procès de sorcellerie en Lorraine: Psychologie des juges." *Tijdschrift voor Rechtsgeschiedenis* 21 (1953): 389–419.

Delcambre, Etienne and Lhermitte, J. *Un Cas énigmatique de possession diabolique en Lorraine au XVIIᵉ siècle: Elisabeth de Ranfaing, l'énergumène de Nancy*. Nancy, 1955.

Delumeau, Jean. *Catholicism between Luther and Voltaire*. Translated by Jeremy Moiser. New York, 1977.

Delumeau, Jean. *La Peur en occident, XIVᵉ–XVIIᵉ siècles*. Paris, 1978.

DeMause, Lloyd, ed. *The History of Childhood*. New York, 1974.

Demos, John P. *Entertaining Satan: Witchcraft and the Culture of Early New England*. New York, 1982.

Demos, John P. "Underlying Themes in the Witchcraft of Seventeenth-Century New England." *American Historical Review* 75 (1970): 1311–26.

Dewald, Jonathan. *The Formation of a Provincial Nobility: The Magistrates of the Parlement of Rouen, 1499–1610*. Princton, 1980.

Dewald, Jonathan. "The Perfect Magistrate: Parlementaires and Crime in Sixteenth-Century Rouen." *Archiv für Reformationsgeschichte* 67 (1976): 285–99.

Diethelm, Oskar. "The Medical Teaching of Demonology in the Seventeenth and Eighteenth Centuries." *Journal of the History of the Behavioral Sciences* 6 (1970): 3–15.

Dintzer, Lucien. *Nicolas Rémy et son oeuvre démonologique*. Lyon, 1936.

Dobbs, Betty Jo Teeter. *The Foundations of Newton's Alchemy*. Cambridge, 1975.
Donegan, Jane B. *Women and Men Midwives: Medicine, Morality, and Misogyny in Early America*. Westport, Conn., 1978.
Douglas, Mary, ed. *Witchcraft Confessions and Accusations*. London, 1970.
Drake, Frederick C. "Witchcraft in the American Colonies." *American Quarterly* 20 (1968): 695–725.
Dupont-Bouchat, Marie Sylvie. "La Répression de la sorcellerie dans le duché de Luxembourg aux XVIᵉ et XVIIᵉ siècles." In Muchembled *et al.*, *Prophètes et sorciers*.
Easlea, Brian. *Witch Hunting, Magic, and the New Philosophy: An Introduction to Debates of the Scientific Revolution*. Atlantic Highlands, N.J., 1980.
Eisenstadt, S. N., ed. *Max Weber on Charisma and Institution Building*. Chicago, 1968.
Eisenstadt, S. N., ed. *The Protestant Ethic and Modernization*. New York, 1968.
Eisenstein, Elizabeth L. *The Printing Press as an Agent of Change*. 2 vols. Cambridge, 1979.
Elias, Norbert. *The Civilizing Process: The History of Manners*. Translated by Edmund Jephcott. New York, 1978.
Ellenberger, Henri. *The Discovery of the Unconscious*. New York, 1970.
Estes, Leland L. "Reginald Scot and his *Discoverie of Witchcraft*: Religion and Science in the Opposition to the European Witch Craze." *Church History* 52 (1983): 444–56.
Estes, Leland L. "The Medical Origins of the European Witch Craze: A Hypothesis." *Journal of Social History* 17 (1983): 271–84.
Evans, Austin P. "Hunting Subversion in the Middle Ages." *Speculum* 33 (1958): 1–22.
Evans, R. J. W. *The Making of the Habsburg Monarchy*. Oxford, 1979.
Evans-Pritchard, E. E. *Witchcraft, Oracles, and Magic among the Azande*. Oxford, 1937.
Fatio, Olivier. "Lambert Daneau." In Raitt, *Shapers of Religious Traditions in Germany, Switzerland, and Poland, 1560–1660*.
Febvre, Lucien. *A New Kind of History and Other Essays*. Edited by Peter Burke. New York, 1973.
Flandrin, Jean-Louis. "Contraception, Marriage, and Sexual Relations in the Christian West." In Forster and Ranum, *Biology in Man in History*.
Flandrin, Jean-Louis. *Families in Past Times*. Translated by Richard Southern. New York, 1979.
Flandrin, Jean-Louis. "Repression and Change in the Sexual Life of Young People in Medieval and Early Modern Times." In Wheaton and Hareven, *Family and Sexuality in French History*.
Folie et déraison à la Renaissance. Brussels, 1976.
Forbes, Thomas R. "Midwifery and Witchcraft." *Journal of the History of Medicine* 17 (1962): 264–83.
Forbes, Thomas R. "The Changing Face of Death in London." In Webster, *Health, Medicine, and Mortality*.
Forbes, Thomas R., ed. *The Midwife and the Witch*. New Haven, 1966.
Forster, Robert, and Ranum, Orest, eds. *Biology of Man in History: Essays from the Annales*. Baltimore, 1975.
Forster, Robert, and Ranum, Orest, eds. *Ritual, Religion, and the Sacred: Essays from the Annales*. Baltimore, 1982.
Foucault, Michel. *Discipline and Punish: The Birth of the Prison*. Translated by Alan Sheridan. New York, 1978.

Foucault, Michel. *The History of Sexuality.* 3 vols. Translated by Robert Hurley. New York, 1978.

Fox, Sanford J. *Science and Justice: The Massachusetts Witchcraft Trials.* Baltimore, 1968.

Frank, Jerome D. *Persuasion and Healing.* Baltimore, 1973.

Freud, Sigmund. *Complete Psychological Works.* Edited by J. Strachey *et al.* 24 vols. New York, 1953–74.

Friedrichs, Christopher R. *Urban Society in an Age of War: Nördlingen, 1580–1720.* Princeton, 1979.

Furse, Margaret Lewis. *Mysticism: Window on a World View.* Nashville, 1977.

Garrett, Clarke. "Women and Witches: Patterns of Analysis." *Signs* 3 (1977): 461–70.

Gatrell, V. A. C.; Lenman, Bruce; and Parker, Geoffrey, eds. *Crime and the Law.* London, 1980.

Gay, Peter. *The Enlightenment: An Interpretation.* 2 vols. New York, 1966–69.

George, Carol V. R., ed. *"Remember the Ladies": New Perspectives on Women in American History.* Syracuse, 1975.

Gibbons, Louis Oliphant. "A Seventeenth-Century Humanitarian: Hermann Loher." In *Persecution and Liberty: Essays in Honor of George Lincoln Burr.* New York, 1931.

Ginzburg, Carlo. *The Cheese and the Worms.* Translated by John Tedeschi and Anne Tedeschi. Baltimore, 1980.

Ginzburg, Carlo. *The Night Battles: Witchcraft and Agrarian Cults in the Sixteenth and Seventeenth Centuries.* Translated by John Tedeschi and Anne Tedeschi. Baltimore, 1983.

Girouard, Mark. *Life in the English Country House.* New Haven, 1978.

Glass, D. V., and Eversley, D. E. C., eds. *Population and History.* Chicago, 1965.

Golden, Richard M., ed. *Church, State, and Society under the Bourbon Kings of France.* Lawrence, Kans., 1982.

Goubert, Pierre. *Cent mille provinciaux au XVIIe siècle: Beauvais et la Beauvaisis de 1600 à 1730.* Paris, 1968.

Goubert, Pierre. "The French Peasantry of the Seventeenth Century: A Regional Example." In Aston, *Crisis in Europe, 1560–1660.*

Green, Robert W., ed. *Protestantism, Capitalism, and Social Science: The Weber Thesis Controversy.* 2d ed. Boston, 1973.

Guazzo, Francesco Maria. *Compendium Maleficarum.* Translated by Montague Summers. New York, 1974.

Guskin, Phyllis J. "The Context of Witchcraft: The Case of Jane Wenham (1712)." *Eighteenth Century Studies* 15 (1981): 48–71.

Hajnal, John. "European Marriage Patterns in Perspective." In Glass and Eversley, *Population and History.*

Hansen, Chadwick. *Witchcraft at Salem.* New York, 1969.

Harding, Robert J. "Revolutions and Reform in the Holy League: Angers, Rennes, Nantes." *Journal of Modern History* 53 (1981): 379–416.

Harner, Michael J. *Hallucinogens and Shamanism.* New York, 1973.

Harris, Marvin. *Cows, Pigs, Wars, and Witches: The Riddles of Culture.* New York, 1974.

Hazard, Paul. *The European Mind, 1680–1715.* Translated by J. Lewis May. Cleveland, 1974.

Heer, Friedrich. *The Medieval World.* Translated by Janet Sondheimer. London, 1962.

Heikinnen, Antero. *Paholaisen Liittolaiset.* Helsinki, 1969.

Henningsen, Gustav. "The Greatest Witch-Trial of Them All: Navarre, 1609–1614." *History Today*, November, 1980, pp. 36–39.

Henningsen, Gustav. *The Witches' Advocate*. Reno, 1980.

Heyd, Michael. "The Reaction to Enthusiasm in the Seventeenth Century: Towards an Integrative Approach." *Journal of Modern History* 53 (1981): 258–63.

Hill, Christopher. *The World Turned Upside Down: Radical Ideas during the English Revolution*. New York, 1973.

Hoak, Dale. "Witch Hunting and Women in the Art of the Renaissance." *History Today*, February 1981, pp. 22–26.

Hoffer, Peter C., and Hull, N. E. H. *Murdering Mothers: Infanticide in England and New England, 1558–1803*. New York, 1981.

Hopkin, Charles Edward. *The Share of Thomas Aquinas in the Growth of the Witchcraft Delusion*. Philadelphia, 1940.

Huizinga, Jan. *The Waning of the Middle Ages*. Garden City, N.Y., 1954.

Huxley, Aldous. *The Devils of Loudun*. New York, 1952.

Jacob, Margaret C. *The Newtonians and the English Revolution, 1689–1720*. Ithaca, 1976.

James I. *Demonology*. London, 1603.

Jones, William R. "The Political Uses of Sorcery in Medieval Europe." *The Historian* 34 (1972): 670–82.

Jordan, Winthrop D. *White over Black: American Attitudes toward the Negro, 1550–1812*. Chapel Hill, 1968.

Kamen, Henry. *The Spanish Inquisition*. New York, 1965.

Kelly, J. N. D. *Jerome: His Life, Writings, and Controversies*. New York, 1975.

Kelso, Ruth. *Doctrine for the Lady of the Renaissance*. Urbana, 1956.

Kieckhefer, Richard. *European Witch Trials: Their Foundations in Popular and Learned Culture, 1300–1500*. Berkeley, 1976.

Kingdon, Robert, ed. *Transition and Revolution: Problems and Issues of European Renaissance and Reformation History*. Minneapolis, 1974.

Kinsman, Robert S., ed. *The Darker Vision of the Renaissance*. Berkeley, 1974.

Kittredge, G. L. *Witchcraft in Old and New England*. Cambridge, Mass., 1929.

Klaits, Joseph. "Witchcraft Trials and Absolute Monarchy in Alsace." In Golden, *Church, State, and Society under the Bourbon Kings.*

Koch, Robert A. *Hans Baldung Grien: Eve, the Serpent, and Death*. Ottawa, 1974.

Kors, Alan C., and Peters, Edward, eds. *Witchcraft in Europe, 1100–1700: A Documentary History*. Philadelphia, 1972.

Kreiser, B. Robert. *Miracles, Convulsions, and Ecclesiastical Politics in Early Eighteenth-Century Paris*. Princeton, 1978.

Kreiser, B. Robert. "The Devils of Toulon: Demonic Possession and Religious Politics in Eighteenth-Century France." In Golden, *Church, State, and Society.*

Kunkel, Wolfgang. "The Reception of Roman Law in Germany: An Interpretation." In Strauss, *Pre-Reformation Germany.*

Langbein, John H. *Prosecuting Crime in the Renaissance*. Cambridge, Mass., 1974.

Langbein, John H. *Torture and the Law of Proof: Europe and England in the Ancien Régime*. Chicago, 1977.

Larner, Christina. "*Crimen Exceptum?* The Crime of Witchcraft in Europe." In Gatrell, *Crime and the Law.*

Larner, Christina. *Enemies of God: The Witch-Hunt in Scotland*. Baltimore, 1981.

Larner, Christina. "Witch Beliefs and Witch-Hunting in England and Scotland." *History Today*, February 1981, pp. 32–36.

Lea, Henry Charles. *A History of the Inquisition in the Middle Ages*. 3 vols. New York, 1888.

Lea, Henry Charles. *Materials toward a History of Witchcraft*. 3 vols. Philadelphia, 1939.

Leff, Gordon. *Heresy in the Later Middle Ages*. 2 vols. Manchester, 1967.

Lenman, Bruce, and Parker, Geoffrey. "The State, the Community, and the Criminal Law in Early Modern Europe." In Gatrell, *Crime and the Law*.

Le Roy Ladurie, Emmanuel. *Carnival in Romans*. Translated by Mary Feeney. New York, 1979.

Le Roy Ladurie, Emmanuel. *Les Paysans de Languedoc*. Paris, 1966.

Le Roy Ladurie, Emmanuel. *Montaillou*. Translated by Barbara Bray. New York, 1978.

Le Roy Ladurie, Emmanuel. "The Aiguillete: Castration by Magic." In Le Roy Ladurie, *The Mind and Method of the Historian*. Translated by Sian Reynolds and Ben Reynolds. Chicago, 1981.

Leventhal, Herbert. *In the Shadow of the Enlightenment: Occultism and Renaissance Science in Eighteenth-Century America*. New York, 1972.

Lewis, I. M. *Ecstatic Religion*. Baltimore, 1971.

Lifton, Robert Jay. *Thought Reform and the Psychology of Totalism: A Study of "Brainwashing" in China*. New York, 1961.

Lougee, Carolyn C. *Le Paradis des femmes: Women, Salons, and Social Stratification in Seventeenth-Century France*. Princeton, 1976.

Lykken, David Thoreson. *A Tremor in the Blood: Uses and Abuses of the Lie Detector*. New York, 1981.

MacDonald, Michael. *Mystical Bedlam: Madness, Anxiety, and Healing in Seventeenth-Century England*. Cambridge, 1981.

Macfarlane, Alan. *The Origins of English Individualism*. Cambridge, 1979.

Macfarlane, Alan. *Witchcraft in Tudor and Stuart England*. London, 1970.

MacLachlan, Hugh V., and Swales, J. K. "Lord Hale, Witches, and Rape." *British Journal of Law and Society* 5 (1978): 251–61.

Maclean, Ian. *The Renaissance Notion of Women*. Cambridge, 1980.

Maclean, Ian. *Woman Triumphant: Feminism in French Literature, 1610–1652*. Oxford, 1977.

Malcolmson, R. W. "Infanticide in the Eighteenth Century." In Cockburn, *Crime in England, 1550–1800*.

Mandrou, Robert. *De la culture populaire au XVIIᵉ et XVIIIᵉ siècles: La Bibliothèque bleue de Troyes*. Paris, 1964.

Mandrou, Robert. *Magistrats et sorciers en France au XVIIᵉ siècle*. Paris, 1968.

Mappen, Marc, ed. *Witches and Historians: Interpretations of Salem*. Huntington, N.Y., 1980.

Marwick, Max, ed. *Witchcraft and Sorcery*. Baltimore, 1970.

Matthews, George T., ed. *News and Rumor in Renaissance Europe: The Fugger Newsletters*. New York, 1959.

Mayer, Milton. *They Thought They Were Free: The Germans, 1933–1945*. Chicago, 1955.

Mayer, Philip. "Witches." In Marwick, *Witchcraft and Sorcery*.

McGowan, Margaret M. "Pierre de Lancre's Tableau." In Anglo, *The Damned Art*.

Michelet, Jules. *Satanism and Witchcraft*. New York, 1939.

Midelfort, H. C. Erik. "Heartland of the Witchcraze: Central and Northern Europe." *History Today*, February 1981, pp. 29–30.

Midelfort, H. C. Erik. "Were There Really Witches?" In Kingdon, *Transition and Revolution*.

Midelfort, H. C. Erik. "Witchcraft and Religion in Sixteenth-Century Germany: The Formation and Consequences of an Orthodoxy." *Archiv für Reformationsgeschichte* 62 (1971): 266–78.

Midelfort, H. C. Erik. "Witch Hunting and the Domino Theory." In Obelkevich, *Religion and the People.*

Midelfort, H. C. Erik. *Witch Hunting in Southwestern Germany, 1562–1684.* Stanford, 1972.

Montaigne, Michel de. *The Complete Works of Montaigne.* Translated by Donald M. Frame. Stanford, 1957.

Monter, E. William. *European Witchcraft.* New York, 1969.

Monter, E. William. "Inflation and Witchcraft: The Case of Jean Bodin." In Rabb and Siegel, *Action and Conviction in Early Modern Europe.*

Monter, E. William. "La Sodomie à l'époque moderne en Suisse romande." *Annales: Economies, Sociétés, Civilisations* 29 (1974): 1023–33.

Monter, E. William. "Pedestal and Stake: Courtly Love and Witchcraft." In Bridenthal and Koonz, *Becoming Visible: Women in European History.*

Monter, E. William. *Witchcraft in France and Switzerland: The Borderlands in the Reformation.* Ithaca, 1976.

Muchembled, Robert. *Culture populaire et culture des élites dans la France moderne.* Paris, 1978.

Muchembled, Robert. *Les Derniers bûchers.* Paris, 1981.

Muchembled, Robert. "The Witches of the Cambrésis: The Acculturation of the Rural World in the Sixteenth and Seventeenth Centuries." In Obelkevich, *Religion and the People, 800–1700.*

Muchembled, Robert; Dupont-Bouchat, Marie-Sylvie; and Frijhoff, William. *Prophètes et sorciers dans les Pays-Bas, XVIe–XVIIIe siècles.* Paris, 1978.

Naroll, Raoul. "A Tentative Index of Cultural Stress." *International Journal of Social Psychiatry* 5 (1959): 107–16.

Newall, Venetia, ed. *The Witch Figure.* London, 1973.

Nicholls, David. "The Devil in Renaissance France." *History Today,* November 1980, pp. 25–30.

Noonan, John T., Jr. *Contraception: A History of Its Treatment by the Catholic Theologians and Canonists.* Cambridge, Mass., 1965.

Notestein, Wallace. *The History of English Witchcraft.* Reprint. New York, 1968.

Obelkevich, James, ed. *Religion and the People, 800–1700.* Chapel Hill, 1979.

Oesterreich, T. K. *Possession, Demoniacal and Other.* London, 1930.

Owen, D. D. R. *The Vision of Hell: Infernal Journeys in Medieval French Literature.* Edinburgh, 1970.

Palmer, Colin A. *Slaves of the White God: Blacks in Mexico, 1570–1660.* Cambridge, Mass., 1976.

Parker, Geoffrey. "Some Recent Works on the History of the Inquisition in Spain and Italy." *Journal of Modern History* 54 (1982): 519–32.

Pearl, Jonathan L. "French Catholic Demonologists and Their Enemies in the Late Sixteenth and Early Seventeenth Centuries." *Church History* 52 (1983): 457–67.

Pearl, Jonathan L. "Witchcraft in New France in the Seventeenth Century: The Social Aspect." *Historical Reflections* 4 (1977): 191–205.

Pennington, Donald, and Thomas, Keith, eds. *Puritans and Revolutionaries: Essays in Seventeenth-Century History Presented to Christopher Hill.* Oxford, 1978.

Peter, Jean-Pierre. "Disease and the Sick at the End of the Old Regime." In Forster and Ranum, *Biology of Man in History.*

Peters, Edward. *The Magician, the Witch, and the Law.* Philadelphia, 1978.

Pfister, Christian. "Nicolas Rémy et la sorcellerie en Lorraine à la fin du XVIe siècle." *Revue historique* 93 (1907): 225–39; 94 (1907): 28–44.

Poliakov, Leon. *The History of Anti-Semitism from the Time of Christ to the Court Jews.* Translated by Richard Howard. New York, 1974.

Pomeroy, Sarah D. *Goddesses, Whores, Wives, and Slaves: Women in Classical Antiquity*. New York, 1975.

Rabb, Theodore K., and Siegel, Jerrold E., eds. *Action and Conviction in Early Modern Europe*. Princeton, 1969.

Rabb, Theodore K. *The Struggle for Stability in Early Modern Europe*. New York, 1975.

Rabelais, François. *The Histories of Gargantua and Pentagruel*. Translated by John M. Cohen. Baltimore, 1955.

Raitt, Jill, ed. *Shapers of Religious Traditions in Germany, Switzerland, and Poland, 1560–1660*. New Haven, 1981.

Ranum, Orest. "Courtesy, Absolutism, and the Rise of the French State, 1630–1660." *Journal of Modern History* 52 (1980): 426–51.

Rappaport, Herbert, and Rappaport, Margaret. "The Integration of Scientific and Traditional Healing: A Proposed Model." *American Psychologist* 36 (1981): 774–81.

Rémy, Nicolas. *Demonolatry*. Edited by Montague Summers. 1595; New York, 1974.

Richet, Denis. "Aspects socio-culturels des conflits religieux à Paris dans la seconde moitié du XVIᵉ siècle." *Annales: Economies, Sociétés, Civilisations* 32 (1977): 764–89.

Robbins, Rossell Hope. *The Encyclopedia of Witchcraft and Demonology*. New York, 1959.

Rojas, Fernando de. *La Celestina*. Translated by L. B. Simpson. Berkeley, 1955.

Rose, Elliot. *A Razor for a Goat*. Toronto, 1962.

Rothkrug, Lionel. "Religious Practices and Collective Perceptions: Hidden Homologies in the Renaissance and Reformation." *Historical Reflections* 7 (1980): 1–171.

Rousselle, Aline. "From Sanctuary to Miracle Worker: Healing in Fourth-Century Gaul." In Forster and Ranum, *Ritual, Religion, and the Sacred*.

Runeberg, Arno. *Witches, Demons, and Fertility*. Helsinki, 1947.

Russell, Jeffry B. *The Devil: Perceptions of Evil from Antiquity to Primitive Christianity*. Ithaca, 1977.

Russell, Jeffry B. *Dissent and Reform in the Early Middle Ages*. Berkeley, 1965.

Russell, Jeffry B. *Satan: The Early Christian Tradition*. Ithaca, 1981.

Russell, Jeffry B. *Witchcraft in the Middle Ages*. Ithaca, 1972.

Saint-André, François de. *Lettres au sujet de la magie, des maléfices et des sorciers*. Paris, 1725.

Schoeneman, Thomas J. "The Role of Mental Illness in the European Witch Hunts of the Sixteenth and Seventeenth Centuries: An Assessment." *Journal of the History of the Behavioral Sciences* 18 (1977): 337–51.

Schormann, Gerhard. *Hexenprozesse in Nordwestdeutschland*. Hildesheim, 1977.

Schwartz, Hillel. *The French Prophets*. Berkeley, 1980.

Sheppard, Thomas F. *Lourmarin in the Eighteenth Century*. Baltimore, 1971.

Shumaker, Wayne. *The Occult Sciences in the Renaissance*. Berkeley, 1972.

Siegel, Friedrich Wilhelm. *Die Hexenverfolgung in Köln*. Bonn, 1959.

Sigal, P. A. "Miracles et guérisons au XIIᵉ siècle." *Annales: Economies, Sociétés, Civilisations* 24 (1969): 1522–39.

Slack, Paul. "Mortality Crises and Epidemics, 1485–1610." In Webster, *Health, Medicine, and Mortality in the Sixteenth Century*.

Spanos, Nicholas P. "Witchcraft in Histories of Psychiatry: A Critical Analysis and an Alternative Conceptualization." *Psychological Bulletin* 85 (1978): 417–39.

Spanos, Nicholas P., and Gottlieb, Jack. "Demonic Possession, Mesmerism, and

Hysteria: A Social Psychological Perspective on Their Historical Interactions."
Journal of Abnormal Psychology 88 (1979): 527–46.
Spanos, Nicholas P., and Gottlieb, Jack. "Ergotism and the Salem Village Witch
Trials." *Science* 194 (1976), pp. 1390–94.
Sprenger, Jakob, and Kramer, Heinrich. *Malleus Maleficarum*. Translated by Mon-
tague Summers. London, 1928.
Stone, Lawrence. *The Family, Sex, and Marriage in England, 1500–1800*. New
York, 1977.
Strauss, Gerald, ed. *Pre-Reformation Germany*. New York, 1972.
Stuard, Susan Mosher, ed. *Women in Medieval Society*. Philadelphia, 1976.
Szasz, Thomas S. *The Manufacture of Madness*. New York, 1970.
Tackett, Timothy. *Priest and Parish in Eighteenth-Century France*. Princeton, 1976.
Teall, John L. "Witchcraft and Calvinism in Elizabethan England: Divine Power
and Human Agency." *Journal of the History of Ideas* 23 (1962): 21–36.
Tentler, Thomas N. *Sin and Confession on the Eve of the Reformation*. Princeton,
1977.
Theresa of Avila, Saint. *The Life of St. Theresa of Avila, Including the Relations of
Her Spiritual State, Written by Herself*. Translated by David Lewis. Westmin-
ster, Md. 1962.
Thomas, Keith. "An Anthropology of Religion and Magic, II." *Journal of Interdisci-
plinary History* 6 (1975): 91–109.
Thomas, Keith. *Religion and the Decline of Magic*. New York, 1971.
Thomas, Keith. "The Puritans and Adultery: The Act of 1650 Reconsidered." In
Pennington and Thomas, *Puritans and Revolutionaries*.
Thomas, Keith. "Women and the Civil War Sects." In Aston, *Crisis in Europe,
1560–1660*.
Thomas, M. Wynn. "Cotton Mather's *Wonders of the Invisible World*: Some Meta-
morphoses of Salem Witchcraft." In Anglo, *The Damned Art*.
Trevor-Roper, H. R. *The European Witch-Craze of the Sixteenth and Seventeenth
Centuries and Other Essays*. New York, 1969.
Trexler, R. "Infanticide in Florence." *History of Childhood Quarterly*, 1 (1973):
98–116.
Trinkaus, Charles, and Oberman, Heiko A., eds. *The Pursuit of Holiness in Late
Medieval and Renaissance Religion*. Leiden, 1974.
Vovelle, Michel. *Piété baroque et déchristianisation au XVIIIᵉ siècle*. Paris, 1973.
Walker, D. P. *The Decline of Hell: Seventeenth-Century Discussions of Eternal Tor-
ment*. Chicago, 1964.
Walker, D. P. *Spiritual and Demonic Magic from Ficino to Campanella*. London,
1958.
Walker, D. P. *Unclean Spirits: Possession and Exorcism in France and England in the
Late Sixteenth and Early Seventeenth Centuries*. Philadelphia, 1981.
Warner, Marina. *Alone of All Her Sex: The Myth and Cult of the Virgin Mary*. New
York, 1976.
Warner, Marina. *Joan of Arc: The Image of Female Heroism*. New York, 1981.
Weber, Eugen. *Peasants into Frenchmen*. Stanford, 1976.
Weber, Max. *Economy and Society*. Edited by Guenther Roth and Claus Wittich.
New York, 1968.
Webster, Charles, ed. *Health, Medicine, and Mortality in the Sixteenth Century*.
Cambridge, 1979.
Wheaton, Robert, and Hareven, Tamara K., eds. *Family and Sexuality in French
History*. Philadelphia, 1980.

White, Lynn, Jr. "Death and the Devil." In Kinsman, *The Darker Vision of the Renaissance*. Berkeley, 1974.

Wilcox, Donald J. *In Search of God and Self: Renaissance and Reformation Thought*. Boston, 1975.

Wilkins, Kay S. "Attitudes to Witchcraft and Demonic Possession in France during the Eighteenth Century." *Journal of European Studies* 3 (1973): 349–60.

Williams, George H. *The Radical Reformation*. Philadelphia, 1962.

Wolf, John B. *Louis XIV*. New York, 1968.

Yates, Francis A. *Giordano Bruno and the Hermetic Tradition*. Chicago, 1964.

Zguta, Russell. "The Ordeal by Water (Swimming of Witches) in the East Slavic World." *Slavic Review* 36 (1977): 220–30.

Zguta, Russell. "Witchcraft and Medicine in Pre-Petrine Russia." *Russian Review* 37 (1978): 438–48.

Zguta, Russell. "Witchcraft Trials in Seventeenth-Century Russia." *American Historical Review* 82 (1977): 1187–1207.

Ziegler, Philip. *The Black Death*. London, 1969.

Index

Witch Cult in Western Europe, The (Murray), 10
Witches
  in art, 74
  baby-devouring by, 97
  men as, 77
  nonconformists as, 19–20
  power to inflict harm, 2
  Satan's need for, 24
  women as, 51–52, 58–59
Witches' Hammer. See Malleus Maleficarum
Witch hunts
  commercial agriculture and, 91–92
  community unity through, 103
  cycle of, 140, 143–46
  demonology, influence of, 46–47
  economic interpretation, 93–94
  internal and external interpretations, 48–49
  irrationality of, 146
  legal reforms and, 92–93, 137–38, 140–42, 146–47
  medieval, 37
  modern analogies to, 157–58
  political nature of, 37, 41, 137
  popular sources of, 86, 94, 102–103
  social conflict and, 50–51
  social order threatened by, 126–27
  spiritual reform and, 71, 84–85, 92
  as stress outlets, 86, 94, 102–103
  superstition as cause of, 8–9
  See also End to witch hunting; Salem trials
Witch pricking, 56–57, 154
Witch prosecutors, 136–39, 140–41
Witch stereotype, 1–3, 4, 17–18, 37, 40
Witch's tit, 2, 56

Witch suspects
  abuse of, 56–57, 149
  aged women as, 72–73, 94–95, 101–102
  ages of, 72–73, 94
  confessions, belief in, 154–55, 156
  occupations of, 95
  rural origins, 56
  women, proportion of, 51–52, 58–59
  See also Beggars; Midwives; Torture
Witch trials
  medieval, 40–42
  of midwives, 100
  pattern of, 39–40
  for possession, 111–13, 114–15
  questionnaires, use of, 141
  reversal of decisions, 42
  sadism of, 73
  saving of souls through, 78–79
  state intervention, 80
  See also Judges; Salem trials; Torture
Wizards, 14, 64–65
Woman-hatred, 5, 52
  in art, 72, 73–74
  Christian tradition of, 66–67
  decline in, 172–73
  in demonology, 67–68
  domestic order and, 69
  in law, 69–70
  medical opinions, 68–69
  sex roles and, 70–71
  sexuality and, 67–69, 73
  spiritual reform and, 72, 84
Women
  aged, 72–73, 94–95, 101–102
  asexual female, concept of, 172–73
  possession and, 125–26
  as witches, 51–52, 58–59
  See also Beggars; Midwives